# The Technological University Reimagined

## GEORGIA INSTITUTE OF TECHNOLOGY,

### 1994–2008

UNIVERSITY

MERCER UNIVERSITY PRESS

*Endowed by*

TOM WATSON BROWN

*and*

THE WATSON-BROWN FOUNDATION, INC.

# The Technological University Reimagined

## GEORGIA INSTITUTE OF TECHNOLOGY,

### 1994–2008

## G. Wayne Clough

President Emeritus, Georgia Institute of Technology

MERCER UNIVERSITY PRESS

*Macon, Georgia*

MUP/ H1014

25 24 23 22 21      5 4 3 2 1


Books published by Mercer University Press are printed on acid-free paper that meets the requirements of the American National Standard for Information Sciences—Permanence of Paper for Printed Library Materials.


Printed and bound in the United States.


This book is set in Adobe Caslon Pro.


Cover/jacket design by Burt&Burt.


Library of Congress Cataloging-in-Publication Data
Names: Clough, G. Wayne, author.
Title: The technological university reimagined : Georgia Institute of
   Technology, 1994-2008 / G. Wayne Clough, president emeritus, Georgia
   Institute of Technology.
Description: Macon, Georgia : Mercer University Press, 2021. | Includes
   bibliographical references and index. |
Identifiers: LCCN 2021025100 | ISBN 978-0-88146-812-0 (hardback)
                              ISBN 978-0-88146-817-5 (eBook)
Subjects: LCSH: Georgia Institute of Technology—History. | Georgia
   Institute of Technology—Reorganization.
Classification: LCC T171.G59 C65 2021 | DDC 607.1/1758231—dc23
LC record available at https://lccn.loc.gov/2021025100

*To my wife of fifty-nine years, Anne Robinson Clough, for believing that I had a talent to share, setting an unshakeable moral compass for our lives, sharing her sense of humor, raising two great kids, and loving me.*

# CONTENTS

# PREFACE

One of the little-appreciated duties of a university president is representing their institution at the inaugurations of presidents of other universities. Given the increased turnover rate for university presidents and the expansion of institutions called universities, this is no small thing. As the scope of the obligation has grown, presidents have turned to willing alumni who have joint ties to both institutions to represent them. But when you know the new president personally, and the university is a neighbor of yours, you do it yourself. So it was that on April 2, 2004, I represented Georgia Tech at the inauguration of Jim Wagner, the new president of Emory University. The event was all that one would expect of an inauguration, but for me there was a lesson in history to be had.

Protocol for the inauguration of a university president calls for the procession of university representatives to be ordered by the date of founding of the universities, oldest institutions first. At an inauguration of a prestigious university like Emory, some of the most historic are represented. When the orchestra struck up Sir Edward Elgar's "Pomp and Circumstance" to begin our procession, men representing Oxford and Cambridge Universities, founded in 1096 and 1209, respectively, led the way. Behind them were representatives of U.S. universities Harvard, founded in 1636, and William and Mary, founded in 1693. Then came those from private U.S. universities from the northeast founded in the early 1700s, and next came southern public universities including the University of Georgia (1785), the University of North Carolina (1789), and the University of Virginia (1819). Representatives from universities with a technical focus cropped up with Rensselaer Polytechnic Institute (1824) and MIT (1861). After this, the ranks of the procession became crowded with those representing great land grant universities, most of them founded shortly after the Morrill Act was passed and signed by Abraham Lincoln in 1862, among them the

University of Illinois (1867), Purdue University (1869), and Ohio State University (1870). Trailing these schools was someone from Johns Hopkins University, founded as the first true research university in the U.S. in 1876. It was as if the entire history of higher education were walking in the procession.

As for the president of Georgia Tech, I was standing back in a spot designated for universities founded in 1885. It felt odd, being so far back in the procession, because none of the schools ahead of me were located as close to Emory as Georgia Tech. None had academic partnerships with Emory like the nationally recognized Emory-Georgia Tech Coulter School of Biomedical Engineering. And I was not just some person representing my university; I was the president. But I was where I was because universities take historical precedent seriously.

Next to me in line was a person in a scarlet red robe representing Stanford University, which shares 1885 as a founding date with Georgia Tech. After exchanging pleasantries with the person from Stanford, I thought about the coincidence that I had connections to both universities. I attended Georgia Tech as an undergraduate in the 1960s and returned as its president in 1994. As for Stanford, I served as a faculty member there for about a decade in the 1970s and 1980s.

Waiting for the procession to begin, I thought about the arc of these two universities. Both had lengthy incubation periods as provincial institutions, but in the 1960s and beyond, they found a new footing. In the decades to follow, a short time in the life of most universities, each attained national prominence, with Stanford leading the way. For Stanford, it helped that in the 1960s and 1970s, California's economy boomed and Silicon Valley took off. Stanford embraced the innovation economy and leapfrogged East Coast universities still tied to their traditional roots. Being on the Stanford faculty at the time, I watched as the train left the station.

Georgia Tech was not quite so fortunate, but it benefitted as Atlanta matured as a city, particularly because the city's leaders chose to back Dr. Martin Luther King Jr. and the civil rights movement. Known as the "city too busy to hate," in the coming decades Atlanta's economy would become the most robust in the Southeast. Along the way, Georgia Tech opportunistically became prominent in areas like logistics and manufacturing. Waiting in the procession for Jim Wagner's inauguration with my colleague from Stanford reminded me that while the destiny of a university is to a degree tied to circumstance, it also depends on the choices and decisions made by the president. Timely choices and decisions influence whether a university grows intellectually and in vitality.

After retiring from Georgia Tech in 2008, I served as Secretary of the Smithsonian Institution, a place that venerates its own history as well as that of our nation. In 2015, I completed my service at the Smithsonian and returned to Georgia Tech to teach part-time. Students would often ask me about my tenure as president, but because the last formally authorized history of Georgia Tech was published in 1985, there was no reference material I could recommend.

It struck me that a lot had happened since 1985, and the people involved, like me, were getting older, running the risk that key events and insights would be lost in time. I decided to help fill part of the gap by writing this book about the years of my tenure as president, 1994 to 2008. I chose to focus on the choices and decisions made that I believed had an impact on the trajectory of the institution.

As with any singular point of view, readers have to take mine with a grain of salt. After all, I am seventy-nine years old as I write this, more than twenty years after some of the events occurred. And I am biased by the thought that I did the best I could under the circumstances of the time. History will be the judge of that.

# Chapter One

# INTRODUCTION

I WAS THE FIRST IN my family to attend the Georgia Institute of Technology. It was not that the Cloughs had anything against Georgia Tech. For generations they had been farmers and timbermen in rural Southeast Georgia. A college education was not part of the equation.

My mother and father had intended to go to college, but the Great Depression threw a wrench into their plans. So they transferred their hopes to their children and saved every penny to send my sister, my brother, and me to college. As a new student at Georgia Tech in the 1960s, I helped out by signing up to be a cooperative education student, alternating terms between studying on campus and working as a railroad surveyor on the way to earning my civil engineering degree. There was no indication that I would become the first alumnus to be president of Georgia Tech.

It was a time when the mores of the Old South were crumbling. Atlanta became the center of the civil rights movement led by Dr. Martin Luther King Jr., and John F. Kennedy was elected president. I was a student in 1961 when Georgia Tech opened its doors to African American students as the first public university in the South to integrate without a court order. Ivan Allen Jr., a Georgia Tech alum, was elected mayor of Atlanta and cast his support for Dr. King. In contrast to George Wallace, governor of Alabama, who personally stood in the door of Foster Auditorium at the University of Alabama to oppose the integration of the university, Allen testified to Congress in support of the Civil Rights Act of 1964. Little did I know that in 2003 I would be one of the pallbearers at his funeral honoring his life's contributions.

As a student at Georgia Tech in the 1960s, I was balancing the challenges of academics with the demands of working on a survey crew, often on rail lines passing through small towns in the Appalachians. Our accommodations were as we could find them, and in diners and pool halls we socialized with local folk. Joblessness and poverty were not far from the surface. The faces we saw recalled those of the Black and White tenant farmers I saw growing up in South Georgia. I was reminded that while I was working my way through school, I was privileged to be where I was. The experience reinforced my intention to make the most of my education at Georgia Tech.

In 1962 I married my high school sweetheart Anne Robinson, who, fifty-nine years later, is still putting up with me. By 1964 I had completed my BS and MS degrees in civil engineering and was offered a job by the U.S. Corps of Engineers in Vicksburg, Mississippi, first at the Waterways Experiment Station and then at the Mississippi River Commission. The engineering experiences offered in Mississippi were among the best, but after living in Atlanta, culturally we were living in a state suspended in time.

Anne and I were welcomed into the community at a luncheon where we were given a book titled *Rebel Victory at Vicksburg*. I may have missed it, but history has it that General Ulysses S. Grant defeated the Confederate forces in Vicksburg. In some ways the war was not over yet in Mississippi because in 1963 civil rights leader Medgar Evers was assassinated outside his home. And in 1964, just before we arrived, three civil rights workers were killed in an incident known today as the Mississippi Burning murders.

We left Vicksburg in 1966 and traveled west of the Mississippi River for the first time to move to Berkeley, California. While Vicksburg and Berkeley were cities in the same country, they were polar opposites culturally. But I was not coming to Berkeley because of its "left-coast politics"; I was there to undertake PhD studies at the University of California in a civil engineering program known for its world-class faculty and leading-edge research. Still, there was no leaving the cultural conflicts behind. The Bay Area was wrestling not only with civil rights but also with the Vietnam War. Both Dr. Martin Luther King Jr. and Robert Kennedy spoke at UC Berkeley, and I was in the audience. Their voices offered us the promise of an America that would bring racial healing and help our country live up to its promise. They asked those of my generation to make a difference.

In 1968, while Anne and I were living through demonstrations and tear gassing on the Berkeley campus, tragically, King and Kennedy were assassinated. It was as if a light went out. In 1971, the song "American Pie" by Don McLean, one of our generation's poet laureates, captured the feeling of the time: "Oh, and there we were all in one place, a generation lost in space, with no time left to start again." But we did start again, although we carried with us a history to which few others could relate.

Fast-forward to 1994. I had served as a faculty member at some of the best private and public universities in the nation and was now the provost and vice president of academic affairs at the University of Washington in Seattle. It was a surprise when I was asked to become president of my undergraduate alma mater, Georgia Tech. Looking back over the somewhat capricious journey of my life, I realized how long the odds were that I would be offered this opportunity. Nevertheless, I hesitated. All four of the universities where my career had taken me encompassed broad ranges of academic programs, and I was not sure I wanted to return to a narrowly focused technological institution.

Three arguments would win the day. The first reinforced expectations: Georgia boy and Tech alumnus comes home to repay the debt he owes to his alma mater, a statement true and deeply felt. Second, my career experiences led me to believe that research universities had become risk averse and had seen their true purposes chipped away. I thought Georgia Tech, with its smaller dimensions but strong academic traditions, might be a place where meaningful change could occur over a relatively short period of time. Third, Anne thought it was a good idea.

In 1994 Georgia Tech was known as a good regional technological university, but it had lost a step when my predecessor stumbled badly

and was forced to resign. Now the university had just two years to prepare to serve as the Olympic Village and host two event venues for the
1996 Centennial Olympic Games. Surviving the Olympics would be
an ordeal unto itself, but I knew my presidency would ultimately be
defined by a small number of decisions about the future of Georgia
Tech that were based on a willingness to embrace calculated risk while
building commitment to underlying core values.

University presidents, no matter how well liked they may have
been during their tenure, are only given a paragraph or two in the history books. What might have been ten or twenty years of a presidency
comes down to a brief summary focused on a few key decisions and
what those decisions did to change the course of the university.

Consider Marion Brittain, who served as president of Georgia
Tech from 1922 to 1944. He led Georgia Tech through the crucible of
the Great Depression, but he is largely remembered for a singular act.
Between 1926 and 1930, the Guggenheim Foundation planned to
make ten grants to endow departments of aeronautics at U.S. universities. As it turned out, these grants ultimately determined which institutions became the best in the nation in this field. However, a funny
thing happened on the way to making the ten grants—they became
eleven. Brittain decided to make a personal visit to the foundation leadership, and he pointed out to them that none of the ten grants went to
a university in the Southeast. Further, he noted, the aeronautics program at Georgia Tech was highly regarded and fully deserving of a
grant. He won the day. Today the Guggenheim School of Aerospace
Engineering at Georgia Tech is ranked number two in the nation by
*U.S. News and World Report*. This level of excellence became possible
because of a decision made by President Brittain in 1930.

When I enrolled at Georgia Tech as a freshman in 1959, it was
segregated. Then President Edward Harrison decided in May 1961 to
integrate voluntarily. Three African American students matriculated
the following September without incident. While I was president,
Georgia Tech achieved the milestone of graduating the largest number
of African American students with engineering degrees in the United
States. This accomplishment traced directly back to a decision made by
President Harrison in 1961.

4

Today Georgia Tech ranks twenty-second in the nation in externally funded research expenditures, and among universities with no medical school, it ranks second only to MIT. This remarkable level of performance was made possible by President Joseph Pettit's decision in the 1970s to emphasize faculty research.

As I look back over my own presidency, the number of decisions made based on personal experience is surprising. Decisions to strengthen diversity and to enhance the educational experience of undergraduates at Georgia Tech were rooted in my days as a student. That experience gave me a unique perspective on what needed to change, and my return as president provided a unique opportunity to make that change happen. I could see to it that all students, then and in the future, would be treated with dignity, would have a rightful chance to succeed and graduate, and would be enriched by their time at Georgia Tech.

Other decisions came as a result of recognizing and responding to unexpected events and opportunities. The germ of the idea behind the full-fledged biomedical engineering partnership between Emory University's School of Medicine and Georgia Tech's College of Engineering came from a conversation between Mike Johns of Emory and Bob Nerem of Georgia Tech during a chance meeting at Atlanta Hartsfield-Jackson International Airport. My decision was to go all in to implement it. While working at Virginia Tech and the University of Washington, I had seen the transformative potential of combining sciences, medicine, and engineering. I wanted to do whatever might be needed to make it work.

The decision to leap across the Downtown Connector and build Technology Square was triggered when Olympic Village preparations forced me to take a roundabout route onto campus through a devastated part of Midtown Atlanta. I realized that the for-sale signs on so many of the properties there were flags of opportunity. Having been on the faculty at Stanford University when Silicon Valley took off, I thought this might the place where Georgia Tech could help Atlanta become known for its entrepreneurial spirit. A subsequent $320 million investment launched one of the most dynamic live-work-play neighborhoods in America.

Even something as small as a comment at a conference led to a significant decision about a fundamental commitment to our values. The comment was about the financial challenges that too often have forced students from low-income families to drop out of college, and it led to the decision to create the Georgia Tech Promise Program. The "promise" was that the cost of their education would not prevent Georgia students from low-income families from graduating from Georgia Tech.

Finally, there were decisions made because duty called—times when the phone rang with a request and I had to say, "Yes, I will do it." For me, those decisions included working with Mayor Shirley Franklin to get Clean Water Atlanta out of the starting gate, advising President George W. Bush on national technology policy, and providing oversight to the Army Corps of Engineers on its plans to rebuild the hurricane protection system for New Orleans in the aftermath of Hurricane Katrina. Although each of these initiatives was different in its own way, all of them helped to demonstrate how Georgia Tech could use its strengths to solve problems facing our community and the nation.

Decisions matter, and this book describes those of my presidency from 1994 to 2008 that I believe made a difference. Taken together, these decisions demonstrated a reimagined future for Georgia Tech. Of course, in the long run history will be the judge. At this point, the only thing I can say with certainty is that my years as president were filled with challenges and opportunities. It was a time when Georgia Tech evolved beyond being a regional player and emerged onto a national and global stage. I was honored to have had a role in making that change possible.

## REFERENCES

McMath, Robert C., Jr., Ronald H. Bayor, James E. Brittain, Lawrence Foster, August W. Giebelhaus, and Germaine M. Reed. *Engineering the New South: Georgia Tech, 1885–1985.* Athens: University of Georgia Press, 1985.

National Science Foundation Higher Education Research and Development Survey Data. "Table 20: Institution Rankings, Ranked by FY2018 R&D Expenditures." *Higher Education Research and Development Survey Fiscal Year 2018.* www.nsf.gov/statistics/srvyherd/.

## Chapter Two

## RIGHTING THE SHIP

John Patrick "Pat" Crecine was president of the Georgia Institute of Technology from 1987 until early 1994. Born in Michigan, he had earned degrees in industrial management, but his career had focused largely on public policy and sociology. He had small acquaintance with either engineering or the Deep South, but this cultural mismatch was only one of a number of things that ultimately crippled his administration.

His contributions to Georgia Tech included leading an academic reorganization; establishing an international campus in Metz, France; and committing Georgia Tech to serve as the Olympic Village and host for two event venues for the 1996 Centennial Olympic Games. But his time at Georgia Tech was marred by controversy, especially in the last two years.

I knew little about the stream of negative publicity that plagued Georgia Tech during this time, because in 1993 I was provost and vice president of academic affairs at the University of Washington in Seattle, about as far from Atlanta as you can get and still be in the contiguous United States. I was enjoying the excitement of working for a comprehensive public university in a vibrant city and a region of great natural beauty. All of the academic units and their deans reported to me—some twenty strong, including the nationally renowned School of

Medicine, which served five states. My wife Anne and I were absorbing this place like sponges, and Georgia Tech was as far from our minds as it was on a map.

Then, early in 1994 Crecine resigned under pressure. His term technically did not end until July, so for most of the intervening months Georgia Tech was effectively left without a president. A presidential search process was instigated shortly after his resignation, and I soon began getting emails from friends inquiring if I would consider becoming a candidate. Initially my answer was no. After all, I had been at my new job for less than a year and was thoroughly enjoying it. However, two months later I received a phone call from a member of the Board of Regents of the University System of Georgia, asking me to reconsider my decision not to be a candidate. At that point I decided to discuss the situation with my boss William Gerberding, president of the University of Washington. He said, "Wayne, you only get one chance to be president of your alma mater, and I will understand if you decide to run." I was the last person to be added to the interview list and the last person to be interviewed. I was offered the position in early summer, and after discussing it with Anne, I accepted.

## FIRST IMPRESSIONS

I knew from the materials sent to me and from conversations with friends that I would face more than the usual share of problems, but I did not fully grasp how bad things were. On my first day on the job in August 1994, I walked into the president's office and found a report on my desk from the Southern Association of Colleges and Schools. SACS, as the organization is affectionately known, controls decisions about accreditation, and they had visited the Georgia Tech campus that spring. They are usually circumspect in their criticisms, but not this time:

> During the past decade Georgia Tech experienced a decline in the effectiveness of services within the business, financial and student service areas…resulting in budget overruns, inaccurate financial information and weak internal controls.
>
> There are…major weaknesses in administrative procedures

and internal controls resulting from long-term ineffective management and management neglect in critical financial areas.

Campus Olympic preoccupation is both a near-term and long-term financial risk.

Deferred maintenance casts a pall over the Georgia Tech campus, its education and research programs, its Dean's effectiveness, the image of the facilities/plant operations, and morale.

It was not a good first impression. But in the next few weeks I would learn that the SACS report actually glossed over many of the real problems. Working late one night in my office at the President's House, I discovered a large manila envelope with the words "To My Successor" scrawled across the front. Inside were about fifteen handwritten pages from Crecine—a long, rambling rant about how bleak things were.

He began by warning that Georgia Tech was in big trouble because of its finances and because of people of influence who were not to be trusted. He said the financial problems included a federal audit of the research program showing that Georgia Tech had overcharged the government by $40 million for "indirect charges," which involved reimbursement for use of facilities related to research activities. Tech was apparently expected to repay the $40 million over the next five years. Next, he pointed out that the facility for the Olympic aquatic competition, which would be staged at Georgia Tech, would require millions of dollars to be converted into something useful after the Games. Of course, there were no "millions of dollars" set aside for this purpose.

In the later pages, he vented about individuals and organizations that he felt had sabotaged his presidency. The swath of his anger spread across the entire Georgia Tech campus and beyond, extending to prominent alumni, state government leaders, and members and staff of the Board of Regents of the University System of Georgia. As I read all fifteen pages, I worried that some of his revelations, if true, would add to my already long to-do list. But I was also saddened that his tenure had ended this way, both for him and for Georgia Tech.

THE TECHNOLOGICAL UNIVERSITY REIMAGINED

## THE FULL LIST

During the early weeks and months of my administration, the list of problems left behind by the Crecine administration grew beyond his handwritten list. It included lingering personnel lawsuits and an audit by the U.S. Equal Employment Opportunity Commission claiming that Georgia Tech was guilty of more than sixty hiring and promotion violations. An effort to automate the university's financial and human resource systems at a cost of more than $20 million had collapsed, leaving Georgia Tech reliant on a financial and personnel system that was on life support.

Fundraising had stagnated. Georgia Tech had hoped to launch its very first national capital campaign to take advantage of the attention and energy surrounding the Olympics. However, given the financial troubles and negative publicity generated by Crecine and his departure, the trustees of the Georgia Tech Foundation had decided to put this idea on hold.

Then there were the Olympics themselves. When I arrived, I was told that by July 1996, slightly less than two years away, the Atlanta Committee for the Olympic Games (ACOG) expected to take over a fully equipped Olympic Village and two event venues. All told, about $230 million of construction totaling 2.3 million square feet was needed.

While I was pondering this challenge, two more Olympic-related matters hit my desk. First, Crecine had diverted $2 million in discretionary funds provided by the Georgia Tech Foundation, normally used for academic purposes, to the construction of the Olympic aquatic venue. His decision had created an uproar among faculty, alumni, and donors who argued that a swimming pool was not the intent of the funds. Second, as the federal security team developed its plans for the Olympic Village, it belatedly noticed that in the middle of campus was a nuclear reactor with fissionable nuclear material in its core. I was not sure how they had managed to overlook the reactor in the first place, but it now became my problem.

The reactor, built in the early 1960s as a teaching and research platform for the nuclear engineering program, had outlived its purpose. But it was still there and still operational. ACOG and the federal

10

security forces indicated in no uncertain terms that they considered it a serious problem. What could be worse than terrorists somehow penetrating Olympic Village security and threatening to blow up the reactor? Decommissioning it would take a long time and cost millions of dollars, and the prospect of finding a place to send the fissionable material was not promising. All I could do at the moment was add the reactor to the long list of things that seemed at times, just maybe, beyond my control.

Just as I was beginning to think the list of problems might finally be complete, a group of faculty and staff requested a meeting with me. They were concerned about crime on campus and the deterioration of the surrounding neighborhoods. They recommended building a high fence around the campus to keep bad elements out. While their concern and the problems they described were real, I knew that the solution lay elsewhere. Georgia Tech needed to become a good neighbor and build bridges, not walls. I did my best to assure them we would put safety high on the priority list, but I avoided saying anything about building a fence.

The full list of problems that fell onto my plate during my early days on the job was long and complicated, and almost every item needed to be resolved somehow in what remained of the two years before the Olympics. There were days—and nights—when I wondered if it could be done. But I kept those thoughts to myself.

Late in my first year as president, University System chancellor Stephen Portch visited South Georgia College in my hometown of Douglas. He knew my father had been mayor at one time, and, being a clever man, he thought that taking me along would be a good signal to send. We planned to spend the night at an economy motel with a restaurant, and when we arrived there, Portch pointed to the motel marquee sign. The top line read, "Welcome Chancellor Portch." Next came, "Catfish, All You Can Eat $4.50." At the bottom a line said, "Welcome President Clough." That seemed to sum up where things stood. I had made the marquee, but I still had work to do if I were to rise above the catfish special.

## A FEW BRIGHT SPOTS

I tend to be a glass-half-full kind of guy, so even as the problems left from the Crecine era piled up, I still felt a bit of optimism. And it was based on more than wishful thinking. For starters, the students enrolling at Georgia Tech were among the nation's best. Their math scores on the SAT were the highest of any public university in the nation, and their verbal scores were not far behind. When I spoke with them, it was obvious that they were bright and talented, and they were looking for me to be a president who understood their hopes and aspirations.

Second, Georgia Tech faculty were beginning to step up and fulfill their potential in research. But I wanted them to understand that gaining a little recognition was not enough. To compete with the best, Georgia Tech would need to do more.

Third, the alumni of Georgia Tech were a special group. Most were remarkably loyal and wanted Georgia Tech to be top notch. Their contributions made Georgia Tech's annual fund one of the most successful in the nation. But to be among the best would require more than routine annual giving.

Finally, there was the state of Georgia. It might seem surprising to include state government on the list of reasons to be optimistic, but particularly during my tenure and even afterward, Georgia continued to be more supportive of higher education than other states. I was fortunate to begin my presidency with Zell Miller as governor. He had served as lieutenant governor for sixteen years before becoming governor, and he knew how to make decisions and get them enacted into law. Earlier in his career he had been a college professor, and he believed in the power of education to improve the state.

Governor Miller made three key contributions to higher education, two of which are well known. The first was the HOPE Scholarship, which at its onset paid for tuition, fees, and books for Georgia residents who attended in-state public colleges and universities, as long as they maintained at least a 3.0 grade point average.

The second was to make state government a partner and driving force in the Georgia Research Alliance (GRA), a public-private partnership to stimulate technology-based economic development. Rather than build technology parks as other states had done, the GRA invested

12

in targeted research areas at six Georgia universities. The list included four public universities—Georgia Tech, the University of Georgia, the Medical College of Georgia, and Georgia State University—plus the private Emory University and Clark-Atlanta University. GRA investments focused on three goals: endowing faculty chairs to attract some of the nation's best scientific talent; providing sophisticated research infrastructure; and supporting the commercialization of research discoveries. Once the GRA was up and running, state budgets provided more than $200 million during the remaining six years of Miller's administration, including the creation of twenty-seven endowed chairs.

Miller's third contribution, probably the least understood, came as a result of a luncheon he asked me to host for him at the President's House at Georgia Tech. I was instructed to invite the presidents of Georgia's three other public research universities—Francis Tedesco of the Medical College of Georgia, Charles Knapp of the University of Georgia, and Carl Patton of Georgia State University. Miller would bring Stephen Portch, chancellor of the University System of Georgia. It was December 8, 1994. I had just arrived at Georgia Tech that August and Governor Miller had just been reelected to a second term in November. The economy was strong, and he was determined that some of the new funds expected to flow into the state's coffers would be invested in higher education. He wanted to make a move in the budget he would submit to the Georgia General Assembly in January, and he was looking to build a case.

After the meeting, all of the presidents at the table remembered his question: "What is the one thing I can do in the next four years that would make the greatest difference for your universities?" Our answer was in unison: improve faculty salaries. Not only were Georgia's faculty salaries not competitive with those at the prominent national universities with which we aspired to compete, but they were even below average for the Southeast. Miller promised us he would seek a 6 percent raise each year for the next four years, and he delivered, even though some legislators fought him tooth and nail. This commitment had lasting value, particularly for Georgia Tech, because we were entering a period in which we would recruit a large number of faculty.

## RESTORING TRUST

For more than two years before my arrival, the faculty and staff of Georgia Tech had been living with the slow-motion collapse of the Crecine administration. They had done their best to keep Georgia Tech on course and fulfilling its obligations to students during that time, but the unrelenting negative headlines had worn them down and made them skeptical of the administration. One of my first jobs had to be restoring trust on campus.

It did not take long to learn that in campus conversations the administration was referred to as "The Hill." Since the central administration buildings and the president's office are located at the highest point on campus, the term was geographically accurate. But as used by faculty and staff, "The Hill" was indicative neither of elevation nor of endearment. Rather it spoke to a separation between the administration and the daily work lives of faculty and staff.

I knew the gulf would always be there to some extent, but I thought it was worth a try to do something about it. So I committed myself to make personal visits to every unit on campus in my first year. Little did I know that this undertaking would require twenty-eight visits. Was all the effort worth it? It's hard to say, but I learned a lot and gained a few points for listening.

My reception varied. The smaller units, especially those outside the university's engineering wheelhouse, welcomed me with open arms. No president in recent memory had ever visited them, and here was their chance to make sure I understood their contributions to Georgia Tech. Almost all of the larger units were courteous, but some saw my visit as an opportunity to tell me they would be just fine continuing as they were, thank you very much, as long as I gave them more resources and kept my fancy ideas to myself. All in all, it was clear there was work to be done to develop a unified vision for the future, and it was good to realize up front that not everybody was going to embrace some of the ideas I had in mind.

## MODEST GOALS BUT STOUT PHILOSOPHICAL ENDS

About the time I embarked on my campus visits, I appointed a task force to develop a new strategic plan, a standard tactic for a new administration to establish its agenda. However, in this case a new plan was very much needed because the existing strategic plan was a top-down document written basically as a wish list. To create buy-in for a new plan, it was important to engage a broader community of students, faculty, staff, and alumni in the discussion. My hope was that the process would help shift campus attention from the problems of the past to the possibilities for the future.

While I thought the planning group needed to develop ideas of their own, my priorities were to reflect what was possible as well as attune our efforts to core values. My list included emphasizing the need for a vibrant undergraduate experience, establishing Georgia Tech's reputation as a place that developed new ideas to solve big problems, and setting aspirations for excellence in programs outside of engineering, including the humanities.

Looking back, the goals of the 1995 Georgia Institute of Technology Strategic Plan were relatively understated, reflecting the challenging circumstances we faced. But this plan was the first step in articulating the connection between the expectations for increasing research and improving our reputation on the one hand and, on the other, creating an institutional respect for teaching and enhancing and personalizing the student experience. The plan stated in explicit terms that the undergraduate student experience not only involved classrooms and laboratories but also embraced independent research with faculty, international study programs, volunteer activities, and opportunities for artistic expression. It spoke to the importance of aesthetics and enhancing the campus to reflect our aspirations.

As for research, the plan addressed three themes: (1) a shift toward collaboration between disciplines and with like-minded institutions; (2) a need to accelerate the process of moving ideas from the laboratory to the marketplace; and (3) an expansion of our intellectual endeavors to include the humanities, public policy, and the social sciences. These were not new ideas for some of our peer institutions, but they were new for Georgia Tech. They would require not only a change in mindset but also new types of facilities and support systems.

The 1995 strategic plan, in and of itself, did not last long. By 1998 it was apparent that our progress was greater than we anticipated, and we began to enlarge our goals. By 2002 an entirely new plan was in place. But the philosophy articulated in the 1995 plan set the stage for a different future for Georgia Tech.

## BUILDING AN ORGANIZATION...FAST

In the sports world, when one team stands to overwhelm another, the game is called a mismatch. That term came to mind as I weighed the work we had to get done against the resources available to do it. For starters, Georgia Tech's organizational structure was out of date. And then there were the people. There were too many of them, and most lacked depth of experience, both in their responsibilities and in never having worked at any university other than Georgia Tech.

With ample time and no pressing deadlines, I would have done things differently. But I had neither. It was blunt instrument time. I began by reducing the number of people working in the office of the president by 40 percent, eliminating most of their job titles at the same time. Recognizing that these departing employees had provided faithful service to Georgia Tech, especially in the last tumultuous days of the Crecine administration, we helped them find jobs elsewhere at Tech or used placement services to assist them in locating employment at other organizations. While this reduction in force may have been difficult for those involved, it was welcomed by the campus at large.

Circumstances dictated moving ahead on multiple fronts at the same time. Developing a new strategic plan had to proceed immediately; critical positions required filling; and if studies were necessary, we had to commission them with dispatch. Although things were a bit chaotic, three guiding principles helped us stay focused: (1) keep the organizational structure flat and emphasize responsible, distributed decision making; (2) build a team of people who were smart, risk takers, quality seekers, and committed to getting results; and (3) find new employees who were acutely aware of what was required to compete with the best.

A baseball manager finds it hard to field a team without a pitcher,

16

catcher, center fielder, and shortstop. That is where I found myself in 1994, and given the rules governing hiring in a public university, I needed to prioritize. First and foremost, I wanted to fill the position of executive vice president for administration and finance. This need had not only been emphasized by the SACS review but was also reinforced by the results of a study of our financial and administrative systems that I had commissioned the firm KPMG to do. Their report provided helpful guidance as to how we should address our problems, but their main conclusion said it all: "Rarely do we hear so consistent a story as the one we heard at Georgia Tech.... Administration and Finance needs a radical overhaul."

Because the existing staff lacked credibility, we conducted a national search. The finalist for the position turned out to be Robert Thompson, a former colleague who had reported to me at the University of Washington. He brought with him more than twenty years of experience and a national reputation for astute management in the world of research universities.

Thompson was not only smart but also ruthless in reducing spending and finding new revenues to support the academic enterprise. He knew how to get infrastructure built and the importance of finding the best architects and engineering talent to do it. At times his bedside manner left more than a little to be desired, but his approach was essential to optimizing a limited base of resources and running a business operation that was respected and efficient. My job was to intervene and reset the playing field when he had stepped on too many toes. He was just too important to lose to internecine warfare.

Sorting out the financial and administrative details was essential, but it was not enough. Two other new positions were needed to accomplish our mission and help increase revenues. First, we needed a leader for our research and development operations who would bring an innovative spirit into play; who could build collaborative university partnerships; and who understood the global connectivity that had come to characterize university research. To set the stage, I reduced the complexity of the existing structure by combining three positions into one—vice provost for research and dean of graduate studies. I wanted to put the big decisions in the hands of one person with an integral understanding of how academic research worked and where the future lay in emerging research.

I had a candidate in mind for this one, someone I knew well: Jean-Lou Chameau. He had been my PhD student at Stanford University, and after graduation he had served on the faculties of Purdue University and Georgia Tech, where he had become chair of the School of Civil and Environmental Engineering. Then he was hired as the CEO of Golder Associates, one of the largest geotechnical engineering companies in the world.

Fortunately, Chameau still lived in Atlanta, and I asked him to have breakfast with me. I told him about our position and explained that he would be provided with funds to invest in new research initiatives. He was quiet for so long that I began to think I had missed the mark. I was about to begin trying to salvage what appeared at the moment to be an awkward situation, when he finally spoke. He said he was ready to return to academia, and this job was a perfect fit for him. I left the breakfast knowing this was one of the best appointments I would make for Georgia Tech, and events would prove me right.

The second of these new appointments was to find someone to direct a national capital campaign. In the turbulent final days of the Crecine administration, plans for a campaign had been put on hold, but financial pressures left no doubt that the delay was temporary. We needed to prepare for a major fundraising endeavor. This position was not easy to fill. It demanded incessant travel; attendance at innumerable events, dinners, and meetings; knowledge of the welter of options in making gifts to universities; an ability to remain coherent while alcohol was served; and an understanding of how to cultivate all manner of donors and their families. I had met such a person when I was dean of engineering at Virginia Tech—Barrett Carson—and he was at a point in his career where he was ready to move on. Negotiations began as we were approaching the Olympics, and we hired him shortly after the Games ended. My only challenge was to tone down his sense of humor, which could be on the sharp side. But we complemented each other: he was a Yankee from Long Island who could ruffle feathers; I was an old boy from South Georgia who could smooth ruffled feathers.

Not all of my appointments were external. We needed someone

on the leadership team who knew the lay of the land from long experience, so I asked Provost Mike Thomas to stay on. He had excellent academic credentials, having been head of Tech's top-ranked School of Industrial and Systems Engineering. Although tainted by his association with Pat Crecine, he was a known commodity on campus and could help launch our efforts in the early stages of my administration.

To make good on my commitments to enrich the undergraduate experience and to restore trust between the faculty and the administration, I created two more new positions. Robert McMath, who was chair of the School of History, Technology, and Society, became vice provost for undergraduate studies and academic affairs, and Dan Papp, who was the founding chair of the School of International Affairs, became the executive assistant to the president. Their appointments signaled a higher level of attention to the non-engineering side of the university, and with their long history as Georgia Tech faculty members and administrators, they proved to be just what the doctor ordered.

In building a team, nothing ever works out exactly as you imagine it at the start, especially in terms of how the members work together. However, I was fortunate to bring the right people on board at the right time. As proof of the quality of those who filled these new positions, I note that two went on to become presidents of other universities; one took an endowed position at another university; and one worked with me for my entire fourteen-year administration, retiring when I left Georgia Tech. Four of them were named Honorary Alumni, the highest award given by the Georgia Tech Alumni Association to non-alumni.

## CLEARING OUT THE UNDERBRUSH

Wins come in different packages. The whole campus celebrates the shiny ones, such as athletic victories, while those in plain-paper wrappers are noticed by only a few. When it came to clearing out the underbrush left by my predecessor, the ones in plain-paper wrapping were far more important in the long run than the shiny ones.

One of the clouds looming over our future was the $40 million that Georgia Tech supposedly owed the federal government, ostensibly because we had overcharged them for indirect cost recovery on research. Not many people knew about this issue and even fewer understood it, but it threatened to stunt our ability to support an ambitious research agenda and build new academic facilities. My secret weapon was Bob Thompson. At the University of Washington, one of his responsibilities had been to negotiate with the federal government in setting the rate of indirect cost recovery for research. I had admired his knowledge of the process as well as his tenacity in standing up for institutional rights. When the federal auditors assigned to Georgia Tech showed up on campus and met Thompson, they learned that a new sheriff was in town.

Thompson had a good sense of humor for a financial guy, but whenever he discussed financial matters, he was dead serious. So I knew something was up when he asked to see me about the indirect cost recovery problem and arrived with a Cheshire-cat grin on his face. In typical Bob Thompson fashion, he explained to me that based on his studies, our problem was not that we had paid the government too little money but that we had paid them too much. This news was so surprising that I made him repeat it to make sure I had heard it right. He said that instead of owing the federal government $40 million, it seemed we could make a case that they owed us money. However, before I could ask how much they owed us, he said we should not be greedy. Instead, he advised that we seek a new agreement that canceled the "debt" we owed and established a higher, indirect cost recovery rate for the future. This way we would lose no time debating the past and move on quickly with a new methodology in hand. This approach ultimately allowed us to create borrowing capacity that would help fund new capital projects.

If Thompson had been the hugging sort, I would have hugged him on the spot. Not only had a cloud been removed, but I could glimpse a genuine ray of sunlight. This win did not merit a headline or even much of a footnote on campus, but it was a game changer for our future.

The second plain-paper-wrapper win came in human resources. The U.S. Equal Employment Opportunity Commission had found Georgia Tech in violation of federal policies in sixty-four hiring and promotion cases. I told the legal and human resources staff that if Georgia Tech was clearly at fault in any of these cases, we should own up and take our medicine. However, if we had reason to believe a case

20

was due to a misunderstanding or an excess of regulatory zeal, we should fight. At the end of the day, we accepted the federal ruling in just six cases, and equitable settlements were quickly reached in all six. Despite this positive outcome, we still adopted new policies to avoid making the same mistakes again. The new policies were based on treating faculty and staff equitably and fairly, and it would serve us well in the future.

The final win in a plain-paper wrapper was so modest that only a few people understood its importance. For years during my predecessor's tenure, administrative personnel had dreaded the annual release of audit results. Accounting and financial operations at Georgia Tech were in such disarray that invariably multiple audit findings were announced, and the media crowded in for an easy feast. Enter Bob Thompson and his team, and in 1996 we quietly celebrated the first clean audit in years. This single event meant that our financial house was in order, and I could now approach potential donors with confidence, knowing our financial management would not be an obstacle.

## FACILITY WOES

As I walked around the campus after arriving in 1994, a sense of nostalgia came over me. So little had changed since my undergraduate days. Many of the buildings where my classes had met were still there, unaltered and worse for the wear. Even the old Highway Materials Building on what used to be the northeast edge of campus was still in service. I had taken undergraduate and graduate civil engineering classes there and worked on my master's thesis research in the high bay area. When I visited it on my early rounds as the new president, an earnest faculty member took me to the high bay area and said we needed to do something about the roof because it leaked in a heavy rain. I hesitated to tell him that the roof had leaked in the exact same place when I had worked in that space thirty years earlier. This leak was just one example of the large-scale problem of long-deferred maintenance that had been identified in the SACS review.

Reshaping the campus would take time, a long time, but it was crucial to get started immediately. We knew we needed a new capital plan and a master plan, but first we needed to assess the state of our existing facility base and understand what would be required to become competitive with our peers. Once again I called on Bob Thompson's experience and contacts in the research university world. Rather than hiring a consulting firm, he knitted together a team of experts whose expertise covered capital planning, campus design, finance, and deferred maintenance. They began by assessing the facilities on our campus and then visited universities we had designated as our "aspirational" peers. On each visit they documented the present status of the university's facilities base and then—the secret sauce—reviewed their plans for the next twenty years. We knew we were aiming at a moving target, so we wanted to know not only how far behind we were at the time but also what it would take to be competitive twenty years in the future.

The report from our team was at once encouraging and discouraging. We learned that the ideas on which our peers were basing their capital facilities plans were consistent with those stated in our new strategic plan, which gave us confidence that we were on the right track. But the report also showed that we would have to find a vast store of new resources if we were to make any progress against the plans they had for the next twenty years. We gloomily concluded that we needed to build one major building per year for the next twenty years to catch up, but state funding would only provide one every five years or so.

As we absorbed the enormity of the task facing us, I began to realize that it also offered an opportunity. If we could mobilize a major building initiative, and in the process configure it to support our goals for next-generation approaches to teaching, learning, and research, we could kill two birds with one stone. As for funding, I believed such a visible challenge would be a perfect rallying cry for our future capital campaigns. It would also scratch my itch to use my civil engineering expertise and consulting experience in the design and construction of large projects to good effect.

## SELLING A NEW MESSAGE FOR THE FUTURE

With the completion of the strategic plan and the capital facilities study, we began the master planning process, laying the foundation for the serious work ahead. As they say in mathematics, all of this logistical work was necessary, but it was not sufficient. The missing ingredients were inspiration and commitment.

The noise of the oncoming Olympics tended to drown out what was really important to our future, but the possibilities were there to see. The importance of biotechnology, biosciences, and nanotechnology was emerging, and we were aligning our strengths to capitalize on their flowering. They would feed off of computing, bioinformatics, and artificial intelligence—strengths we were also developing. In addition, policy and business strategy would no longer be the exclusive province of old-boy networks but would be driven by technology. Although we were starting out behind other better-established universities, they were locked into more traditional pathways. Our position gave us the flexibility to chart a new course toward these emerging and converging new fields.

Our challenge was to build a narrative about the opportunities that lay ahead for Georgia Tech. Seizing them would require new facilities and new faculty, and it was up to me to sell the excitement offered by the possibilities. We needed to develop a cadre of believers in our ideas who could speak for us, and to identify donors who found our aspirations inspiring.

In the two years leading up to the Olympics I made fifteen extended trips out of state, along with dozens more within the state, to meet with alumni and friends of Georgia Tech. I discovered that what they knew of Georgia Tech in those days was based on what they had read or seen in the news—mostly about football and the problems surrounding the Crecine presidency. I hated to waste time on either of these topics in my conversations, because I might only have fifteen minutes to make my case before the meeting ended, but it could not be helped. Before I could even think about asking for a gift, most people needed to be reassured that our accounting systems were now accurate and that gifts to Tech would go where they were supposed to go.

Looking back, it is obvious to me that my visits were useful in building relationships. Sometimes my job was mostly listening, such as the time I visited Gary Jones, a Tech alumnus who had been successful in the financial sector in New York City. He was involved with Georgia Tech, serving on the advisory board of the new Ivan Allen College, which at that time included the School of Industrial Management. I visited Jones in his office next to a trading floor in Manhattan, and when I asked him for his opinions, he pulled out a yellow legal pad with five handwritten pages of issues he wanted to talk about. But he did it with a smile. He had clearly thought about the problems he saw and the opportunities he felt were being lost, and he talked about them without hesitation. I liked him immediately.

Scraping my way through those early days, I was reassured by encounters with exceptional people who were willing to invest in our ideas, poorly developed though they were at the time. Al West was one of them. I "inherited" him from the Crecine presidency, as he was serving on the Georgia Tech Advisory Board when I arrived. I was impressed by all I knew about him. He and I were about the same age and were Southerners. He was a pioneer in developing digital platforms to serve as a "back office" for large financial institutions, including Goldman Sachs. I liked him because he was open to new ideas, and he was more than willing to let you know his opinions, always delivered with nuance and a shrewd smile. We would become friends well beyond the bounds of our Georgia Tech connection.

On my early trips it was impossible to leave out California because so many Georgia Tech alumni lived there, and high on our list was Michael Tennenbaum. He had grown up in a modest home on St. Simons Island and worked his way through Georgia Tech as a cooperative education student, like me. He earned his MBA at Harvard University, had a successful career on Wall Street, and then formed his own investment firm located in Southern California. Like Jones and West, Tennenbaum was not shy about offering his opinions and giving advice. I might not have agreed with all of his positions, but his advice always helped shape issues and ideas. Jones, West, and Tennenbaum were the type of alumni living outside of Atlanta who helped bring wide-ranging experience into our discussions about the future of Georgia Tech.

After working my way through my list of visits, I came to two conclusions. First, Georgia Tech alumni, as products of a demanding technological education, expected me to bring an organized, disciplined approach to the table. Second, they could be divided into three groups: (1) those who wanted to be reassured that Georgia Tech had its financial house in order and would ensure that any future gift they made would be used as agreed upon; (2) those who wanted to see new ideas and aspirations that looked to the future; and (3) those who needed to be convinced I was not going to be a flash in the pan.

As the Olympics approached, it was apparent we still had a long way to go, but I felt the ship of state had been righted. We had brought our many financial problems to heel, built a first-rate executive team, completed many planning efforts that were essential to setting our course for the future, developed relationships that would bear fruit in the coming capital campaign, and established a philosophical basis for what it would take to become a great institution. Now all we had to do was get the Olympics out of the way.

## REFERENCES

Barlament, James. "HOPE Scholarship." *New Georgia Encyclopedia*, April 30, 2019. https://www.georgiaencyclopedia.org/articles/education/hope-scholarship.

Eby-Ebersole, Sarah, ed. *Signed, Sealed, & Delivered: Highlights of the Miller Record*. Macon: Mercer University Press, 1999.

*Georgia Institute of Technology Strategic Plan*. Atlanta: Georgia Institute of Technology Office of Publications, GT96-195, 1996.

KPMG Peat Marwick LLP. *Georgia Institute of Technology: Administration and Finance Organizational Review*, Atlanta, October 12, 1995.

Robichaud, Kathleen. "Georgia Research Alliance." *New Georgia Encyclopedia*, May 22, 2013. https://www.georgiaencyclopedia.org/articles/education/georgia-research-alliance.

Southern Association of Colleges and Schools. *Report of the SACS Commission on Colleges Reaffirmation Committee: Georgia Institute of Technology*, Decatur, May 26, 1994.

*Chapter Three*

# THE CENTENNIAL OLYMPIC GAMES

"The International Olympic Committee has awarded the 1996 Olympic Games to the city of...Atlanta." With these words, spoken in Tokyo on September 18, 1990, Juan Antonio Samaranch, president of the International Olympic Committee (IOC), launched celebrations in Atlanta. It was an understatement to say the selection of Atlanta was a surprise. The frontrunner had been Athens, Greece, because these Games would mark the one hundredth anniversary of the first modern Olympics, held there in 1896. Toronto was considered the closest competitor with a strong bid backed by the Canadian government. Atlanta was a dark horse, thought to be well back in the pack. However, its bid brought several unique assets to the table: William P. "Billy" Payne, an irrepressible lawyer whose idea it was to bring the Games to Atlanta; former United Nations Ambassador Andrew Young; and a computer-generated "flyover" of the venues developed by Georgia Tech in lieu of the stodgy physical models used by others.

Billy Payne was a man with a smile and a knack for working tirelessly to sell a dream. He is remembered for telling the Olympic selection committee that the average temperature in Atlanta in the summer is seventy-five degrees Fahrenheit, a slight fudge that enabled him to avoid mentioning that daytime temperatures often peaked as much as twenty degrees higher. Andrew Young, a civil rights icon who was formerly a congressman, U.S. ambassador to the United Nations, and mayor of Atlanta, joined Payne as an enthusiastic supporter of the Olympic bid. His connections and contacts as a citizen of the world gave him standing with the IOC that no one else in Atlanta had.

Georgia Tech's "flyover" was an eye catcher. Viewers could visualize how the proposed Atlanta event venues would work together to create a seamless experience for Olympic visitors. Today's apps enable users to create flyovers on their personal computing devices, but in 1990 few people had ever seen one. It had "wow" power and highlighted for the Olympic Committee Atlanta's world-class telecommunications capabilities, available through CNN, BellSouth, and Georgia Tech's cutting-edge computing technology.

Although Samaranch's announcement brought joy and jubilation to those in Atlanta who had worked on behalf of the bid, it was the first time most of the faculty and students on Georgia Tech's campus realized they might be involved. As for me, I was the dean of engineering at Virginia Tech at the time, with no reason to think it would have any impact on my life.

## FACING REALITY

When Atlanta was named the host city, what had been a hypothetical exercise suddenly became a reality. A largely inexperienced group of enthusiastic boosters began to realize they now had a steep hill to climb. They had less than six years to develop multiple competition venues, figure out how to accommodate two million visitors who would descend on the city for the Games, and raise most of the funding to do it from private sources.

The Games actually consisted of two events spread over two different date ranges. The Centennial Olympic Games would formally begin with the opening ceremonies on July 19, 1996, and run for thirteen days, ending with the closing ceremonies on August 4. They were to be followed by the Paralympic Games for disabled athletes, scheduled to take place from August 16 to August 25. More than 10,000 athletes from 197 countries would compete in the Olympic Games, while almost 3,300 athletes from 100 countries would compete in the Paralympics. Georgia Tech would find itself intimately involved in both events.

Part of Atlanta's appeal was that the geography of its proposal was relatively compact. Most of the competition venues for both the Olympic and the Paralympic Games would be concentrated in or near Atlanta, and the athletes competing at these venues would be housed in the city. The original idea was to spread housing for the athletes across several Atlanta university campuses. However, control and logistical issues changed the plan to one consolidated Olympic Village—the Georgia Tech campus. During the Olympic Games, the village was expected to provide services for 16,000 athletes, trainers, and coaches and to house about 12,000 of them—almost double the number of beds on campus at the time. After the Olympics, Georgia Tech would also serve as the village for the Paralympics Games.

To accommodate the housing requirements for the Olympic Village, seven new residence halls were built on property to the west of Hemphill Avenue on the northwest side of the Georgia Tech campus. But still more beds were needed. The solution was a large housing complex built on land directly across North Avenue from the campus— close enough to be wrapped into the security perimeter of the village. These projects provided much more additional student housing than Georgia Tech could swallow in one gulp, so the complex on the south side of North Avenue was ceded to Georgia State University after the Games. During subsequent years, this arrangement proved impractical because Georgia State's campus was some distance away in downtown. Late in my tenure as president, we negotiated a deal to transfer the North Avenue Apartments to Georgia Tech. By this time, we had absorbed all the other Olympic housing for our student body, and the additional space was welcome.

For Georgia Tech president Pat Crecine, serving as the Olympic Village was not enough. He successfully argued that the campus should host the competition venues for aquatics and boxing as well. Of these, boxing was the less worrisome since it involved a welcomed renovation of the existing basketball arena.

The venue for aquatics was a different matter entirely. It called for the construction of a large, specialized, outdoor aquatic structure designed for Olympic competition—a facility that would require significant modification at a significant cost in order to be useful to Georgia

Tech post-Olympics. The consensus within the Georgia Tech community was that the Aquatic Center was a bridge too far and that locating it on the Tech campus made little sense. Not to be dissuaded, Crecine, a swimmer, fought an uphill, sometimes bitter battle to make it happen. Along the way he incurred the enmity of numerous people who already were questioning his leadership.

Security prior to and during the Olympics was the joint responsibility of Atlanta Committee for the Olympic Games (ACOG) and state and federal authorities. Having met the people in charge, I was convinced they had expertise. However, as an outsider who had arrived after the key decisions were made, I wondered who had thought it made sense for Georgia Tech's relatively small campus to serve not only as the Olympic Village but also as host to two event venues. After all, the "Munich massacre" during the 1972 Olympic Games had made security the single most important objective for the village. On that occasion, Palestinian extremists had broken into the Olympic Village, killed two Israeli athletes, and captured nine more. After the nine had been held hostage for days in the glare of international publicity, they were killed in a shootout. Yet ACOG and the IOC had agreed to snug two Olympic venues into the village on the Georgia Tech campus, each attracting thousands of visitors.

Technically, it was not my problem, but I knew if a terrorist attack succeeded on my campus, Georgia Tech's name would be forever linked with it. How such decisions could have been made was enough to give me pause and raise questions in my mind about the judgment of Crecine, the leaders of the Olympic movement, and ACOG. The Olympics posed many problems that caused me to worry, but because I had no control over this one in particular, it kept me up at night.

## THE PLAYERS

The local organization for the Atlanta Olympics was split into two entities: the Atlanta Committee for the Olympic Games (ACOG) and the Metro Atlanta Olympic Games Authority (MAOGA). The first was responsible for venue construction and operating the Games; the second was responsible for financial oversight. Georgia Tech had interests in both sides of the Olympic house. ACOG made policy decisions that would affect us leading up to and during the Olympics. MAOGA was critical to all matters related to financial obligations as they pertained to Georgia Tech.

The Olympic venture for Georgia Tech was framed by the yin of the challenges and problems that came with our commitment and the yang of the enthusiasm of student, staff, and alumni volunteers in support of the Games. Fortunately, I had most of my new executive team in place and discovered that a number of people from outside our campus would come to our aid.

Of course, Bob Thompson, executive vice president for administration and finance, was central to protecting our interests. Then there were the "two Bills," hired not long after the success of the Atlanta bid was announced. Both were ex-military guys who had served in the U.S. Army Corps of Engineers on major projects around the world, including in combat zones. The senior of the two was Bill Ray, retired general, and his next in command was Bill Miller, retired colonel. They were in charge of the construction of the Olympic facilities that fell within Georgia Tech's purview, as well as managing logistical matters such as parking. Having worked for the Corps of Engineers myself, I knew that, given our circumstances, their experience and dedication were what we needed. After meeting them, I was confident that despite the long haul required by all the work the Olympics demanded, these two would get it done or die trying.

Like most people, my knowledge of past Olympics consisted of stories about host committees plagued by fiscal mismanagement, inadequate funding, and debt that lingered after the Games had ended. Would the Atlanta Olympics prove to be the exception? ACOG had promised that the Games would be self-supporting and funded by private sources. I hoped it would prove true, but experience suggested it might be wishful thinking, and no friendly government with deep pockets stood behind this bid.

Standing between us and the possibility that ACOG would not meet its commitments was A. D. Frazier, ACOG's chief operating officer. Frazier was not only a top-flight financial expert who had been chairman and CEO of the Chicago Stock Exchange but had also worked as an executive in Jimmy Carter's presidential administration.

31

He understood and appreciated how much Georgia Tech had put on the line to make the Olympics successful. Given the fluidity of the financial situation of ACOG and MAOGA, it was reassuring to have him telling us that at the end of the day Georgia Tech would be made whole.

Gary McConnell, the director of the Georgia Emergency Management Agency (GEMA), would prove to be another stalwart ally. He interceded on our behalf more than a few times regarding the nuclear reactor and matters related to parking and security. He was an island of stability in a sea of otherwise confused ACOG employees.

Finally, we needed help to deal with ACOG's politically motivated actions. The pressures of the Olympic Games caused natural tensions between Georgia Tech and ACOG, but the heat intensified when ACOG officials tried to circumvent our negotiators and use external political pressure to force us to cave on core principles. Fortunately, University System of Georgia chancellor Stephen Portch and his staff stepped into the breach and helped us push back. They created the space we needed to keep the playing field level.

## FINANCING THE GEORGIA TECH OLYMPIC FACILITIES

"Georgia Tech made out like a bandit because the Olympics paid for so many new buildings." I heard this a lot and wished it were true. However, of the $233 million spent on our campus for the Olympics, Georgia Tech itself put up $160 million—almost 70 percent. Of our share, $147 million came from bonds borrowed on state credit through the University System of Georgia, and the remainder came from Georgia Tech's discretionary funds and philanthropic giving.

The bulk of these funds—$194 million of the $233 million—went into housing. Prior to the Olympics, Georgia Tech had a housing capacity of a little less than 7,000 beds for its student body of 13,000. Dormitories accounted for about 6,000 beds, and houses owned by fraternities and sororities made up the rest. The dormitories tended to be old, with more than a few built by the Works Progress Administration during the Great Depression. Some of the available funds gave these existing dormitories a face-lift for the Olympics. Fraternities and sororities benefitted by renting their houses to guests from smaller countries, who found the houses a perfect fit for their Olympic teams and were willing to pay a premium for them. By encouraging their alumni to add to the revenue from the rents, many Greek chapters were able to undertake renovations or even a complete rebuild of their houses.

The principal housing investment on the Georgia Tech campus came in the form of seven state-of-the-art residence halls clustered on the northwest side of campus, which added 2,500 beds to our housing capacity. Our plan was to pay for the bonds used for their construction with monies from the rent charged to the students who would occupy them after the Olympics. The rest of the additional housing required by the Olympics was built directly across North Avenue from our campus, with Georgia State University taking ownership to house their students.

Before I arrived at Georgia Tech, a deal had been negotiated to use our basketball arena, Alexander Memorial Coliseum, as the boxing venue. ACOG felt that the arena could be used essentially as it was but was willing to put up $1.5 million for improvements. When I arrived, the Georgia Tech Athletic Association asked me for permission to undertake a campaign to raise additional funds from alumni and corporate interests to permit a more significant $12 million renovation. I agreed because I believed that the publicity surrounding the Olympics would help stimulate interest in the campaign and because the expanded renovation plan added air conditioning. We used the coliseum for commencement ceremonies, and spring and summer graduations were hot, humid affairs.

While everyone was happy about the improvements the Olympics would bring to Alexander Memorial Coliseum, the Aquatic Center was a different story. The idea of building it in the first place was unpopular in many circles, and converting it to a student recreation center post-Olympics required a stretch of the imagination. Nevertheless, the immediate task before us was to build the facility to Olympic specifications. Chosen to design it were Bill Stanley and Ivenue Love-Stanley, a husband-wife team. They had been among the first African Americans to earn degrees in architecture from Georgia Tech, and Ivenue Love-Stanley was the first African American woman to become a

33

licensed architect in the Southeast. Their joint firm, Stanley, Love-Stanley, P.C., was one of the largest African American architectural firms in the South.

The facility was to include an open-air, state-of-the-art swimming pool and diving well, with a roof that sheltered both the pools and the spectator seating. Designing it was not an easy task. Providing 11,000 spectator seats with good sight lines required temporary stands that rose high above the pools, pushing up the roof to seventy feet in height. However, the high, expansive roof provided a unique opportunity. Georgia Power stepped up to provide a $5 million array of solar cells to cover the roof, which generated power for the operational needs of the Olympic Games and for Georgia Tech afterward. While many buildings have rooftop solar arrays today, they were unusual in 1996, and the Aquatic Center array was the largest in the world at the time.

To their credit, ACOG put up the $20 million needed to construct what the Olympics required by way of an aquatic facility. However, Georgia Tech, with an eye toward its future use as an enclosed recreation center, wanted a more substantial foundation than was needed for the open-air Olympic structure. Tech was responsible for the additional $2 million cost, and Pat Crecine drew these funds from an account provided to the president by the Georgia Tech Foundation. The funds were technically under the discretion of the president, but they were normally used for academic purposes. The decision to divert them to the Aquatic Center was not well received and became one more item on the growing list of issues that led to Crecine's downfall. Following the Olympics, the Aquatic Center remained an open-air facility, useable only in the warm weather, until funding could be arranged to convert it to a new purpose.

## THE STUDENT FACTOR

As the impact of Georgia Tech's role in the Olympics began to take shape and grow before their very eyes, students and faculty became increasingly concerned about how Tech would accommodate their needs. After all, the campus was relatively small for a university of its size, and Olympic obligations would impact essentially every building.

Tech students are by and large a patient lot, but many of the undergraduates attended the university on a thin budget and a tight time schedule. Georgia Tech also had a large Cooperative Education Program in which undergraduate students alternated between work experience and on-campus studies. The summer academic term was particularly critical for many of these students to stay on track toward graduation.

Then there were the graduate students and their faculty advisors, who faced the prospect of a prolonged period with no access to their laboratories, not only impeding their educational progress but also putting some ongoing experiments at risk. A related question was how academic buildings with expensive specialized equipment and ongoing experiments were to be protected from the thousands of people with Olympic Village access, some of whom would not be athletes and might have other motives in mind.

The Crecine administration initially decided the easiest solution was the best solution. They called for the summer term of 1996 to be cancelled entirely and told students they would have no access to campus during the Olympics. This news landed like a lead balloon, and both students and faculty objected strenuously. The growing tide of complaints, especially from students, resulted in a compromise: the essential courses for the summer term would be compressed and squeezed into a four-week period between the conclusion of the Olympic Games and the start of the fall academic term. This idea was awkward for the faculty, and it meant classes would take place concurrently with the Paralympics Games, with some non-laboratory courses shifted off campus to Grady High School on the east side of the Midtown neighborhood. However, it addressed the primary need for the undergraduates. Left hanging were the graduate students who needed access to laboratories and computers for their research. Eventually, under pressure from the students, Crecine promised that "no student would have his or her time to graduation affected by the Olympics." This promise was easier said than done.

The problems raised by ongoing research proved more difficult than those posed by academic coursework. Negotiations involved graduate students, faculty, the Crecine administration, and ACOG, and they resulted in an agreement to create a "research zone" on campus to be carved out and isolated from the Olympic Village. The research zone would have its own security entrance, separate from those used for Olympic purposes, and only designated Georgia Tech faculty, staff, and students would be permitted to enter. While this solution satisfied the graduate students and research faculty, it was considered less than desirable by Olympic security officials, who felt it offered another point where a possible security breach could occur.

Lingering issues notwithstanding, in March 1996 sophisticated security fences to guard the village began to go up. Not long afterward, access to campus was gradually limited to secure entrance points. On June 30, 1996, ACOG formally took control of the Olympic Village, and on July 6 the first national teams with their coaches and trainers arrived. ACOG continued to control the entire campus for several days after the Games concluded on August 4, to allow the village occupants to leave and equipment to be removed. Georgia Tech regained control over a portion of it on August 8, with just two days to prepare for the arrival of more than 4,000 students for the compressed summer academic session.

As the summer session began, sections of the campus were cordoned off and secured for the Paralympics, which began on August 16. The Aquatics Center and Alexander Memorial Coliseum were used as Paralympic venues, and the athletes were housed in the new Olympic dorms on the west side of campus. The Paralympic athletes were allowed to mingle with the Georgia Tech students on the rest of the campus, and the Kessler Fountain emerged as a favorite gathering place. Finally, after the Paralympics closed on August 25, we regained full control of the campus.

## DEALING WITH SECURITY ANXIETY

Security during the Olympics was a primary concern, but the palpable sense of fear on campus began well before the Olympic Games. In 1993, a Yale University computer scientist named David Gelernter opened a mailed package that blew up in his face, seriously injuring him. The package had been sent by someone known as the Unabomber, who had a reputation for disliking modern technology. Two more such bombings occurred in 1994 and 1995 before Ted Kaczynski was

36

identified as the Unabomber and arrested in California in April 1996. During this same time frame, members of Congress received letters containing a white powder later identified as anthrax bacteria.

In early 1995, Georgia Tech held campus awareness programs to help employees who handled or opened mail to recognize suspicious packages. While this effort was well intended, it fed a sense of paranoia. Any white powder in a mail delivery generated alarm, and within weeks fire trucks began arriving on a regular basis, their blaring sirens and flashing lights heralding the advent of first responders to investigate what office assistants feared could be anthrax bacteria. It did not take us long to realize that ordinary talcum powder was often used in packaging to prevent products from sticking together. A common use was to keep latex gloves from binding to each other, and almost all of our engineering and science departments used latex gloves in the course of their research. In the run-up to the Olympics, our diligent first responders never discovered anthrax bacteria, but they identified a lot of talcum powder.

Aside from white powder, bomb threats became such a common occurrence that we acquired the services of a bomb-sniffing dog and handler. We also trained faculty and staff to take their brown-bag lunches, briefcases, and backpacks with them when they evacuated a building. If left behind, such objects had to be examined individually, which prolonged the time it took to clear the building and made investigations even more intrusive.

The growing concern about bomb threats reached a climax on Saturday morning, August 5, 1995. Driving across campus, I encountered a police roadblock near the Wenn Student Center. A crowd had gathered, and I asked a man standing at the front what was happening. He said a suspicious package had been found in the student center mailroom, and the Atlanta Police bomb squad was investigating. As we watched, a police truck arrived towing an odd-looking steel tank. I saw a Georgia Tech policeman and spoke with him. He explained that apparently a mailroom employee had found a poorly wrapped package with lots of stamps attached that contained a heavy cylindrical object—the perfect depiction of a mail bomb. Within the next thirty minutes, a policeman in protective armor brought out the suspicious package, placed it in the steel tank, and blew it up.

The next day we learned that the police had blown up a barometer that belonged to faculty in the School of Earth and Atmospheric Sciences. A balloon had lifted the barometer high into the atmosphere to make measurements. Its packaging had included an ample supply of postage stamps and a note asking whoever found it after it fell to the ground to mail it back to Georgia Tech. The finder had done exactly that and mailed the barometer, but it did not survive the explosion. In a later incident, another package found near the Georgia Tech Athletic Department was blown up and then discovered to have contained a set of fencing swords.

We eventually decided it was too disruptive to blow things up and have the fire department come to campus every time a semblance of white powder was found in the mail. So we worked with staff and faculty and gradually managed to strike a balance between panic and a more measured response. We also learned that some of the bomb threats had been pranks by students around finals time. We began to track down the phone numbers of threatening calls and convinced students that such behavior could lead to expulsion. But it was clear that until the Olympics were over, life on campus would not be the same.

## RAINING BULLETS

It was Independence Day, July 4, 1996, just before the Olympic athletes began arriving on campus. By this time, National Guard troops were on duty at the entrance to the President's House, and during the day my wife Anne and I talked with some of them. It was hot and humid, and we learned that ACOG had not provided any bottled water—that was reserved for the 16,000 people using the Olympic Village. So we filled some glasses with ice water for our guardsmen. One of them, Sergeant Thomas Bentley, standing about six foot four, told us he was from Madison, Georgia, and that he was quartered in the Fulton County jail during the Olympics. Sergeant Bentley was not complaining; he was not the type. Rather, he was one of those people you immediately liked.

At 11:30 that night, the phone rang at the President's House. When I picked it up, a man said, "Mr. President, we believe one or more snipers may have positioned themselves in the trees around your house. Turn out the lights and hit the deck. We will be there in two minutes. We will knock three times, hesitate, and then knock two more times. Do not open the door until you hear the password, 'open sesame.'"

Dutifully I relayed this news to my wife Anne to the best of my ability, telling her to get out of bed and lie on the floor. Then I remembered that JV, our dog, was downstairs and decided to creep down the interior stairs and bring him up to the bedroom. Before I could reach him, I heard three knocks on the front door, followed by two knocks. I walked gingerly to the door and said, "Password?" A moment later I was relieved to hear, "Open sesame."

Opening the door, I saw five heavily perspiring men clothed in black garb and body armor and carrying big weapons. I told them the house had three floors, but the leader was mainly interested in the basement. After I explained how to access the basement through the kitchen, he ordered three men to proceed there. A moment later it occurred to me to tell the leader about the second set of stairs to the basement. I led the way down those stairs with the remaining two men behind me, guns at the ready. As we rounded the corner at the bottom of the stairs, the three who had gone down by the kitchen peered around their corner, guns pointed at me. Seeing a laser light on my chest, I surprised myself with the speed of my calm response: "Okay, I'll just take my dog and go back upstairs, and leave the search to you guys."

Not long afterward, as Anne, JV, and I huddled in our upstairs bedroom, we saw beams of light piercing the trees behind the house. We gradually realized they came from a helicopter whose propeller downwash was blowing the treetops. Looking out, we saw the red berets of soldiers who were spreading out among the trees with guns drawn. Next I heard the voice of the leader of the original group of five, calling me to come downstairs. He said they did not find anyone in the house, but that did not mean no one was there. I was not sure if I should feel reassured, but he added that they would remain nearby in case of trouble. After another hour, the soldiers concluded no one was to be found. As they were leaving, they told me what had triggered the search. A National Guardsman standing in our driveway had been shot, and while lying there he had heard bullets coming through the trees.

The next day we learned that the guardsman who had been shot was our friend, Sergeant Bentley. He had been hit in the chest above his bulletproof vest and knocked down. However, the bullet that struck him had fallen from the sky. It had been fired upward from an AK-47 rifle by someone who was celebrating our nation's Independence Day. The other bullets he had heard while lying on the driveway, which he interpreted as being fired by snipers hiding in our trees, had also been falling from celebratory shots.

Sergeant Bentley was rushed to Grady Hospital, where they found the bullet that hit him lodged in his belt. Fortunately, all he sustained was a large bruise. When he returned to duty a few days later, he told us that when the bullet hit, it felt like someone had thrown a brick at him from close range.

We were glad that the mystery was solved and that Sergeant Bentley was going to be fine, but I remained concerned that someone firing a military weapon into the air could rain bullets on our campus. Later I learned that federal Olympic security forces used the bullet patterns found near our house to locate a public housing project from which they had been fired. Based on interviews there, they even found the culprit. There were no more such incidents during the Olympics, and not long thereafter the public housing units were torn down.

### THE NUCLEAR REACTOR:
### A LONG GOODBYE

In 1957, Georgia Tech was authorized to build and operate one of the first nuclear reactors in the South under the regulatory oversight of the Atomic Energy Commission (now the Nuclear Regulatory Commission). Built for the nuclear engineering program with funding from the state of Georgia and a grant from the National Science Foundation, it began operation in 1964. Located in the middle of campus, the reactor's nuclear fuel rods and surrounding cooling system were housed in a distinctive white-domed containment structure whose appearance seemed to proclaim, "Nuclear reactor inside." It was still operational when I arrived in 1994, but its utility had diminished. Reactor technology had moved in a different direction, and growing public opposition had halted the construction of new nuclear power plants.

That the reactor posed a safety issue for the Olympic Village seems obvious today. However, for some reason it did not occur to the Olympic decision makers until after the Georgia Tech campus was designated the Olympic Village and I became president. This situation was not good, and it did not get any better when I was told the fuel rods in the reactor were made of "highly enriched" uranium, sometimes referred to as "weapons-grade." While the reactor was not about to explode anytime soon, I could see the headlines: "Georgia Tech nuclear reactor fueled by weapons-grade uranium endangers lives of two million Olympic visitors."

We began to consider our options to deal with this messy state of affairs. None of them were good. The most decisive choice would have been to decommission the reactor. However, preliminary estimates indicated that this process would cost $20 million to $30 million and take years, neither of which we had. Although decommissioning became my ultimate goal, we had to find another way to deal with the problem in the short term.

Then another unanticipated twist appeared like a skunk at a picnic. I remember the day clearly. Our reactor safety officer asked to meet with me and promptly told me I needed to understand that we were on track to relicense the reactor. After I picked myself up off the floor, I asked, "Why relicense if we are trying to get rid of it?" In an even tone he replied that we had to relicense if we wanted to decommission the reactor. Apparently, in the world of nuclear policy, you could not decommission an unlicensed nuclear reactor.

No sooner had I added the relicensing problem to my you-have-got-to-be-kidding list than I learned that the Nuclear Regulatory Commission required public hearings as part of the relicensing process. Now here was a truly interesting prospect. People were already lining up to ask us to shut the reactor down before the Olympics. In addition, a group known as Georgians Against Nuclear Energy had filed an intervention against relicensing and was threatening legal action against us. The hearing requirement was a catch-22 that would put me in the position of publicly supporting the relicensing of the reactor even as I was working behind the scenes to close it.

I began to feel like a fly caught on sticky paper when we were whipsawed yet again by two factions that emerged publicly to oppose decommissioning the reactor. The first was a group of Georgia Tech nuclear engineering faculty who believed that with proper investment the reactor could be useful in the potential development of nuclear fuel for ships. The second was a heartrending humanitarian cause. In addition to housing a nuclear reactor core, our reactor structure also contained a cobalt-60 source that was used for research on irradiated materials. Cobalt-60 was in the news at the time because recent medical research had shown it was a possible candidate for treating one of the worst forms of brain cancer, glioblastoma. People with the disease and their loved ones began to lobby Georgia Tech to adapt our cobalt-60 source to address this need. I gathered the reactor team to ask about this medical application and discovered they had already considered this possibility. Fortunately for me, the conclusion was that our over-the-hill reactor could not be converted into a place where sophisticated cancer treatments could be performed.

It was apparent that neither argument for continuing to use the reactor in the future was persuasive, but both groups continued to press their case. I did not have much sympathy for the faculty group, but I did for the families of those who had contracted glioblastoma. Nevertheless, we had to inform them that we were unable to do what they wanted. The only olive branch we could offer these families was that the cobalt-60 itself would not be destroyed and could be moved to another location better able to serve their needs.

Independent of the relicensing issue, we still had to deal with the safety, and the perceptions of safety, of the reactor during the Olympic Games. Something had to be done to reduce the threat of a terrorist attack. The easiest approach would have been to remove the fuel rods and store them on-site in a heavy container, but nobody liked that idea. When no other simple alternative seemed acceptable, I came to the conclusion it was time for us to press for outside help. It would have to come from the federal government. After all, the Department of Energy (DOE) through the Atomic Energy Commission had encouraged the development of the reactor in the first place, and they were the only ones who had facilities for storing nuclear materials.

We got a boost from an unexpected and unwelcome source. On October 26, 1995, a clever investigative reporter from a television program called "Current Affairs" climbed a security fence that surrounded part of the reactor site. To make his point that security at the reactor could easily be compromised, he danced around inside the fence while the cameras recorded the scene. Actually, he was not inside the secure zone for the reactor but rather in a laboratory area used by faculty and students. He neglected to mention this fact in his report. As soon as our security people learned what was happening, the reporter and his television crew were escorted off campus, but the deed was done. The segment ran on "Current Affairs" in a national broadcast on November 14. Although the publicity was less than positive, it caught the attention of those who could help us.

On November 17, 1995, we took the only step we could on our own and announced that the reactor operation was being shut down for the Olympics. With the help of GEMA's Gary McConnell and eventually Vice President Al Gore, we convinced the DOE to remove the fuel rods and take them to a nuclear storage facility in South Carolina. We were asked if we wanted the fuel rods back after the Olympics. Our reply: "Probably not."

Finally, on February 20, 1996, I was notified that the DOE had successfully removed the fuel rods and shipped them to South Carolina. However, the problem of what to do with the cobalt-60 source still remained. There was no longer enough time to move it before the Olympics. In mid-June, the DOE helped us place it inside a heavy cask, which was stored inside the reactor shell. As a final security measure, ACOG worked with GEMA to position a number of large trucks loaded with heavy materials around the reactor site to protect against the use of vehicles or car bombs in a terrorist attack.

The contentious relicensing hearings trudged along in the days leading up to the Olympics, but no decision was reached before the Games. We finally received authorization to relicense the reactor in May 1997, and on July 1 we announced the decommissioning of the reactor. This process, and the final demolition of the structures on the site, would take until 2015 to complete.

## THE RUN-UP TO THE OLYMPIC GAMES

In addition to the challenges posed by bomb threats, potential anthrax bacteria in the mail, and the nuclear reactor, we had ongoing debates with ACOG officials over details about logistics, housing, parking, and faculty access during the Olympics. People on both sides were nervous and under stress, given the demanding pace of the work and the large stakes involved. Still, thanks to the good will of key players and hard work by the Georgia Tech team, progress was steady and encouraging.

The first milestone was the dedication of the Aquatic Center on August 1, 1995. While it was only a small part of the Olympic construction on the Georgia Tech campus, this facility was important because it was the first element to be completed. Dignitaries who participated in the dedication included Billy Payne, CEO of ACOG; Bill Campbell, mayor of Atlanta; and Stephen Portch, chancellor of the University System of Georgia. To kick things off, a diver did a back flip off the ten-meter platform. Earlier I had stood on the platform myself, and looking down, I had concluded that platform diving was not in my future.

As these things go, the dedication went well. However, Mayor Campbell caught my attention when he said, "After the Olympics this facility will become a wonderful community pool for Atlanta." It was then that I realized some deal must have been made that I did not know about. I understood the possibility that the pool might occasionally be made available to local swim teams for training during off hours, but there was no way it could serve as a "community pool" for thousands of Atlanta kids and at the same time be part of a campus recreation center. It took several months to clear up this misconception.

The Aquatic Center was also the first new Olympic competition venue to be tested, as we hosted the Pan Pacific Swimming Championships there a few days after the dedication ceremony. My most vivid memory from that occasion was standing by the side of the pool as the synchronized swimming teams from multiple nations walked by. Somehow, I had been under the impression that synchronized swimming was not much of a sport. However, on that day I gained a new appreciation for what it took to compete. I am six foot one, but most of these women were taller than I was and far more muscular. The Pan

Pacific athletes also tried out the new housing complex across North Avenue from campus, a fortunate test that uncovered some construction errors that needed to be corrected.

There were two more dedication events prior to the Olympic Games. The first, on April 23, 1996, was small in the scheme of things. It was the dedication of the Olympic Welcoming Plaza, the location where each of the 197 teams would be welcomed to the Olympic Village. It was raining cats and dogs that day, but it was nice to get another notch in our belt.

The last and most important of the dedications was held on June 30, 1996. My role was to turn over the symbolic key to the campus to ACOG officials as they took control and formally established the Olympic Village. In addition to a large crowd, the dignitaries included Governor Zell Miller, Lieutenant Governor Pierre Howard, Mayor Bill Campbell, and, on behalf of ACOG, CEO Billy Payne, COO A. D. Frazier, and Russ Chandler, who had been named mayor of the Olympic Village.

The day was so unbearably hot that two people standing in the sun passed out. It reminded all of us that the summer daytime temperature in Atlanta was usually considerably higher than the average of seventy-five degrees Fahrenheit Payne had quoted to the Olympic site selection committee.

After the dignitaries and I made remarks, Billy Payne gave me an Olympic torch. Normally people earned one by running a leg in the Olympic torch relay. Although I had not participated in the relay, I had paid my dues more than a few times over in helping Georgia Tech complete its preparations for the Olympics. All in all, it was a nice touch and I very much appreciated it—especially since a member of the Georgia Tech mechanical engineering faculty, Sam Shelton, had designed the internal mechanism of the torch.

As the ceremony concluded, I had an odd, wistful feeling. I had just turned over control of my campus, one I had worked so hard for two years to improve, to a group of people who knew little to nothing about it.

Once ACOG had control of the campus, their security forces began to close it to outside access, other than for those whose credentials allowed them to pass through one of two heavily guarded gates. The security system used fingerprints as the means of identification, and Anne and I had gotten our credentials on March 29.

With the closure of the campus, I was now largely cut off from the ACOG officials who would run the Olympic Village. It felt awkward and worrisome. If there was a degree of satisfaction to be had at this stage, it came from having delivered on our promise to complete $230 million worth of new construction and renovations. I was grateful to Bill Ray, Bill Miller, and my executive team for all the work they had done to bring our preparations to reality.

## THE OLYMPIC GAMES

Olympic teams, especially those from smaller nations, began arriving at the Olympic Village on July 6, nearly two weeks before the Games began on July 19. The early arrivals were in part due to a desire to let the teams acclimate to the village and the Olympic venues but also because of the liberal amenities offered in the village itself. Olympic athletes were provided with free dental and medical care, all the food they could eat, and recreational opportunities, including the latest in computer-based video games. Many of the young men and women from smaller nations had never had access to dental care, and the lines to see the dentists were long. As for food, the athletes burned lot of calories in training, and when I dropped by the food tent it was not uncommon to see a young man walk by with one plate holding five steaks and another holding mounds of potatoes.

There was no question that the athletes and their trainers also enjoyed the video games, recreational swimming pool, and musical performances that were provided, but I discovered that not everyone else agreed. Security had banned vehicle access to the Olympic Village, so I often walked across campus from the President's House on the northern edge to my office on the southern edge. It was good exercise, but the weather was hot and humid and I wore a coat and tie to the office. It was a little galling when ACOG employees zoomed by me in golf carts, never offering a lift. One day a dignified man wearing clothes from an African country joined me in my walk. We talked about the Olympics and the village, and I asked him his impression. He said he was a coach for runners and was disturbed by all the distractions in the village. As he put it, "My runners are losing all of their discipline." As we parted, I thanked him for our conversation and asked who he was. He said he was Kip Keino from Kenya and was glad to have met me. Little did I know I had been walking alongside a distance-running legend and two-time Olympic gold medalist.

## OPENING DAY, JULY 19

Not only was July 19 the opening day of the Olympics, but President Clinton, First Lady Hillary Clinton, and their daughter Chelsea were coming to campus to see the Olympic Village. For some reason that to this day I do not understand, ACOG officials decided that no one from Georgia Tech, not even me, would be invited to participate in this visit—not even when the President and First Lady made their formal presentations in the theater of our Ferst Center for the Arts. I was incensed, especially for the employees of Georgia Tech who had worked so hard to get to this point.

Because I had met President Clinton before, my staff made calls to the protocol office of the President. The protocol office told us President Clinton would consider it an insult not to be able to pay his respects to the president of Georgia Tech when he was on the campus. Further, we were told the President wanted to acknowledge the role of Georgia Tech in the Olympics in his remarks at the Ferst Center. Although ACOG officials attempted to bypass his wishes, Clinton's staff intervened to ensure that I would be seated in the front row for the ceremony. The final coup occurred when we received a desperate call from ACOG only an hour or so before the ceremony. They asked if we could find some Georgia Tech staff to help fill the theater for what would otherwise be a sparsely attended ceremony. In the end, the theater was filled to capacity with Georgia Tech staff, along with the Georgia Tech president, who all cheered raucously when First Lady Hillary Clinton and then President Bill Clinton acknowledged the contribution of Georgia Tech to the Olympics. Afterward, the Clintons invited me back to the "green room" of the Ferst Center for a personal meet and greet. I still treasure the photograph I have of me with President and First Lady Clinton and their daughter Chelsea. I remember clearly talking Georgia Tech football with President Clinton, who told me he thought we were going to have a good year. (We had five wins and six losses.)

That night, the opening ceremonies were held at the Centennial Olympic Stadium, the site for the track and field events. Anne and I attended and were impressed as teams from nation after nation walked by to the music of "Summon the Heroes," composed by John Williams. The most moving part of the ceremony was the lighting of the Olympic torch by the great boxer Muhammad Ali, whose hands shook as he lit the torch because he was suffering from Parkinson's disease.

## THE CENTENNIAL OLYMPIC PARK BOMBING

The next few days went by in a blur as Anne and I hosted visitors in the President's House and attended events on behalf of Georgia Tech and the Olympics. Finally, on July 27 we had only one event on the schedule for the day—to attend the China-USA basketball game to be held in the evening at the Georgia Dome near Centennial Olympic Park. Late in the day we welcomed our son Matthew and his friend, Andy Kaufman, who came to stay with us for a few days and take in some Olympic events.

The basketball game proved to be a bit of a yawner as the USA team, which featured Shaquille O'Neal, John Stockton, Karl Malone, Scottie Pippen, and Charles Barkley, defeated the Chinese team in a rout. As Anne and I left, a band was preparing for a late-night concert in the park. We arrived home about midnight. At 1:30 a.m., while the band was still performing, a bomb exploded, killing one person and injuring 111 others.

The next morning, as I was having my second cup of coffee on the back deck of the President's House, I was surprised to see soldiers in red berets with guns appear and begin combing through the shrubs. It seemed time to ask a nearby lieutenant what was going on. He replied that they believed a bomb had been placed on our property by a "Caucasian and a Black Cuban" who reportedly had been seen leaving our property that morning. Although that report sounded alarming, it struck me as odd. I told him my son and his friend had left not long ago on their way to see several Olympic events. The officer asked me if

48

they had a backpack. At the time I did not know that the Olympic bomber had used a backpack to carry the bomb, but I explained that my wife had made peanut butter and jelly sandwiches for Matt and Andy and packed them in a backpack. Still, I could see the officer felt he might be on to something. So I went on to say that it was just possible the "Caucasian and Black Cuban" could have been my son and his friend, who had a dark beard and a deep tan from his work as a construction supervisor. After an hour or so, the lieutenant came back and reported that they had not found a backpack on the property and had concluded it was a false alarm.

It would take seven years before the actual Centennial Park bomber, Eric Rudolph, was captured hiding out in the mountains of North Carolina. The legend of the "Caucasian and Black Cuban," however, lives on whenever our family gets together and shares memories of the Olympics.

By the time of the closing ceremonies, we were exhausted and glad to see the Games end. Atlanta and ACOG had taken their share of criticism about over-commercialization and transportation glitches, and as a result of a general predisposition that Southerners lacked sophistication. Juan Antonio Samaranch, who always before had praised Olympic host cities for the "best ever Games," could only summon up "most exceptional Games" for Atlanta. Everyone seemed too tired to debate the issue, and we had work to do to prepare for the 4,000 students who would shortly arrive for the summer academic session.

## IN RETROSPECT

The Centennial Olympic Games were an experience of highs and lows. Looking back almost twenty-five years later, the highs are the most memorable. In the track and field competition two Georgia Tech students, Derrick Adkins and Derek Mills, were standouts. Adkins ran the 400-meter hurdles and Mills was a member of the 400-meter relay team. Both brought home gold medals and were perfect ambassadors for the university. Having the mathematical bent of an engineer, I enjoyed pointing out that if Georgia Tech had entered in the Games as a country, we would have been tied with Ireland and Sweden for twenty-eighth place in the gold medal count, ahead of 168 other countries, including Great Britain.

Then there was my administrative team, a group that fulfilled all of our commitments on time and on budget in the face of adversity and challenges. And, although we had had our differences with ACOG, A. D. Frazier made good on his promise to see to it that Georgia Tech was made whole after the Olympics. This task included repairing damage to our new residence halls caused by some of the teams and replacing trees that had been cut down for security reasons.

The principal legacy of the Olympics for Georgia Tech was clearly the seven new residence halls. These, plus those obtained later from Georgia State University, provided an opportunity to create learning communities. We concentrated the freshmen in one area and provided specialized support services for students who were at risk of losing their way in the transition to college. Language houses helped prepare students to study abroad; honors students were grouped for in-house study programs; and localized food services and fitness facilities helped create the feel of a neighborhood. The impact was long lasting.

Not to be overlooked was the decision by the City of Atlanta to demolish Techwood Homes and Clark Howell Homes just to the south of our campus. These public housing projects, built in 1935 and 1940 respectively, had provided shelter and homes for citizens of Atlanta and Georgia Tech students at a time when it was much needed. However, over time both housing projects had deteriorated and become places where poverty and crime festered. A grant from the U.S. Department of Housing and Urban Development just prior to the Olympics replaced Techwood Homes with Centennial Place, an attractive new neighborhood designed to serve an economic mix that included both low-income and market-based housing. Clark Howell was similarly replaced soon after the Olympics.

Last but not least among the highs was Centennial Place Elementary School, a math-science magnet school created by the Atlanta Public Schools to serve the children of Centennial Place and nearby neighborhoods. More than 80 percent of the students were African American, and a high percentage came from low-income families. I was pleased to sign Georgia Tech on as a partner, providing Tech student volunteers who not only helped pupils learn but also maintained the school's digital systems and updated software for the faculty.

Centennial Place Elementary School became one of the highest-performing schools in the Atlanta Public Schools system. In 2001, I was honored to be the speaker for the graduation of the first class of students to have attended Centennial Place School for all of their elementary grades. Watching those children walk down the aisle to receive diplomas under the admiring gaze of their parents was a special moment. For me, it represented hope for the future and the best of the spirit of the Olympic legacy.

## REFERENCES

Clough, G. Wayne. "Georgia Tech's Olympic Legacy." *Georgia Tech Alumni Magazine* 73, no. 1 (Spring 1997): 96–101.

Fralick, Melissa. "Our Olympic Legacy." *Georgia Tech Alumni Magazine* 92, no. 2 (Summer 2016): 100–105.

French, Steven P., and Mike E. Disher. "Atlanta and the Olympics: A One Year Retrospective." *Journal of the American Planning Association* 63, no. 3 (1997): 379–92.

Hertel, Nolan E. "History of the Georgia Tech Research Reactor." Presented at the Nuclear Engineering 50th Anniversary Celebration: Colloquium on History and Contributions of Nuclear Engineering at Georgia Tech, November 2, 2012.

Myerson, Allen. "Marathon Man of the Atlanta Games." *The New York Times*, February 25, 1996.

Sachs, Kevin. "Bombing at the Olympics: The Overview; Olympic Park Blast Kills one, Hurts 111, Atlanta Games Go On." *The New York Times*, July 28, 1996.

Weisman, Robert. "Atlanta Selected Over Athens for 1996 Olympics." *The New York Times*, September 19, 1990.

*Chapter Four*

# BIOTECHNOLOGY AND BIOSCIENCE

The twenty-first century is said to be the "Age of Biology," supplanting the "Age of Chemistry" of the twentieth century. Many date the beginning of the Age of Biology to 1953, when James Watson and Francis Crick published their findings on the double-helix structure and the function of deoxyribonucleic acid (DNA). Developments soon took off, with the development of DNA sequencing, genomics, and protein sequencing in the 1970s and 1980s. The term came into the broader public lexicon in 1990, when a plan to sequence the DNA of humans was announced. It became known as the Human Genome Project.

The year 1990 was also when I became the dean of the College of Engineering at Virginia Tech. One of my first undertakings was to meet young faculty who were working in areas that were at the cutting edge. A faculty member in chemical engineering caught my attention when he said his research was in the emerging field of cell and molecular biology. A chemical engineer working on problems in biology seemed odd to me. Even more unusual, his research collaborators were a group of young faculty in the College of Veterinary Medicine. They explained how their combined efforts were expected to lead to new cures for diseases by reaching into cells and changing the way genes responded to their environment. While the topic was fascinating, what stayed with me was the broader idea that engineering had a role to play in what heretofore had been largely a scientific enterprise.

I invested in the work of those faculty, and it paid off, not only in the form of new developments of great promise but also in drawing attention to the College of Engineering. The experience convinced me that cell and molecular biology offered remarkable possibilities for engineering, and, more importantly, for humankind.

Upon becoming provost and vice president for academic affairs at the University of Washington (UW) in 1993, I found myself in the middle of a growing movement in biotechnology and biosciences that combined the School of Medicine, the School of Engineering, and a group of related science departments. Not unrelated was the emergence of Microsoft, whose founders, Bill Gates and Paul Allen, made early large gifts to this new field.

One of the gifts by Gates in 1992 had allowed the UW to recruit Leroy Hood from the California Institute of Technology to create the Department of Molecular Biology. Hood, a pioneer in using technology to advance molecular science, went on to win the National Medal of Science, and he became one of the few people to be named a member of all three national academies—medicine, engineering, and sciences. Soon after I arrived on campus, I made it a point to meet him. Hood explained his vision for cellular and molecular biology at the UW and its potential for the world. After that, I spent time with him as often as possible to deepen my understanding about where this new field was going. It struck me as a revolution waiting to happen.

Not long after I met Hood, the UW College of Engineering, seeking to capitalize on this new initiative, asked me to support a large proposal to be submitted to the Whitaker Foundation to create a biomedical engineering program. I offered to help. The Whitaker Foundation was created by Uncas A. Whitaker, a highly successful engineer who had bequeathed a portion of his fortune to encouraging the development of biomedical engineering programs. The UW seemed to be a strong contender, given the well-established ties between its engineering and medical schools, but when the three winners were announced, the UW was not one of them. The surprise on the list was the Georgia Institute of Technology, a newcomer with a proposal to create a PhD program in bioengineering in collaboration with the Emory University

School of Medicine. That caught my attention.

## LEARNING THE LAY OF THE LAND
## AT GEORGIA TECH

One of the first things I did upon arrival as president of Georgia Tech was ask who was leading the biotechnology effort. The name Robert Nerem popped up immediately. He was a member of both the National Academy of Engineering and the Institute of Medicine (now the Health and Medicine Division of the National Academies of Sciences, Engineering, and Medicine). He had been lured to Georgia Tech to fill an endowed faculty position funded by a Georgia Tech alumnus named Parker H. "Pete" Petit. I knew then that it was important to get to know Nerem and Petit, and to understand the nature of the relationship between Georgia Tech and Emory University.

The connection between the two universities dated back to 1987, when the Emory/Georgia Tech Biomedical Technology Research Center was created. Mutual research interests and complementary expertise had led the two presidents to provide a joint seed fund to enable faculty from both institutions to work together in early-stage research in biomedicine and biotechnology. Bill Todd, assistant vice president for health affairs at Emory, and Don Giddens, a leading biomedical engineering researcher at Georgia Tech, developed the agreement creating the center. Once the center was up and running, it did not take long for the funding to boost collaborative research between faculty from the two universities. The crowning achievement was the Whitaker Grant in 1993.

By the time I arrived at Georgia Tech in 1994, both Todd and Giddens had moved on to other jobs. Todd had become the founding president of the Georgia Research Alliance, a public-private partnership created by Governor Zell Miller to grow the research capabilities of Georgia's research universities in targeted fields. Giddens had gone to Johns Hopkins University as dean of the Whiting School of Engineering. However, as fate would have it, both of them would play influential roles in the future plans for bioengineering and biosciences at Georgia Tech.

Early meetings with Nerem and the Georgia Tech principals who were working in biotechnology reinforced my belief that we had the requisite parts to build a program that was competitive at the national level. The partnership with the Emory School of Medicine was unique and would offer a strategic advantage. However, while Georgia Tech had undisputed power in engineering, we lacked bench strength in biosciences and in the emerging field of computational biology.

For decades, Georgia Tech's biology program had been a stepchild whose main function was viewed as teaching engineers what they needed to know about biology. The 1995 National Research Council rankings of PhD programs placed Georgia Tech 112th among 113 programs in molecular biology. In cell and developmental biology, we ranked 176th out of 179 programs. These rankings were actually optimistic, given that our general PhD program in biology was barely up and running and we did not offer PhD degrees in these specific fields, but they showed how far we had to go. Becoming nationally competitive was more than just a goal for our biology efforts in themselves. It was a necessity if we were to succeed in the long run in interdisciplinary fields like biotechnology and biosciences.

As for computing, although it was another of Georgia Tech's strengths, there was little interest in computational biology at this point. Yet it was clear to me that computational biology, or bioinformatics, was a field of great promise, particularly as new developments pushed biosciences and biotechnology toward greater use of massive databases and computer modeling. It was one place where we could begin a stealth march on the competition, if we could just harness our computing expertise in the service of biotechnology.

Developing expertise in biosciences and bioengineering would require money. We would need to hire new faculty and provide resources to support their research. Where these funds would come from was not clear at the time, but the opportunity was too great to miss. I believed we could make it happen if our investments in our larger goals for biotechnology were structured in a way that brought biosciences and bioinformatics along.

## FEELING OUR WAY ALONG

On a university campus, any "great leap forward" usually begins with a discussion of program space, and that held true for biotechnology at Georgia Tech. In fall 1994, shortly after I arrived on campus, Bob Nerem and his leadership team presented a proposal to me to create new space for their program by renovating an area in the existing building of the School of Mechanical Engineering. The project had an $8 million price tag. Although it was not obvious where we might get the money, the cost did not strike me as the real problem. More important were two other concerns. First, the proposed space was in one of the oldest buildings on campus, which was not suited for high-end biotechnology work. Second, if this program had as much potential as I thought it did, it would need much more space than requested in the proposal.

I asked Nerem and his team to come back with a more aggressive plan. Several weeks later they returned with a proposal to build an $11 million addition to the Mechanical Engineering Building. Although this idea still left much to be desired, it seemed the only option we had at the time. We agreed to work together to raise the money from private sources. Fundraising for this project moved slowly, which actually turned out to be fortuitous.

## THE GAME CHANGER

The next ten months proved to be critical in building institutional capacity for Georgia Tech. The first breakthrough came when we resolved the contention that Georgia Tech had overcharged the federal government for indirect costs on research grants during the Crecine administration. Thanks to Senior Vice President for Administration and Finance Bob Thompson and his team, who renegotiated our indirect cost recovery rate, we were no longer burdened with the prospect of a long-term payback to the federal government. We now had an important source of future funding to grow our research enterprise, particularly our facilities. Deep in federal policy was a provision that allowed funding from indirect cost recovery to be used for construction of and improvements to research-related buildings and facilities.

Indirect costs were recovered on an annual basis, and one year's income was not enough to fund a major capital project. However, this revenue stream could be used to pay back bonds borrowed for such projects. Thompson was well aware of this tool from his experience at the University of Washington.

That Georgia Tech had not tapped into this resource meant we had bond-payment capacity lying fallow. Further, if we managed to grow our federally funded research programs, our capacity to pay for research facilities using this approach would increase commensurately. Our plans to expand our research portfolio and facilities in biotechnology and biosciences seemed a perfect fit.

At the same time that we were contemplating space needs for biotechnology and biosciences, the early work on our campus master plan was beginning to identify potential sites for the construction of new buildings. The most promising area for development was on the north side of campus, and it offered enough land for an entire quadrangle of potential new buildings. The only thing standing in the way on the site was the old Highway Materials Building—the very place where I had taken courses as a student.

This building had long ago outlived its purpose, and the pesky roof leak that had plagued its occupants in my student days still persisted. Removing it would be a pleasure. The only obstacle was finding replacement space for the civil and environmental engineering laboratories that were housed there. Fortunately, we were acquiring additional land on the west side of our campus at the same time. We offered to develop a state-of-the-art structures laboratory for the School of Civil and Environmental Engineering there, and they were pleased to accept.

Now the game had changed. Instead of thinking about housing the bioengineering and bioscience program in a small building addition squeezed into the historic area of campus, we could consider constructing an entirely new building. And it would be on a site that could accommodate several more future buildings for related programs in science and engineering.

Equally exciting was the pioneering vision that Nerem and his colleagues were developing for their new building. It would not only be Georgia Tech's most advanced building for bioengineering and bioscience research, but would also house a mix of engineering and science faculty to encourage innovative interdisciplinary research. This colocation of disciplines, a remarkable idea in its own right, also offered an opportunity to jump-start the process of upgrading our bioscience program. The building would house what appropriately became known as the Institute for Bioengineering and Bioscience (IBB).

## MAKING THE SALE

To sell the plan, I needed a firm estimate of the cost of the biotechnology building and an equally firm schedule showing we could pay back the bonds we would borrow. The preliminary design produced a cost estimate of $50 million, which was a large investment for Georgia Tech at the time. The risk potential was further elevated by the fact that it would serve an emerging program still in its early days.

Bob Thompson and his team set about ensuring that indirect cost recovery would provide the capacity to pay back the bonds required to build a $50 million building. Once he had confirmed that we were on sound financial footing, he found a willing agency, our own Fulton County, to issue us the $50 million in bonds. We now had in hand the preliminary design, the cost estimate, a source for the bonds, and a plan to pay for the building. It was time to sell the project.

I believed the new plan had the right attributes, but I would need to convince key Georgia Tech advisory boards as well as Chancellor Stephen Portch of the University of System of Georgia and his governing body, the Board of Regents. The place to begin was with the Georgia Tech boards, since their support was necessary before approaching the Board of Regents.

I was convinced that this building would be an easy sell, so I was surprised when more than a few influential Tech alumni expressed reservations. Perhaps I should have expected it. Many were still shell-shocked by the highly public demise of the Crecine administration and believed we needed a period of calm before undertaking any new big ideas, particularly with the Olympics approaching. Others were not well acquainted with biotechnology and did not appreciate either the long-term potential of the field or Georgia Tech's ability to become a major player. Finally, some were concerned about borrowing $50 million based on a payback scheme that was untested at Georgia Tech.

As was often the case when I was struggling to get buy-in for a new initiative, someone who understood the importance of what was at stake stepped forward. In this case it was alumnus Pete Petit who had earlier funded Bob Nerem's endowed chair. After hearing about the project and talking to Bob Nerem, he informed me in April 1996 that he wanted to donate $5 million in support of the new building. His gift was important not only for its financial impact but also because of its endorsement of our plan. At the time, Petit, who was widely admired for his business acumen, was one of the few Georgia Tech alumni who had built a career in biotechnology. His support helped persuade the doubters that this investment would create new opportunities for Georgia Tech.

My executive team and I were elated by the news of the Petit gift. However, because Bob Thompson had already convinced me that indirect cost recovery funds would cover the bond payments for the building, I suggested that Petit consider a different purpose for its use. With his agreement, his gift became the first permanent endowment to support the programs of the Institute for Bioengineering and Bioscience. A subsequent gift led to the naming of the building for Petit.

With Georgia Tech support falling into place, we were ready to take the biotechnology building idea to Chancellor Portch and the Board of Regents. My request to them involved no state funding; we simply needed their permission to take on the risk. The chancellor and the regents gave a tentative go-ahead, contingent on our keeping them informed of progress and any changes in plans.

Having no state funding in the project had a hidden benefit. We could manage the construction of the building ourselves rather than having to turn over control of the project to a state agency. This capability made it possible to use what was then a new approach called "design-build," in which the design and construction processes were linked. In my previous career as a civil engineer, I had used this method to speed up project completion. Having in-house control and using design-build meant we could complete construction as much as a year faster, perhaps even more, than if we had been forced to take a conventional approach on the state's timetable.

Oddly, the amount of time it takes to build a facility is often not seen as important at universities. However, I knew that every year we could gain by advancing a building project meant a year in which we could become more competitive in research and in hiring new faculty. If we could extend this impact across multiple building projects, it would compound the effect. Finally, advancing the time to completion also meant reducing the chances of getting caught in a building materials inflation cycle that could cause a project to be downsized midstream.

It would take several more years until the new site could be prepared and the biotechnology building built. But the die was cast, and there would be no looking back.

## WHY ESCALATOR CONVERSATIONS
## CAN BE IMPORTANT

As an engineer/scientist, I always believed you made your own fate by hard work and a willingness to take calculated risks. But as I grew older and looked back over my life, I was surprised by the number of events that had seemed at the time to be coincidences. In Taoism, Lieh-Tzu put it this way: "How we explain coincidences depends on how we see the world. Is everything connected, so that events create resonances like ripples across a net? Or do things merely co-occur and we give meaning to those co-occurrences based on our belief system? It is all in how you think."

One of those "co-occurrences" happened in 1996, when an escalator at the Hartsfield-Jackson Atlanta International Airport brought two men together as they returned from a conference in Washington, D.C. The men in question were Georgia Tech's Bob Nerem and Mike Johns, who had recently become executive vice president of health services at Emory University. Before joining Emory, Johns had been dean of the Johns Hopkins University School of Medicine, which had close ties to the university's Department of Biomedical Engineering. This department, ranked number one in the nation, reported to the dean of the Whiting School of Engineering, the aforementioned Don Giddens.

We had already come to know and appreciate Mike Johns, as he was an early supporter of the new Institute for Bioengineering and Bioscience. However, it was his impromptu meeting with Nerem on an escalator that lit the fuse for taking the collaboration between Emory and Georgia Tech to an entirely different level. Johns remembered the conversation this way: "As we were coming up the escalators I said, 'Hey Bob, I really think Emory and Georgia Tech need to come together and form a biomedical engineering department. We don't have an engineering school and you guys don't have a medical school. This is something we can do together.'" When news of this idea arrived in my office, I pinched myself to make sure I was not dreaming. The notion that a public university could partner with a private university to create a jointly funded and administered academic department was almost outlandish. But Johns had perfectly captured the strengths the two institutions would bring to the table.

With the Olympics bearing down on us, it would take time to bring an idea birthed on an escalator into focus. Boards of governance, faculty, and advisory boards on both campuses would need to be brought into the discussion to ensure there were no roadblocks, but the concept had my full support.

Although I complained that the Olympics took an inordinate amount of my time, I had to give them credit for creating an opportunity to approach Don Giddens about his future. His son Eric, a Georgia Tech graduate, and Eric's wife Rebecca were both world-class kayakers. Eric had made the U.S. Olympic team for the Atlanta games, and Giddens came to Atlanta to see him compete. Tech Provost Mike Thomas, a longtime friend of Giddens, met with him to explore his interest in returning to Georgia Tech to lead the effort to create a new biomedical engineering department. Thomas returned with good news. Giddens was interested.

## BUILDING THE ACADEMIC FOUNDATION FOR THE EMORY/GEORGIA TECH PARTNERSHIP

While Georgia Tech and Emory University had worked closely in developing the Emory/Georgia Tech Biomedical Research Center, no joint academic degree programs existed when I arrived on campus. This deficiency was corrected in 1995, when Georgia Tech was formally added to the Emory MD/PhD program through a biomedical engineering component. Students in this program would earn an MD at Emory and a PhD in bioengineering at Georgia Tech.

In the months after the Olympics, we followed up on the escalator meeting between Nerem and Johns and on the Olympics meeting between Thomas and Giddens. With assurances from both Georgia Tech and Emory University that we were serious about creating a joint department of biomedical engineering, Giddens returned to Georgia Tech in 1997. One of his first assignments was to chair a committee established by Thomas and Tom Lawley, dean of the Emory School of Medicine, to create a plan for the new department that was acceptable to both universities. Everyone agreed that the plan they developed met the governance needs of both universities and offered both of them an exciting opportunity. The new department was formally established in late 1997 with Giddens as its head. He reported jointly to the dean of the Emory School of Medicine and the dean of the College of Engineering at Georgia Tech. Giddens immediately set about hiring new faculty, and for the time being they were to be housed in the new building for the Institute of Biotechnology and Bioscience.

Arranging parking for faculty on the campuses of the respective institutions proved to be more elusive. It took more than a decade to resolve this matter, proving the old adage that parking is the among the most important of all campus issues.

To complete the birthing process for the new department, Georgia Tech added doctoral, master's, and bachelor's degrees in biomedical engineering. No sooner had the degree programs been created than students came in droves. We were hard pressed to add faculty fast enough to meet the demand.

The very idea of a joint biomedical engineering department and degree program between a public and a private university attracted national attention. Its innovative appeal and the substance behind it led to immediate recognition in the rankings. We leapfrogged established programs in the *U.S. News and World Report* rankings to land at number two, just behind Johns Hopkins—and ahead of Duke University, a program that was in business even before I had worked there as a young assistant professor in the late 1960s.

## THE PETIT BIOTECHNOLOGY BUILDING

By 1997, we were well into final design for the building to house the Institute for Bioengineering and Bioscience. It would be one of the most sophisticated ever built at Georgia Tech, with sixty fume hoods and the capacity to add sixty more as needed. Faculty offices would surround the laboratories, which would be visible through large glass windows. In accordance with the IBB concept, the offices would house science and engineering faculty side by side.

However, before construction could begin on the new building, we had to demolish the old Highway Materials Building. This building had resisted removal for years, and it had one more trick up its sleeve: it was filled with asbestos. On hearing this news, I thought back to my days as a master's degree student, working in a little cubbyhole office up on the graduate student mezzanine of the building. When I arrived each day, I had to clean little bits of gray fluffy material off my desk. I now knew it was asbestos that had floated down from the ceiling. Our safety people assured me that I would have needed many more years of exposure to be at any risk, but it did make me wonder.

Because removing the Highway Materials Building would represent the start of something big, we decided to declare a Demolition Day. I was just one of many Georgia Tech alumni who had studied and worked in this old building, and everyone who showed up on Demolition Day got to whack the building with a sledgehammer. On my swing, I punched a hole in the siding, but the building did not budge.

A few of us were given mementos of the day. Mine was an old surveying instrument that had been found stored away in the building and had not been used for years. The crew had mounted it on a finished wood base that gave it an elegant touch. I still have that surveying instrument and enjoy the memories that return when I look at it.

Using design-build, construction of the Petit Biotechnology Building proceeded apace, and it was dedicated in 1999. A highlight was the unveiling of "The Cell Wall," a beautiful mural in the atrium created by Karen Ku, an accomplished artist and wife of one of the IBB faculty, David Ku. The ceremony represented not only the completion of the building but also the beginning of a new era at Georgia Tech.

## SUCCESS BUILDS ON SUCCESS

Now we had two overlapping groups out of the gate: those conducting biotechnology research in the Institute for Bioengineering and Bioscience and those developing the new Department of Biomedical Engineering. You could sense the pace picking up.

In 1997, even before they occupied their new building, faculty were hard at work on securing a grant from the National Science Foundation for an engineering research center (ERC). Any competition to win an ERC always attracted the best universities. To succeed you needed a great idea, industry collaboration, university commitment to long-term goals, matching funds, and the involvement of stellar faculty. The IBB bid was focused on the engineering of living tissue, an effort led by Bob Nerem and his team with collaborating faculty at Emory. It was a long shot, but we had an innovative idea, strong faculty, a unique partnership with Emory, and the prospect of a new building whose design could be tweaked to support the grant if necessary. Still, we would be going up against well-established competition backed by old money.

It was pleasant surprise when notification came that we were among the finalists and warranted a site visit. We hosted the visiting committee in 1998, just as the new biotechnology building was being outfitted. Joining us to meet the NSF panel of experts was Georgia Tech alumnus Bill Todd, president of the Georgia Research Alliance, a public-private partnership to support the state's research universities in targeted fields, including biotechnology. We knew the panel would press us on our commitments, especially our ability to meet the requirements of cost sharing, which would be considerable for such a large grant. When the panel raised the issue, Bill Todd stepped up and said, "If you will, I will." The room was silent for a moment, and then the head of the visiting committee said, "You mean if we make a multi-million-dollar grant, you will see to it that Georgia Tech and Emory can meet the matching requirements?" Todd said, "Yes."

There are moments in life when you instinctively know something significant has just happened. That was one of them. I could see in the eyes of the visiting committee that they knew it too. Within months we would learn that the National Science Foundation had awarded a $12.5 million grant to the Institute for Bioengineering and Bioscience at Georgia Tech, working in partnership with Emory. The ERC would be named the National Engineering Research Center for the Engineering of Living Tissues. With the recognition this grant brought, our biotechnology efforts swiftly moved from minor league to national player status.

For a number of years I had the privilege of serving on the National Science Board, the governing body for the National Science Foundation. In the foyer just outside the board room, the foundation highlighted innovative projects they had funded. I took delight in pointing out to my fellow board members the poster about the Georgia Tech-Emory National Engineering Research Center in the Engineering of Living Tissues.

## THE COULTER PARTNERSHIP:
### A DIFFERENCE MAKER

Georgia Tech had not been in the game long enough to have many alumni who were invested in the biomedical world, but there was one who had succeeded in biomedical engineering before hardly anyone used the term. Oddly enough, we did not even know him, although we should have.

By 1998, Georgia Tech's first comprehensive capital fundraising campaign was gaining traction. Campaign-related research had identified an alumnus named Wallace H. Coulter, who had created a very successful biomedical instrument company. He had recently sold it to Beckman Instruments and left the company. Oddly, we had never contacted him before. We also had no line item for biomedical engineering in our campaign plan because the program did not yet exist when the plan was completed in 1996. However, we had hired an experienced fundraiser, Marta Garcia, to help with prospects for engineering gifts, and we encouraged her to reach out to him.

Not long after Garcia became aware of Coulter, she attended a meeting with key alumni to identify prospective donors. There Michael Tennenbaum, a good friend with a big Rolodex, gave her the contact information for Sue Van. Van had been the CFO for the Coulter

Corporation and was one of Coulter's closest and most trusted associates. Getting to know Wallace Coulter and Sue Van would turn out to be singularly important and lead to a valued lifelong friendship.

Wallace Coulter was a native of Arkansas who had entered Georgia Tech to study electrical engineering in the depths of the Great Depression. After two years at Tech, he ran out of money and left in 1934 before earning his degree. He found a job with GE X-Ray, which changed his life dramatically. He was sent to work in the Far East, spending time in the Philippines, Singapore, and China. In Shanghai he fell in love with all things Chinese, especially history and art, and began what eventually became a world-class collection of jade art.

The start of World War II forced him to return to the United States, and after the war he worked in electronics in Chicago. He had enjoyed tinkering since boyhood, so he set up a lab in the basement of his home. He was soon on the path to becoming one of the most prominent biomedical instrument inventors in the world.

Coulter was not just an inventor but also a humanitarian motivated by a desire to reduce the costs of healthcare and help cure diseases that others neglected. His humanitarian concerns took precedence over making a profit. Over time he acquired eighty-five patents, the most impactful of them for the Coulter Counter. This device had many applications, but it became a standard tool in hospitals to count and size red blood cells rapidly, a task previously done manually. It was so revolutionary it became the gold standard for what is known as a "complete blood count"—a common part of today's medical evaluation of our health.

I had learned about the Coulter Counter as a master's degree student at Georgia Tech because I had used it to measure soil particle counts in fluids. Little did I know that one day I would come to know Wallace Coulter. At the time, I had marveled at the device he had invented for its simplicity, accuracy, and eye-appealing aesthetics. I like to think that Wallace Coulter preceded Steve Jobs in understanding how such elements could come together to make a great design.

Sue Van is a story unto herself. She is an immigrant from China whose family threaded the difficult transition from a country devastated by World War II to a new life in the United States. Nothing proved easy in their new country. The family had little money, and discrimination reared its ugly head. However, her parents and family persevered, and Van earned her BS and MS degrees at universities in the Washington, D.C., area. She joined the Coulter Corporation in 1975 and never looked back, becoming Wallace Coulter's key partner in running the company.

The Coulter Corporation was so important to Beckman Instruments that soon after Beckman bought it in 1997, the company changed its name to Beckman Coulter Diagnostics. After the sale, Wallace Coulter set aside $100 million from the proceeds to be distributed to his employees based on years of service. A substantial portion of the remainder was used to establish the Coulter Foundation, with Sue Van serving as president. One of the primary purposes of the Coulter Foundation was to support biomedical engineering programs, with a focus on accelerating the process of translating discoveries and inventions into practice. Unfortunately, Wallace Coulter passed away in 1998 before he could see the culmination of his foundation's relationship with Georgia Tech.

Jean-Lou Chameau had been named dean of the Georgia Tech College of Engineering in 1997, and he became the point person in developing our relationship with Sue Van and the Coulter Foundation. Over the next few years, working in consultation with Don Giddens, both parties came to realize that Wallace Coulter's legacy was a natural fit with the new Department of Biomedical Engineering. Coulter was one of the greatest biomedical entrepreneurs of our time as well as a Georgia Tech alumnus, and our department represented an entrepreneurial approach to the field. In 2001, it was named the Wallace H. Coulter Department of Biomedical Engineering at Emory University and Georgia Tech, and the Coulter Foundation provided a gift of $25 million to support fellowships and faculty chairs and to help fund translational research. To highlight the personal connection between Georgia Tech and Wallace Coulter, exhibition space was added in the executive offices to house a number of pieces of art from his famed Chinese jade collection.

In 2006, Wallace Coulter became the first person to receive a posthumous honorary doctorate from Georgia Tech. I was proud to be the president who presented it to Sue Van, who accepted on his behalf. It took seventy-two years, but he finally earned his Georgia Tech degree.

## A HOME FOR THE COULTER DEPARTMENT
## OF BIOMEDICAL ENGINEERING

Rapid growth in the faculty and activities of the Institute for Bioengineering and Bioscience soon made it clear that we needed another building to house the Coulter Department of Biomedical Engineering. Fortunately, there was space on the new quadrangle adjacent to the Petit Biotechnology Building, a location that would allow synergy between the faculties of the two programs to continue.

Funding for the new building came from institutional resources, the Coulter gift, and a new gift from the Whitaker Foundation. In honor of the new gift the building was named for Uncas Whitaker— like Coulter, another legend who helped lay the groundwork for the development of the field of biomedical engineering.

The Whitaker Building, like the biotechnology building, was designed to reflect the culture of the new department. In this case, one of the differentiating factors was something called "problem-based learning" (PBL), which the Coulter faculty had agreed to use in teaching undergraduate biomedical engineering majors. This educational approach involved learning through hands-on experience with complex, real-world problems and working in collaborative teams. To accommodate PBL, the building included multiple breakout rooms where student teams could work and, in a first for Georgia Tech, walls that students could write on as they brainstormed.

I have to admit that I was a bit of a skeptic about PBL, but it was the faculty's choice, and I liked people who wanted to break out of old conventional molds. Time would prove the biomedical engineering faculty right, as students loved learning with the new approach, and it became one of the signatures of the Coulter Department.

We broke ground for the Whitaker Building in 2002, and it was completed in 2003. Once again I marveled at how fast things could move when a good idea was driving the pace.

## A ROLLING STONE GATHERS NO MOSS

With facilities, faculty, and funding falling into place, we had reason to believe that the next few years would be a time to settle in and begin harvesting the crops from the seeds that had been planted. That proved true in a sense, but we had no time to rest on our laurels. The rapid development of our biotechnology and biomedical engineering research and education programs created a new dynamic that encouraged continuous innovation. In addition, a new wave had arrived that had a name: nanotechnology.

Nanotechnology referred to research that focused on manipulating atoms and molecules to customize them. This futuristic development had been foreseen in 1959 by the Nobel-Prize-winning physicist Richard Feynman. In his seminal lecture, "There Is Plenty of Room at the Bottom," he had predicted that nanotechnology would open new horizons for research discoveries. It took more than a few years for Feynman's insights to take hold, but nanotechnology gained traction in the late 1980s and early 1990s. The first applications appeared in the development of a new generation of computer chips, energy devices, and materials. However, at Georgia Tech it quickly spread to biotechnology and bioengineering, and it soon became a second research thrust in addition to tissue engineering.

The clean rooms Georgia Tech had built for the development of new computer chips gave the university a built-in advantage for experimentation in nanotechnology. These rooms assured there would be no contamination as researchers worked at the molecular and atomic scale. Nevertheless, dramatic growth in the application of nanotechnology in Tech's research endeavors meant it did not take long for a large new clean room facility to appear on our drawing board. The Marcus Nanotechnology Building, built adjacent to the biotechnology and molecular engineering quadrangle toward the end of my presidency, features 30,000 square feet of clean room space.

The first payoff for employing nanotechnology in biosciences and biotechnology was not long in coming. In 2004, the National Institutes of Health (NIH) made a $10 million grant to Emory and Georgia Tech to create an interdisciplinary research center focused on developing a new class of nanoparticles for molecular and cellular imaging. This

70

grant was significant not only in its size but also because it was one of the first NIH grants to fund nanomedicine applications. It caught the attention of many people. Before this grant, Georgia Tech had barely registered on the radar screen of NIH activities. Now, working with Emory, Tech was suddenly making waves in the big leagues.

The Emory-Georgia Tech team notched two more victories in 2005. A second NIH award of $11.5 million supported research in the use of nanotechnologies to analyze plaque formation in its early stages. Shortly thereafter, the National Cancer Institute of the NIH named Emory and Georgia Tech as a National Center of Cancer Nanotechnology Excellence, supported by a $19 million grant. Georgia Tech and Emory named the new center the "Emory-Georgia Tech Nanotechnology Center for Personalized and Predictive Oncology." With these awards, the Georgia Tech-Emory partnership was no longer the new kid on the block; it was now seen as competitive not only in what was unfolding at the moment but also in understanding where things were going in the future.

## LOOKING BACK IN AMAZEMENT

By the time I retired as president of Georgia Tech in 2008, I stood in awe of the accomplishments of the Emory-Georgia Tech partnership in biomedical engineering and biosciences. The research funding kept mounting, with NIH awarding a $31 million grant to form a new partnership among Georgia Tech, Emory, and other research and healthcare institutions in the Atlanta area.

While the funding was important, what really mattered was the substance of the research and the opportunity the Coulter Department offered to our students to earn degrees in biomedical engineering. Georgia Tech was now working at the forefront of some of the most challenging and promising areas of biomedical research. Beyond the powerful research agenda, the rise of the Coulter Department into the top ranks of biomedical engineering programs in the country in a very short time was a stunning accomplishment. As it shot up through the rankings, undergraduate enrollment quickly increased from less than 100 in the late 1990s to more than 900 in 2008 when I retired. Young women made up half its student body—a rarity for an engineering program.

The "spin-off" effect from the new Coulter Department and the Institute for Bioengineering and Bioscience helped to lift related programs in biology and molecular sciences to new heights. Engineering programs felt the impact as well, with the School of Chemical Engineering changing its name to the School of Chemical and Biomolecular Engineering to reflect its expanded reach. The College of Computing also enlarged its scope over time as programs in bioinformatics and health system informatics emerged to complement biotechnology and biosciences.

What had begun in 1994 as a discussion about renovating a space in an old building to house our nascent biotechnology program became a juggernaut that helped lift Georgia Tech into the ranks of the nation's best universities. To be truthful, while I envisioned some of the possibilities that biotechnology and biosciences offered, I underestimated what would actually happen. What I did not anticipate was how so many talented people would join our efforts, how enthusiastic Emory would be about the partnership, and how so many donors like Pete Petit, the Whitaker Foundation, and the Coulter Foundation would step up to make a difference in the early days. Credit for what was accomplished is due to so many people, whom I have listed in the acknowledgements of this book.

As for Sue Van, she and I connected again after I retired from Georgia Tech in 2008 and was named the Secretary of the Smithsonian Institution. I was proud to inform her that the National Museum of American History (NMAH) had one of Wallace Coulter's first Coulter Counters in its collection of medical devices. Even as we talked about ways to publicly recognize the contributions of Wallace Coulter, the NMAH was developing a new exhibition to tell the story of American enterprise. The intent of the exhibition was to highlight Americans who, in the process of making groundbreaking inventions, demonstrated what was best about our country. The exhibition opened in 2017 with support from the Coulter Foundation, and it included a segment on medical devices that featured Wallace Coulter, Georgia Tech alumnus extraordinaire.

## REFERENCES

"About the Petit Institute." Parker H. Petit Institute for Bioengineering and Bioscience. Georgia Institute of Technology, August 24, 2013. http://ibb.gatech.edu/history/.

"The Georgia Tech and Emory Connection." Parker H. Petit Institute for Bioengineering and Bioscience. Georgia Institute of Technology. https://petitinstitute.gatech.edu/georgia-tech-and-emory-connection.

"Leroy Hood: Leading the Systems Biology Revolution." *Lasker Foundation Newsletter*, June 8, 2020.

Stavrides, James. "The Dawning of the Age of Biology." *The Financial Times*, January 19, 2014.

"Wallace H. Coulter Biography." Wallace H. Coulter Foundation. https://whcf.org/wallace-h-coulter/wallace-biography/.

## Chapter Five

# THE SAM NUNN SCHOOL OF INTERNATIONAL AFFAIRS

When Georgia Tech established the Ivan Allen College of Management, Policy, and International Affairs in the academic reorganization of 1990, the youngest of its schools was International Affairs. While traditional international affairs programs were based on diplomacy and intergovernmental relations, Georgia Tech hoped to use its reputation to help this new school carve out an innovative niche around issues in which technology played a role. Even so, it would still have to prove its merits against well-established programs at comprehensive universities with deep connections to the federal government and global diplomacy, such as Harvard, Georgetown, and Princeton universities.

The School of International Affairs had its roots in the old "service departments," whose job had been to provide engineering majors with lower-level courses in the liberal arts and sciences that were required for a bachelor's degree. During the second half of the 1900s, these departments gradually morphed into more robust academic programs whose faculty came to fit the same academic and research profile that characterized the rest of Georgia Tech. Upper-level courses began to emerge, paving the way for new degrees. Prior to 1990, these new degrees were in the sciences and mathematics, but the creation of a School of Social Sciences opened the door for disciplines such as public policy, international affairs, and the history of technology to become more robust.

When the School of International Affairs was created, it was one of the first professional schools of international affairs to be established at a major technological university. Only four years old when I arrived as president in 1994, it was just beginning to find its way. However, I believed that if it could become successful, it would add a unique dimension to Georgia Tech. I was no expert on international affairs, but I had traveled the world as an earthquake engineer, visiting sites where tremors had caused enormous damage and loss of human life. My job had been to make recommendations about structural design changes that would improve safety and increase the rate of recovery from earthquake disasters. While it was apparent that improvements in engineering design would help, the challenges went beyond the technical and required the combined efforts of multiple levels of governments and even multinational organizations. Making positive changes in such circumstances called for a new kind of talent—people who understood technology but also were able to communicate across cultures and understood how to develop and implement effective policies. It seemed to me that graduates from our new School of International Affairs could be such individuals.

Beyond graduating people with special skills to address international issues, I felt that this new school could provide Georgia Tech with two other advantages. First, our academic scope was limited compared to other nationally ranked universities, even those with a focus on technology. A major in international affairs could attract students who were interested in technology but who wanted a more humanities-based education. Second, if Georgia Tech was to fulfill its potential as an institution of global standing, it needed to have an academic unit that saw its primary mission through an international lens.

I was fortunate to have Dan Papp as my first executive assistant from the faculty. He had been the founding chair of the School of International Affairs, and he helped me better appreciate how far the program had come in a relatively short time. One thing already stood out: some of our brightest undergraduate students were choosing international affairs as their major. Still, for all of its potential, the school needed something to lift it to a greater level of national and international prominence.

## A FATEFUL BREAKFAST

On December 9, 1995, I was invited to a breakfast with Georgia's U.S. senator Sam Nunn and two of his friends, Gordon Giffin and Charlie Brown. Giffin was a lawyer with the firm of Long Aldridge & Norman (now McKenna Long & Aldridge). Brown was a Georgia Tech alumnus who had become prominent for planning and developing large mixed-use projects. Giffin had worked as the chief counsel for Senator Nunn in the mid-1970s, and Brown was Nunn's lifelong friend and golfing buddy. While I did not know the senator as well as Giffin and Brown, I admired his ability to deal with complex issues and cross party lines, as well as his sterling reputation for integrity. We all shared interests in basketball and golf, but the breakfast was about much more than that.

Nunn was now in the latter stages of his fourth term as a senator and confided that he was not going to run for reelection. The purpose of our meeting was to discuss possibilities for him to be involved at Georgia Tech in some way after he retired from the U.S. Senate. He also mentioned that he would be having similar discussions with Emory University, where he had earned two degrees, and the University of Georgia, which had a strong program in public policy and governance.

Samuel Augustus Nunn was well known to us at Georgia Tech. He had grown up in Perry, Georgia. In addition to being an excellent student, he had been a star athlete in high school as a golfer and a short but able point guard on the Perry High School basketball team that had won the state championship. He had enrolled as a freshman at Georgia Tech in 1956, hoping to play on the basketball and golf teams while studying management. Unfortunately, his plan had two problems. First, he was not good enough to make the basketball team, and second, he found himself in over his head in mechanical drawing, a required course for all Tech students in those days. I myself had struggled with a lack of aptitude for mechanical drawing, so I sympathized. In a graduation speech at Tech years later, Nunn pointed out that he had flunked his first attempt at mechanical drawing and was grateful to receive a "D" the second time around. His encounter with mechanical drawing turned out to be a learning experience of another sort—he transferred to Emory University where he excelled, earning his undergraduate and law degrees.

A Democrat who was elected to the U.S. Senate in 1972, Nunn became widely known for his work in national defense and global economics and for his ability to work across the aisle with Republican colleagues. He served with distinction as chair of the Senate Armed Services Committee from 1987 to 1995. In 1991, Nunn joined forces with his colleague Senator Richard Lugar to pass the Soviet Threat Reduction Act, designed to dismantle nuclear weapons left in the hands of countries that had been satellites of the former Soviet Union. Ultimately known as the Nunn-Lugar Cooperative Threat Reduction Program, it led to the elimination of more than 7,600 nuclear warheads. Many believed Nunn and Lugar should have won the Nobel Peace Prize for their efforts to make the world a safer place for all of us. Beyond his leadership in the Senate, Nunn became active in policy circles, especially with the Center for Strategic International Studies (CSIS), a respected think tank. He continued to serve as chair of the board of CSIS for many years after his Senate career ended.

As we talked at our breakfast, it became clear that Nunn's expertise and experience in defense and global economic policy aligned perfectly with several of the areas we hoped to develop in our School of International Affairs. He spoke about how science and technology had grown in importance during the Cold War and about the critical need for engineers and scientists who could speak to the issues facing decision makers and politicians. He saw that Georgia Tech had elements in place to contribute, given its history of working on defense research and economic development and the strength of the students it attracted. It was almost as if he were making the case for the mission of the School of International Affairs. I could see even then how he could serve as a role model for the students we wanted to enroll in both our undergraduate and graduate programs.

We left the breakfast with nothing settled but with an understanding that, from Georgia Tech's perspective, there were strong avenues of programmatic alignment that could possibly be used to build a role for the senator.

## DEVELOPING A PROPOSAL

It was time to get back to campus to test the waters. Fortunately for me, Dan Papp was perfectly placed to run the traps on this matter. Clearly we needed to consult with Linda Brady, the chair of the school, and with the faculty. Were they comfortable with continuing the dialog with Senator Nunn? The feedback was positive, so we began to develop a proposal, consulting with Giffin and Brown about ideas for the relationship.

Going in, I felt we were at a disadvantage. Senator Nunn had earned two degrees at Emory University, and the University of Georgia had long-standing programs in public policy. But that cloud also had a silver lining. As the home of Jimmy Carter's Presidential Library and the Carter Center, Emory already had a prominent political name associated with it. Similarly, the University of Georgia's most visible center of public policy had been named for long-term Georgia senator Richard B. Russell, whose name was well known and respected but also carried with it the baggage of his support for segregation. Georgia Tech had an unnamed School of International Affairs that had little in the way of a track record but a lot of potential.

A lead for our proposal would be to offer to name our school for Senator Nunn. However, given his background, we knew we would need to offer something deeper than a relationship in name only. To have value, our proposal would need to fit the senator's personal goals while at the same time matching our aspirations for the School of International Affairs. Fortunately, we already had a framework that matched well with his appreciation for the growing need to combine international policy issues with expertise in engineering and science. Although the youth of our school could be seen as a disadvantage, its newness offered the opportunity for Senator Nunn's vision of the future to have a bigger impact on its shape and direction than would have been possible with a well-established program.

We also understood that our proposal should address Nunn's desire for collaboration among Emory University, the University of Georgia, and Georgia Tech. This aspect did not present a problem because these universities were better established in the field, and we would gain recognition by working with them and combining resources as appropriate. Much could be accomplished through an annual series of events and symposia with Senator Nunn that rotated among the three universities, with Georgia Tech coordinating the activities.

Offering to name the school for Sam Nunn would require work. Prior to that time, the naming of facilities and programs for individuals had been mainly the provenance of the Athletic Association. However, the ice was broken in 1990 when the Crecine administration named the new College of Management, Policy, and International Affairs for Ivan Allen Jr., a Georgia Tech alumnus and the former mayor of the City of Atlanta. Because Ivan Allen stood for integrity, public service, and support of civil rights, his name was an excellent choice for the college. We believed that attaching Senator Nunn's name to the School of International Affairs would send a similar message about our shared values and provide a visible statement about our intentions for the future.

At the next meeting with Giffin and Brown, I presented the outlines of our proposal. They were supportive and agreed to bring it to Senator Nunn. By late spring 1996, Nunn had agreed with the concept. Of course, once "decided," these things take time to negotiate and steer to safe harbor, given all the details and different parties involved.

## CLOSING THE DEAL

My job was to keep the agreed-upon arrangement confidential while key players to the process were informed. They included members of Georgia Tech advisory boards, University System of Georgia chancellor Stephen Portch and the system's Board of Regents, President Bill Chace of Emory University, and President Charles Knapp of the University of Georgia. With a bit of luck and hard work, the concept came together just as the Olympics were arriving on our doorstep.

We knew that any attempt at an announcement would be lost in the swirl of Olympic press coverage. So we allowed the whirlwind of the Olympics to pass and then held a public ceremony on October 7, 1996, to announce officially the naming of the School of International Affairs for Senator Sam Nunn and to designate him a distinguished professor at Georgia Tech. It was a landmark day for the Sam Nunn School of International Affairs, Georgia Tech, and Senator Nunn, who said it best: "Technology and science are outrunning the world of law, religion, human relations, and government and international relations. Bridges must be built between the world of science and the world of human relations—bridges which can give shape and purpose to our technology and breathe heart and soul into our knowledge."

I felt an underlying element of satisfaction in the naming because the Nunn School made its home in the Ivan Allen College, and I could see the strong parallels between the lives of the two men. Both were native Georgians, Georgia Tech alumni, and exemplary public servants. Both had made a difference in our lives—Mayor Ivan Allen in supporting the civil rights movement and Martin Luther King Jr., and Senator Sam Nunn in making our world a safer place by negotiating a treaty that reduced the threat of nuclear war. Both were role models for Georgia Tech students, proving that their degrees had opened the door to a life of public service.

## 1996–2000: THE VECTOR TILTS UPWARD

The announcement of the naming of the school for Senator Nunn made waves that resonated throughout the field of international affairs. However, at the time the school only offered a BS in International Affairs and enrolled just 180 students. It was also not yet a member of the all-important Association of Professional Schools of International Affairs (APSIA), whose thirty-eight members included programs at such American universities as Harvard, Georgetown, Duke, and Michigan as well as related programs in Singapore, France, Korea, and Russia.

We had a lot of ground to make up, but it came quickly, both on campus and in the profession. Nunn School enrollment expanded rapidly, and by 2000 it was more than three hundred, including fifty-four students enrolled in the new MS in International Affairs degree program. Faculty increased from ten in 1994 to fifteen in 2000.

In accordance with Senator Nunn's wishes, the Nunn School worked with its counterparts at Emory University and the University of Georgia to establish the biennial Sam Nunn Policy Forum that rotated among the three universities. The Bank of America provided the funding to support the forums, which brought in national and international leaders to discuss issues ranging from nuclear threats to international monetary policy.

All of these achievements were well and good, but third-party confirmation was needed to prove that the Nunn School was really on its way. It arrived in short order, when the school was admitted to the APSIA on its first try in 1998. Membership in this prominent organization gave the Nunn School much-needed credibility and allowed its leadership to rub shoulders with the heavyweights.

Then came the news that the European Commission, governing body of the European Union, had selected the Nunn School as one of eight international affairs programs in the United States to house a European Union Center of Excellence. The center came with a grant of $600,000 and the mission of understanding the role of the European Union in the economy of the Southeast as well as how technology is linked to innovation. Georgia Tech was asked to serve as a point of contact for the thirty universities and colleges then in the University System of Georgia where mutual studies were performed.

## STEADY AND RAPID MATURATION

During the remainder of my tenure as president, from 2001 to 2008, the Nunn School, now under the leadership of Bill Long as chair, continued to grow both in size and reputation. A PhD program was added in 2007, and by 2008 the school's enrollment exceeded 420 students. The faculty proved adept at securing grants and contracts, including a renewal of the European Center of Excellence grant.

The Nunn School also assumed a significant role in the larger initiative underway at Georgia Tech to expand its international profile and study-abroad programs. In 2001, the school partnered with the Department of Modern Languages to create an interdisciplinary BS in International Affairs and Modern Languages, offering our students another option in the humanities. Then these two academic units joined with the Office of International Programs to roll out Tech's International Plan in 2006. This innovative program offered undergraduate students in any of twenty-seven majors the opportunity to incorporate international studies into the academic work for their degree, earning a special designation on their diplomas.

All of these achievements were signs of steady progress, but it was

82

a $1.3 million grant from the prestigious MacArthur Foundation in 2003 that spoke volumes about how far the Nunn School had come in its short life. The MacArthur Foundation funded grants at nine universities to establish programs designed to help mid-career scientists and engineers become leaders in the field of international security policy. In addition to Georgia Tech, the universities included MIT, Carnegie Mellon, Harvard, Stanford, and Cornell. Professors John Endicott and Seymour Goodman, along with Senator Nunn, were among the faculty leading the effort. The program attracted some of the brightest young scientists and engineers in the country to Georgia Tech to pursue a new direction in their careers. It allowed the Nunn School to demonstrate that it was capable of working on a par with some of the best schools of international affairs on a topic of importance that was critical to our nation's future.

In 2006, the program was renewed for five more years with another grant of $1.8 million. The visibility of the MacArthur program was not only important for the Nunn School but also demonstrated that Georgia Tech was making progress toward its larger goal of excellence in the liberal arts as well as in engineering, science, and business.

The partnership between Senator Nunn and the school named for him turned out to be fortuitous. When we approached Nunn in 1996, he knew this new school was a work in progress, but he saw the potential. As hoped, the Nunn School today has become widely known for its ability to bring a technological perspective to bear on matters of national security, monetary policy, cybersecurity, international trade, and international conflict. It also has proven to be a resource on the Georgia Tech campus, helping educate students in other degree programs about the nature of issues that link countries around the world, including climate change, telecommunications, and governance.

In the years following the naming of the school, Senator Nunn continued to be active at the highest levels of national policy-making. He maintained an active role with the Center for Strategic and International Studies, and in 2001 he was named the founding CEO of the Nuclear Threat Initiative (NTI), a position he held until 2017. Originally created to reduce the threat of nuclear war, the NTI expanded its mission under Nunn's leadership to include cyber-security and biosecurity. He brought the fruits of these activities to his work with students and faculty, and his active involvement on campus gave the Nunn School and Georgia Tech greater visibility at a national level.

Often joining in at the School of International Affairs was Nunn's colleague, U.S. representative John Lewis, whose congressional district included Georgia Tech. He was just one of the distinguished affiliated faculty and influential guests who participated actively in seminars, classes, and conferences—a list that grew longer as the Nunn School progressed. These individuals had long and productive careers in industry, our nation's military, government, and banking. Their participation in the school's activities came in large part because of the involvement of Senator Nunn and their respect for him. I am pleased to say that as I write this book, I am active with the school as well, through lectures and seminar programs.

It was my good fortune to play a role in helping develop the Nunn School of International Affairs into a substantive and highly respected program. I am grateful to those whose hard work brought a new dimension to Georgia Tech's reputation and proved that my confidence in the future of the school was not misplaced. I will always be indebted to Senator Sam Nunn for his friendship and willingness to take a chance on a new program and a new president.

## REFERENCES

"Celebrating 20 Years as the Sam Nunn School of International Affairs." Ivan Allen College of Liberal Arts. Georgia Institute of Technology. https://iac.gatech.edu/news/item/584833/celebrating-20-years-sam-nunn-school-international-affairs.

"MacArthur Foundation Selects Georgia Tech for Prestigious Three-Year Grant: MacArthur Fellowship to Strengthen Scientific and Technical Advice on International Peace and Security Policy." Georgia Institute of Technology press release, January 27, 2003. https://news.gatech.edu/2003/01/28/macarthur-foundation-selects-georgia-tech-prestigious-three-year-grant.

McMath, Robert C., Jr; Ronald H. Bayor; James E. Brittain; Lawrence Foster; August W. Giebelhaus; and Germaine M. Reed. *Engineering the New South: Georgia Tech, 1885–1985*. Athens: University of Georgia Press, 1985.

Pavri, Tinaz. "Sam Nunn (b. 1938)." *New Georgia Encyclopedia*, July 17, 2018.

https://www.georgiaencyclopedia.org/articles/government-politics/sam-nunn-b-1938.

Rast, M. C. "Georgia Tech Opens New EU Academic Center." *Global Atlanta*, September 22, 2008. http://www.globalatlanta.com/georgia-tech-opens-new-eu-academic-center/.

*Chapter Six*

# THE UNDERGRADUATE EDUCATION EXPERIENCE

Georgia Tech alumni of my generation remember a freshman assembly at which a dean said, "Look to your left, look to your right; only one of you will graduate." We were too naïve to question why someone thought this message was helpful or why a 33 percent graduation rate made any sense. The dean provided no tips on how to be the one of the three who survived. Given my lack of academic discipline at the time, the early odds were that I would become one of the two who did not make it.

My freshman dormitory and the civil engineering building where I studied were equally grim. Built during the Great Depression in the 1930s by the Works Progress Administration, they had not been renovated since. Students of my day had good reason to refer to graduating from Georgia Tech as "getting out."

I was grateful that Georgia Tech challenged me academically, but after I left my horizons expanded. All of the universities where I worked were more comprehensive than Georgia Tech, with robust social science and humanities programs. Although my discipline was civil engineering, I sought opportunities for conversation with students and faculty from fields outside engineering. As an assistant professor at Duke University, I participated in a biweekly discussion and dinner group composed of students and faculty from different colleges and living units across campus. As a professor at Stanford University, I volunteered as a freshman advisor and enjoyed the challenge of meeting bright students who had multiple interests beyond engineering. Even as an academic administrator at Virginia Tech, I taught a course in the Honors College focused on great books of both science and the humanities. Experiences at Duke, Stanford, Virginia Tech, and the University of Washington helped me understand what it took to create an educational experience that encouraged the kind of well-rounded intellectual growth that engineers and scientists needed to compete successfully in a globally connected world.

## ASSESSING WHERE WE STOOD

When I came back to Georgia Tech, I learned that circumstances for undergraduates had improved somewhat since my days as a student. However, a pervasive notion still existed that it should be intentionally hard to graduate from this school, even if the difficulty had nothing to do with academics.

Compounding this attitude was a lack of opportunities for personal growth for students. Only one hundred students studied abroad each year, and fewer than sixty undergraduates were engaged in research. Elective music or arts programs were bare bones. While serving as the Olympic Village would improve student housing with the construction of new residence halls and the renovation of old ones, the existing long-range capital plan had no provisions for new classrooms or student fitness and wellness. Bottom line: undergraduate students were not a priority at Georgia Tech.

Georgia Tech paid a price for this approach. Having finally moved into the top fifty universities in the 1995 *U.S. News and World Report* rankings, Georgia Tech stood out for two reasons. On the positive side, the test scores of entering freshmen at Tech were the highest of any public university in the top fifty. However, the graduation rate for these bright students was 66 percent, dead last among the top fifty. How could Georgia Tech be first among public universities in the quality of its students but last in its ability to graduate them?

Then there was the news from *The Princeton Review*. Although this source was considered suspect because it was just a survey of students regarding how they felt about their university, it had public impact. People paid attention to the results. The reviews showed Georgia Tech students to be loyal in general but downright uncomplimentary about the living and learning environment on campus. Even though the evidence was unscientific, it was a strong hint that we had problems.

It struck me that Georgia Tech was a place at war with itself—wanting to be seen as a great institution but at the same time holding fast to an approach to undergraduate education that was stuck in the past. The conclusion was obvious; the way forward was not.

Some attributed this culture to the days immediately following World War II, when the GI Bill enabled veterans to flood the campus. The faculty dealt with this surge by weeding out the less competent and industrious students early on so that the numbers for upper-level courses would be more manageable. The surge of GI Bill students was over by the time I came to Tech as a freshman in 1959, but my own experience supported this view.

One of my calculus teachers was known for berating students, causing them to drop out of his class. As we headed into the last week of the term, only eight of us remained of the initial thirty-five students in the class. None of us believed we had the test scores to make better than a "C" or a "D" in the course, and an "F" was a distinct possibility, but we were stuck because the drop deadline had passed. I studied hard for the last weekly test and felt good about how I had done. On Monday the professor came into the classroom with the tests in his hand. As he threw them into the trash can, he said, "This is what I think of your tests. You can fish them out at the end of class if you like."

After class ended and the professor left, I did fish out my exam and found I had earned a barely passing mark. Angry and determined, I decided to go all out for the final exam. I memorized every one of the solutions for the advanced problems listed at the end of each chapter of the calculus textbook—including developing the proof for the formula to determine the volume of a toroid (a donut-like shape). When I opened the final exam, the toroid problem was the first question. Under ordinary circumstances I would have permitted myself a little smile, but experience with this professor had taught me never to be hopeful.

The next week, as I walked to the professor's office where he had posted the grades by student ID number, I was expecting the worst. I thought I saw a "B" by my ID, but I pulled out a ruler to make sure that grade really aligned with my number. I was happy, but I knew no one should have to go through what I had gone through to earn a "B." Needless to say, the Georgia Tech of those days was not designed to encourage student success.

When Joseph Pettit arrived from Stanford as president in 1972, he set about lifting Georgia Tech's reputation as a research university. He provided incentives for faculty to do research and publish but offered little in the way of comparable encouragement for them to become good teachers. Good teaching was not discouraged; it was simply not recognized or rewarded, and no real effort was made to change the culture.

President Pettit died in office in 1986, and when John Patrick Crecine arrived to succeed him, he understood that things needed to change. Unfortunately, he quickly became embroiled in numerous struggles, and when he sought to improve the graduation rate, he was accused of lowering academic standards.

From my point of view, it was time for Georgia Tech to rethink the undergraduate education experience. It was not a question of lowering academic standards but of providing the remarkably bright students who earned their way onto our campus with the enriched educational opportunities they deserved.

## LOOKING FOR ANSWERS

That the undergraduate educational experience left something to be desired was obvious. Low retention and graduation rates reflected a poor understanding of our students and a systematic lack of opportunities for creative expression. Even the physical infrastructure, with its shabby classrooms and out-of-date recreation facilities, demonstrated that Georgia Tech cared little about its undergraduates. It was clear to me that if we were serious about improving undergraduate education, it would take time and a concerted effort to make it right.

## UNDERSTANDING OUR STUDENTS

As I was seeking to understand the new generation of Georgia Tech students, someone suggested taking a look at the annual survey of freshmen done by the Cooperative Institutional Research Program at the University of California, Los Angeles (UCLA). This longitudinal survey, begun in the mid-1960s, had grown to include almost 238,000 freshmen entering more than 450 institutions by fall 1994. Georgia Tech was a founding participant in the survey, and more than 70 percent of entering Tech students regularly contributed to it. However, it was not clear to me that Tech ever did much with the results.

As I perused the UCLA survey, three things about Georgia Tech freshmen stood out. First, students said they chose to attend Georgia Tech because they thought it would help them get a job that paid well. Second, while their math SAT scores were among the highest in the nation as expected, their verbal SAT scores were also high—highest of any university in the state of Georgia and among the highest in the nation. Third, more than 50 percent indicated that they had played a musical instrument in high school, but few expected to pursue this talent at Georgia Tech.

What the first of these findings said to me was that we needed to help our students learn to see beyond materialistic goals. Then there was the question of how to encourage their latent talents in the arts and humanities. This exercise was not merely esoteric but had a practical end. We knew creativity thrives when people use both the left and right sides of their brains. If we could encourage balanced growth for our students, they would be more likely to reach their full potential and become better engineers and scientists.

## MOVING BEYOND PRECONCEPTIONS

Before we could establish a plan to enrich undergraduate education, we needed to understand why so many students left Georgia Tech without graduating. Most alumni, myself included, believed that Tech's low graduation rate was primarily the result of its high academic standards. However, Sandra Bramblett, the director of institute research and planning, disabused me of this preconception. In one fell swoop she debunked the "flunking out" myth with data showing that the majority of students who left early were actually in good academic standing.

Reading exit interviews done with these students was like taking a cold shower. Many had initially enrolled in engineering and then later concluded that it was not their cup of tea. Not finding any alternative majors of interest, they left for universities that offered more options than Georgia Tech. A second group left because they perceived the campus to be impersonal, the faculty to be uncaring, and opportunities for personal growth to be lacking. Finally, there was a minority who actually did leave because of poor academic performance. Yet, as I absorbed the impact of Bramblett's findings, I began to believe our lack of support systems had probably contributed to their academic distress.

## A COMMITMENT TO CREATE A NEW CULTURE

In the middle of the Great Depression, President Franklin Delano Roosevelt spoke to his staff about what to do in the face of a host of challenges. "It is common sense to take a method and try it," he said. "If it fails, admit it frankly, and try another. But above all, try something!" Although the approaching Olympics presented a plate full of challenges, we knew it would be to our detriment to wait until after the Games to begin the effort to improve undergraduate education.

One of the first changes was personal. I never believed that SAT scores should be the deciding factor in who received a scholarship, nor did I believe they predicted who would become a good engineer. However, in 1994 the SAT held sway at Georgia Tech. When it came to awarding Georgia Tech's premier scholarship, the President's Scholarship, no prospective student with less than a 1300 combined SAT score could even be considered. I asked a simple question: "Are you are telling me that a student with a 1300 combined SAT score but no extracurricular activities would be selected for a President's Scholarship over one whose combined SAT score was 1299 but was captain of the football team, leader of the debate team, and president of the senior class?" The answer was yes. I replied, "You know, this does not make sense." The next day we dropped the SAT score requirement and ramped up consideration of extracurricular activities in choosing President's Scholars.

Next on the list were the criteria used for admissions. The first order of business was to reduce the weight accorded to SAT scores and devise a system similar to the one used at the U.S. Naval Academy, which included credit for extracurricular activities. The idea was to look beyond the score of a test and see the whole person. We also included a requirement for an essay and recruited dozens of alumni to read them and participate in interviews of those students who were applying for scholarships. In the end, students with the highest SAT scores were still likely to be admitted, but in the main this more holistic approach meant we were admitting students who were more well rounded and open to new possibilities. I had to chuckle when a few faculty accused me of "lowering standards," especially as time showed that the SAT scores of students who were admitted using this new process steadily increased. The lesson was that SAT scores do not need to serve as the deciding factor in choosing quality students for admission. If you admit the right students, the SATs will take care of themselves.

Beyond admissions, we laid out our underlying philosophy for changing the playing field for undergraduate education in the 1995 strategic plan and then enlarged and reinforced it in the subsequent 2002 plan. The 1995 plan spoke to "Enriching Educational Opportunities" and "Improving Student Life." In the 2002 plan, these two goals were combined into one, "A Student-Focused Education," while a separate section, "A Diverse Community," emphasized the importance of diversity in our faculty, staff, and student body.

The title of the 2002 strategic plan, *Defining the Technological Research University of the 21st Century*, not only captured its essence but also stated an aspiration against which to test our plans and progress at every turn. Regarding the educational experience we sought to provide to our students, the plan stated:

> The student body is the soul of Georgia Tech and the mark of our success. To our undergraduate and graduate students alike, we owe a relevant, learner-centered education that prepares them for life and leadership.... Georgia Tech will nurture a community of scholars that seeks rich opportunities for lifelong learning both inside and outside the classroom. Georgia Tech's rigorous curriculum and co-curricular activities will continue to challenge our students to grow as intellectual and social beings, preparing them for success on

their chosen path.

Reflecting the experience of seven years of work under the 1995 plan, the 2002 strategic plan stated our goals with a clearer focus:

Improve retention and graduation rates to levels that are comparable to our peers.

Provide opportunities for diverse learning experiences both in and out of the classroom including art, drama, recreation, extracurricular activities and athletics.

Offer international education and internships that enable students to work or study abroad. At least one-third of Georgia Tech's students should have such experience by the time of graduation.

Increase by 50 percent the number of undergraduates who have research experience upon their graduation.

Build a campus that understands that diversity reaches across racial and socioeconomic boundaries and embraces the life experiences of each individual.

Soon after we finished the 2002 strategic plan, we began looking ahead to our once-a-decade accreditation review by the Southeastern Association of Colleges and Schools, coming up in 2005. In preparation we needed to develop a Quality Enhancement Plan (QEP), a requirement intended to prod schools to plan for the ongoing improvement of their educational endeavors. Institutions typically responded by proposing marginal enhancements that could be implemented with minimal cost and effort. But we had now been working for almost a decade on improving the undergraduate experience and were gaining traction. Something was in the air at Georgia Tech, and we felt it was time to stop nickel-and-diming our future plans.

Our QEP focused on expanding study abroad and undergraduate research opportunities. We set ambitious expectations—that 50 percent of the graduating class of 2010 would have studied abroad, and 60 percent of them would have engaged in structured research. In 2004, about 2,560 students received bachelor's degrees. Applying these

94

targets to that class would have meant that 1,280 of them would have studied abroad and more than 1,530 would have participated in research. While we had made significant progress, the new goals represented a quantum leap. And, beyond the two focal points of our QEP, we had additional strategic plan goals to achieve.

High aspirations are nice, but resources and people are required to make things work. That was my job. We needed to (1) expand extracurricular options; (2) increase our limited set of majors, particularly in the liberal arts; (3) create a culture that was welcoming and supportive of all students, regardless of ethnicity, gender, or sexual orientation; (4) design buildings that offered support for undergraduates, accommodated group projects, and encouraged informal discussion; and (5) encourage good teaching.

## MAXIMIZING EXTRACURRICULAR OPTIONS

Of all the papers written about undergraduate education, few examine the impact of extracurricular activities on academic performance. Yet it was a potentially rich vein that had been overlooked at Georgia Tech. Adding opportunities for well-designed extracurricular activities was our chance to kill two birds with one stone. First, students would have a better way to develop the social networks that would help sustain them through inevitable hard times. Second, in many cases these activities could be shaped to support larger academic goals. An added advantage was that changes in extracurricular activities did not have to go through the faculty governance channels required for academic changes and thus could be implemented more quickly.

### Study Abroad, Phase I

As I talked with alumni about expanding study abroad programs, an older alumnus wryly commented that in his day, a trip to South Carolina was a study abroad. When I arrived as president in 1994, things were better than that, but not by much. Next-to-no studying abroad on the part of Tech students was not for lack of interest. The culprits were cost, a dearth of opportunities, and a highly prescriptive engineering curriculum with little elbow room for extras. If we could just find a way around these barriers, we could add another notch in our belt toward defining the technological university of the twenty-first century.

As we searched for solutions, time and time again we came up against the issue of scale. Sending students abroad, particularly engineering students, required dedicated facilities on site, careful supervision, educational programs that met university accreditation standards, and student participants to make it work. This combination was not in ready supply.

Part of the solution was to create a portfolio of opportunities that gave our students options that fit their needs. These ranged in duration from a summer to a semester to a year and involved formal courses, internships, cooperative education, and volunteer experiences. We also encouraged fundraising to provide financial assistance to students who needed it to study abroad.

Despite early progress, the sticking point continued to be the reluctance of engineering students, who comprised the majority at Georgia Tech, to participate. Attention turned to the new Georgia Tech campus in Metz, France (now known as Georgia Tech Lorraine, or GTL), which had been opened during the Crecine presidency. The Metz campus had been founded for research and graduate education, but its classrooms, offices, residence halls, and location made it ideal for undergraduate study abroad. In addition, Georgia Tech controlled it, and it had an engineering focus.

But using this campus for study abroad was not as easy as it appeared. The graduate education and research programs served French students and were highly valued by the Province of Lorraine. The growth and development of these programs had to continue, even as an undergraduate element was added. The challenge was to find a way to blend our aspirations for undergraduates with those for graduate studies and research so that GTL would work for everyone.

In the end, it came down to people who had the passion, the cultural and political connections, and the know-how to make it all work. On the Georgia Tech side were the early leaders at Metz—first Teddy Puttgen and then Yves Berthelot—and, back in Atlanta, Dean of Engineering then Provost Jean-Lou Chameau and Vice Provost Steve McLaughlin. That Berthelot and Chameau were both French and Puttgen was Swiss was an asset. We were also fortunate to have the best of allies among the political leadership in Metz and Lorraine— Jacques Faudon, the deputy mayor of Metz who became the first president of GTL, and the remarkable Jean-Marie Rausch, mayor of Metz and president of the region of Lorraine. The talents and vision of this French-American team carried the day.

We began in 1998 with a summer undergraduate program on the Metz campus, taught by Georgia Tech faculty from Atlanta who spent the summer term at Metz. About one hundred students participated initially. This number grew as schools and departments increased their capacity to offer financial support for their students to study at Metz.

Not to be left behind, our graduate and research programs in Metz also celebrated an important milestone in 1998, when we formalized an agreement between GTL and the Centre National de la Recherche Scientifique (CNRS), a French national entity similar to the National Science Foundation in the United States. This agreement allowed GTL to obtain research funding directly from the French government, a capability no other American university had.

To celebrate our new accomplishments, I visited GTL in summer 1998 to meet the inaugural group of undergraduate students and faculty and to sign the documents finalizing our new relationship with CNRS. As the day drew to a close, we hosted a reception with all of our students, including our French graduate students. In a moment of inspiration, I encouraged our French and American students to join me in singing Georgia Tech's "Ramblin' Wreck" fight song. Of course, our French students had no idea what a fight song meant. Our American students explained and helped them with the words, which include "Like all the jolly good fellows, I drink my whiskey clear; I'm a Ramblin' Wreck from Georgia Tech and a hell of an engineer." Our French students did their best with the song. But afterward, seeing that we were serving wine, several came up to me and asked, "Where do we find the whiskey clear?"

With the basic building blocks in place in Europe, it was time to get to work on Asia. Because of existing personal relationships and institutional strengths, we focused our attention on Singapore for logistics and on Shanghai for electrical engineering and undergraduate studies. We were successful in establishing partnerships with the National

University of Singapore and with Shanghai Jaio Tong University. I will never forget receiving an honorary doctorate from Shanghai Jaio Tong University, presented by their two presidents, one an academic and the other representing the Communist Party. By 2000, we had platforms in Singapore and Shanghai that served different and useful purposes.

*Study Abroad, Phase II*

By 2000, the number of undergraduate students studying abroad annually had risen to more than 600, a six-fold increase from 1994. But we realized that if we were to achieve the level of participation we were hoping for, we would need to step up our game. At the same time, I found my presidential role evolving towards greater emphasis on fundraising and national policy engagement. Fortunately for me, the team we had assembled by then was both self-reliant and committed to helping Georgia Tech achieve its goals.

During the next few years, my colleagues proposed two seminal initiatives that made it possible to consider the extraordinary goal we set in our QEP. First, we made the decision to go to a year-round undergraduate study abroad program at Georgia Tech Lorraine in Metz, France, including a commitment to add full-time faculty there. We began this effort with fall semester 2006.

Second was the International Plan, launched in 2005 as part of our QEP. The goal of the International Plan was to enable students to pursue their chosen major in a global context. Requirements included completing at least twenty-six weeks of international experience, developing proficiency in a language other than English, and taking a series of internationally oriented academic courses. Satisfying these requirements led to a special designation on a student's diploma. We believed this program would offer participating students a competitive edge upon graduation. The only question was whether it would attract enough students to make it viable. Our concern was soon allayed as students signed up in significant numbers from its beginning.

It was not until I returned to campus in 2016, after stepping down from leading the Smithsonian, that I realized the significance of the International Plan. When I was asked to speak to the incoming class of International Plan students, many of those already in the program showed up as well. Amazed by the size of the group, I learned that the program had grown to more than 800 active students.

Study abroad programs not only proved popular with our students but also provided a means to enrich their lives and expand their career options. What was unique about Tech's approach was the creation of opportunities for engineering and science majors to participate while staying on track to graduate in four years. As a result, our efforts soon drew attention from others. In 2007, Georgia Tech received the Senator Paul Simon Award from the Association of International Educators for excellence in internationalization efforts, a rare honor for a technology-focused university. The International Plan was subsequently honored in 2010 with an Andrew Heiskell Award from the Institute of International Education for injecting an international aspect into engineering education.

When I left Georgia Tech in 2008, 1,200 students were taking part in study abroad programs each year, double the number from 2000 and twelve times the number from 1994. A wonderful unexpected side benefit was that the number of students taking modern language courses had quintupled even though Tech had no formal requirement for language study. As of the writing of this book in 2020, more than 2,000 Georgia Tech students study abroad each year, and the number of engineering and science majors among them is higher than at any other university in the nation.

*Undergraduate Research*

Undergraduate research was a sister initiative to study abroad and had a similar history. When I arrived at Georgia Tech as president, no one seemed concerned that the number of students who participated in either one was tiny. Not much regarding such activities had changed since my undergraduate days in the "dark ages" of the 1950s and 1960s. As a student, I was never told anything about the possibility of studying abroad. However, in the case of undergraduate research, I had personal experience.

As a cooperative education student at Tech, I alternated quarters between academic study and working on a job related to my major. As it turned out, my final quarter on campus as a senior occurred during a summer term. Unfortunately, engineering economics, one of the last required courses I needed to graduate, was not offered in the summer. Fortunately, along the way I had worked for Bill Schultz, the chair of the School of Civil Engineering, and he was willing to help. Somehow he managed to substitute an undergraduate research project for the engineering economics course to satisfy my graduation requirements. My advisor for this project was a post-doctoral fellow named Sam Martin, who was to join the faculty in the fall. He proved to be an ideal mentor to his naïve mentee who knew nothing about research.

Sam Martin was working on a beach erosion research project funded by the U.S. Navy. He asked me to design an experiment to investigate two factors involved in causing a sand particle to be lifted out of its bed: the slope of the bed and the speed of the water flowing over it. I used a water flume and sand made of artificial particles to do the experiments. Having never done such experiments before, I had more than a few questions. Martin was always available for my questions, but he never gave me any answers. Instead he provided me with references and sources of information. As he put it, "In research you have to learn to find the answers yourself by thinking about the problem and seeing what other investigators have done." At times I was frustrated, but Martin wanted me to learn why it was important to think independently, and also to savor the answer when I found it. I never knew if my modest project helped Martin's research, but he helped me see the joy that comes from research, and that changed my life.

Based on my own experience as a student and later as a faculty member, I was convinced that the opportunity to do research would enliven the undergraduate experience. In addition, it offered the means to connect the research agenda of our graduate programs to the teaching agenda of our undergraduate programs. The question was whether many if any of our high-flying research faculty would be willing to bring undergraduate students onto their research teams and give them the kind of experience I had had with Sam Martin.

The answer was not long in coming when I met with Charlie Liotta and Chuck Eckert, two faculty whose reputations were among the best on campus for their research and teaching. Liotta was a scientist and Eckert was an engineer, but they worked as a team. Both said they would be glad to incorporate undergraduates into their research, but they advised me to put my money where my mouth was. The problem was that they could not justify paying short-term undergraduates out of their funded research because their projects had a longer trajectory to become productive.

Given their advice, we established a modest fund to prime the pump. The results of our pilot program were encouraging. It was a pleasure to see how many students showed an interest early on, but it truly warmed my heart to see some of the best faculty at Georgia Tech become engaged.

As with our study abroad initiative, time and experience helped us understand how to sharpen our undergraduate research efforts. Our initial efforts, begun after the Olympics, were encouraging but did not produce the number of students we hoped. To jump-start further progress, we added more funding for faculty and students and created the Undergraduate Research Opportunities Program (UROP) with its own professional staff.

The combination of committed funding and full-time staff focused on undergraduate research broke the dam. By 2008, 1,200 students were engaged annually in undergraduate research. As I write this book in 2020, this number has risen to more than 2,500. These days, undergraduate research is considered so important that it is used as a parameter in some university rankings. The 2020 *U.S. News and World Report* rankings listed Georgia Tech eighth in the nation for undergraduate research programs.

*The Sound of Music*

Music is not the first thing you think of when someone says "Georgia Tech," but the first Glee Club was formed all the way back in 1906. As the *Atlanta Constitution* reported in 1907, "One of the great social organizations that helps to make the thorny path at Tech tread easier is a musical club organized...under the suggestive title, Tech Glee Club." A year later in 1908, fourteen students joined together to form the Georgia Tech Band.

When I arrived in 1994, the Music Department was home to a small but thriving collection of student music groups. However, given that the UCLA freshman surveys showed that half of our students brought musical talents with them from high school, I had reason to believe the need was underserved. I discovered, for example, that the Men's Glee Club had been disbanded, reportedly because women could not participate. I thought this reason specious—after all, the real problem was not men versus women but too little singing altogether. Who among us has not been moved by the beauty and passion of singing groups ranging from Welsh coal miners to women's acapella chorales?

It did not take long to prove the point. When we hired conductor Jerry Ulrich, a renaissance of both men's and women's singing groups was upon us, and the Glee Club, the oldest in the South, was reconstituted. As we expanded musical opportunities, we never had to solicit or encourage participation. Everything we offered quickly filled. Choral groups, glee clubs, jazz groups, chamber groups, bands, and symphonic orchestras spread the sound of music across campus. The marching band grew exponentially when we purchased the musical instruments from the Olympics after the Games were over. I was proud to note that we now had twenty-four tubas and twenty-four students who could play them. But what was most gratifying was that the students taking part in the new music offerings were majoring in engineering, science, computer science, and business. We knew we had tapped into something important.

The Glee Club went on to national recognition, and I was present when they performed at Carnegie Hall. After singing a medley of classical pieces, school songs, "Brown Eyed Girl," and "Amazing Grace," they received a standing ovation, and not a dry eye was in the house.

This account of our efforts on behalf of music has a personal footnote. After I left Georgia Tech, the Glee Club surprised me twice by showing up at the Smithsonian—first when they happened to be performing in Washington and later in a special performance at my retirement reception. On the latter occasion, alumni who had sung in the Glee Club traveled from places as far away as Seattle to participate. I was overwhelmed by the tribute, but what was most impressive was the reaction from my Smithsonian colleagues. They just could not believe students from Georgia Tech could sing so incredibly well.

*Poetry@Tech*

How many dawns, chill from his rippling rest
The seagull's wings shall dip and pivot him,
Shedding white rings of tumult, building high
Over the chained bay waters Liberty
      — ("To Brooklyn Bridge" by Hart Crane)

Tom Lux loved the poem "To Brooklyn Bridge" by Hart Crane, and he found a new role for it when he became the first holder of the Bourne Chair of Poetry at Georgia Tech. He used the analogy Crane offered to catch the attention of the hundreds of engineers and would-be poets who took his classes. As he said, "Writing a great poem is like designing a great bridge."

Lux grew up a farm kid with a strong constitution and a deep, booming voice. He became prominent on the New York City poetry scene while teaching at Sarah Lawrence College. He loved words and Red Sox baseball, and he wrote award-winning poetry books. Listening to him read poetry was an experience never to be forgotten. So how did he come to be the founder and longtime head of the Poetry@Tech program?

It began in 2000, in the waning days of our first national capital campaign. No one was asking for gifts to support a poetry program, but two donors stepped forward anyway. Henry Bourne Jr. had been a Georgia Tech faculty member in electrical engineering who then served in the administration of President Pettit and became acting president after Pettit died. He liked to say he fell in love with poetry when he was a student at MIT and heard Robert Frost read, and he was supportive of efforts to enhance the teaching of liberal arts at Georgia Tech. Bruce McEver had graduated from Georgia Tech with a degree in chemical engineering, but James Dean Young, a professor in the English Department, had encouraged him to write. He went on to earn an MBA from the Harvard Business School and established a successful investment firm in New York City. In his spare time he wrote poetry and took classes with Tom Lux. The two of them hit it off.

The connective tissue in the equation was Kenneth Knoespel, chair of the School of Literature, Culture, and Communication in the

103

Ivan Allen College, who knew Bourne and McEver. Bourne made the first move, creating an endowment for the Margaret T. and Henry C. Bourne Jr. Chair in Poetry. According to Knoespel, Bourne described the Frost poetry reading at MIT as one of the most important experiences of his life. He said, "That's the experience I want Georgia Tech students to have as well!" Then McEver and Knoespel hatched the idea of complementing the Bourne Chair with the H. Bruce McEver Visiting Chair in Writing to be held by a poet-in-residence for two years at a time.

With the creation of two endowed chairs and McEver's encouragement, Tom Lux began to see that Georgia Tech was serious about establishing a poetry program and offered a unique opportunity to build something special. In 2002, he left Sarah Lawrence College after teaching there for twenty-seven years and became the first Bourne chairholder and founding director of Poetry@Tech. At Georgia Tech, Lux continued to write poetry, but he also had an overpowering belief that Poetry@Tech could help change people's lives. His courses for Tech students, who were novices at creative writing, came to be regarded as among the most unique poetry classes taught at any university. He organized poetry readings that were open to the public, and he crisscrossed Atlanta and neighboring cities to speak about and read poetry at high schools and middle schools. In 2006, poet Travis Denton joined Lux to help with the growing offerings of Poetry@Tech, bringing with him *Terminus*, a poetry journal that today publishes the works of poets nationwide.

So many people wanted to attend the inaugural poetry reading organized by Tom Lux that it was held at Georgia Tech's Ferst Center for the Arts, whose theater can seat 900. The lineup of poets was amazing to behold: Rita Dove, Billy Collins, Stephen Dobyns, and Lucille Clifton. The joy was palpable, and many understood that they might never see these highly regarded poets together in the same room again. During my tenure as president, more than 10,000 people attended poetry readings organized by Lux. My wife Anne and I were often among them. For me they were a delight to experience, and I took pleasure in seeing the light in the eyes of students and of friends who came with us. The readings were also a chance for Lux to introduce young poets, especially those from Georgia. They grew into one of the nation's largest and best-known poetry reading series.

In 2017, Tom Lux passed away, and Georgia Tech and Atlanta were poorer for it. Fortunately, Poetry@Tech is endowed and still going strong today under the leadership of Travis Denton and prize-winning poet Ilay Kaminsky, with the continued support of Bruce McEver. Nevertheless, its creation was so implausible that some today might be tempted to wonder how it ever happened. For any who might be dubious that so many highly regarded poets actually came to Georgia Tech, especially in the program's early days, the story of Poetry@Tech is documented through a digital archive of most of the readings through the years and in the minds of the students who experienced a once-in-a-lifetime event. I was glad to be there to see it.

Study abroad, independent research, music offerings, and poetry readings all enriched the lives of our students. Our commitment to these extracurricular activities also drew wider attention, including from Pulitzer Prize winner Thomas Friedman. In the 2006 update to his book, *The World Is Flat,* in a chapter titled "The Right Stuff," he captured the impact we were striving for. "Very few presidents of premier technology universities boast about their tubas as much as their test tubes," he wrote. "But Clough has reason to boast, because my guess is that by making Georgia Tech sing—and by making other user-friendly additions to the undergraduate teaching system, and by making education overseas easily available for Georgia Tech students—he is producing not just more engineers but the right kind of engineers."

## ROUNDING OUT THE UNDERGRADUATE MENU

Enriching our extracurricular offerings was a great improvement, but it was not enough. The academic side of the house was too important to ignore. Exit interviews of students told a consistent story: the narrow set of majors and academic options offered at Georgia Tech was a primary reason for transferring out. There was no question that the number of undergraduate majors offered at Tech was small compared to that at comprehensive universities. However, a closer look at our peer technological institutions revealed that even they offered more majors than we did. It was not only a competitive issue in attracting students, but it also showed that we were not providing the range of opportunities for intellectual growth that our students deserved.

Adding majors was not a quick or simple matter. Protocol required our strategy for expanding our academic programs to follow a deliberate organic process rooted in Georgia Tech's broader directions and growth. In addition, changes had to be made within the parameters and according to the procedures of accreditation and faculty governance, and in many cases they required approval by the Board of Regents of the University System of Georgia.

Fortunately, we had another option that could be implemented in the meantime: add depth and breadth using minors. A minor is an eighteen-unit program of academic study outside of a student's major, and it often encourages an interdisciplinary viewpoint. The courses for minors are adapted to reduce the need for prerequisites, so an engineer could take an upper-level liberal arts course, or a liberal arts major could take an upper-level engineering course. Minors offer students the chance to get credit on their diplomas for broadening their education. They work especially well at a school such as Georgia Tech, where more than 80 percent of the students bring advanced placement credit with them, giving them some flexibility in designing their curriculum.

Although expanding the minors we offered did not inherently address the problem of students who were looking for alternatives to engineering as a major, it did give engineering students a chance to expand their horizons. The minors we added to enrich the education of engineers included engineering and business, music, East Asian studies, pre-law, science fiction studies, and women, science, and technology. On the reverse side of this equation, we added minors that offered non-engineering students a chance to expand their technological knowledge in areas such as energy systems, computing and media, sustainable cities, and robotics.

It did not take long for new majors to grow out of our expanding programs. Georgia Tech's blossoming extracurricular activities in music immediately generated interest in more formal programs of study. We began with a Certificate in Music (1995) and then a music minor (1998) and a Master of Science in Music Technology (2006). Shortly after I left Georgia Tech in 2008, a Bachelor of Science in Music

106

Technology and a PhD in Music were added.

The creative genius behind Georgia Tech's venture into the space between music and computing was Gil Weinberg, who arrived in 2003 after earning his PhD in media arts and sciences from MIT. I was fascinated by Haile, Weinberg's robotic musician, which made its debut in 2006. Haile was not only more adept than a human at sophisticated rhythms but was also able to improvise by using artificial intelligence to recognize and adjust to surrounding music in real time. Weinberg became the founding director of the Center for Music Technology at what became the Georgia Tech School of Music and went on to create additional robotic musicians, prosthetics for musicians who were amputees, and music-making digital apps.

New majors appeared in other fields as well, many of them interdisciplinary. As our joint program with Emory University grew, it was natural to add a new undergraduate degree in biomedical engineering as described in chapter four. The growing application of computing to other fields spawned new degrees that went beyond conventional computer science, including fields such as computational media and digital media.

Finally, initiatives such as new minors, the International Plan, and the active involvement of U.S. Senator Sam Nunn were driving enrollment growth in the Ivan Allen College of Liberal Arts and defining another natural area for new degrees. We created interdisciplinary degrees that combined economics with international affairs, modern languages with international affairs, and modern languages with global economics, reflecting the growing connectivity of the world economy.

Even with these changes, Georgia Tech remained a university in transition when I left. With the steady, rapid infiltration of technology into business, entertainment, sports, policy, and international affairs, adding more new degrees was only a matter of time.

## IMPROVING DIVERSITY

Georgia Tech, originally a White, male bastion, had made a commitment to diversity long before I arrived as president. Female students were admitted in 1952 and African American students in 1961. Both of these steps were clearly the right thing to do, breaking down walls of prejudice and affirming that any student who had the ability to compete and succeed at Georgia Tech should be able to do so. However, making admission possible for women and African Americans did not mean they would want to enroll in any numbers.

One of the most enlightened steps Georgia Tech took was to create the Dual Degree Program in the early 1970s with the historically Black institutions of the Atlanta University Center. Participating students from one of these colleges took three years of coursework at their home campus, then transferred to Georgia Tech for two years of engineering coursework. At the end, a student earned a liberal arts degree from their home institution and an engineering degree from Georgia Tech. The program embraced the women of Spelman College as well as the men of Morehouse College, allowing Georgia Tech to address both ethnic and gender diversity at the same time. When I arrived as president, I asked how the students from the Atlanta University Center did upon transferring to Georgia Tech. The answer was "exceedingly well." Georgia Tech was fortunate to collaborate with such strong colleges.

Johnetta Cole and Walter Massey, presidents of Spelman and Morehouse colleges respectively, became lifelong friends, and they helped me build relationships in the African American community of Atlanta. While we were all in office together, the three of us worked to reinforce the vitality of the Dual Degree Program. Later we all reconnected through the Smithsonian Institution while I was serving as its secretary.

In addition to the Dual Degree Program, Georgia Tech established a series of initiatives to support the success of minority students, beginning with the Office of Minority Education (OMED). Originally focused on African American students, OMED later expanded to include students from all groups that were underrepresented on the Georgia Tech campus. While I was president, we were fortunate to appoint Gordon Moore as the director of OMED, and he still holds that position as I write this book. OMED was nationally recognized for its role in improving retention of minority students after they arrived at Georgia Tech.

My goal was to strengthen and expand diversity on campus by

building on programs like the Dual Degree Program and OMED. To some extent, this task required new resources, and several leaders on campus rose to the challenge. In 1998, a group led by Electrical Engineering Professor Gary May, himself African American, won a $3.2 million grant from the National Science Foundation to support engaging minority students in undergraduate research and preparing them to continue on to graduate school. Named FACES (Facilitating Academic Careers in Engineering and Science), this initiative became so successful that the funding was renewed multiple times, and May won recognition with a national award for mentoring presented by President Barack Obama.

Then, in 2001, a Georgia Tech team led by Jean-Lou Chameau, dean of the College of Engineering, won a $3.7 million ADVANCE award from the National Science Foundation to encourage female students to consider faculty careers, and to support women faculty at Tech, including their efforts as role models and advisors. Like the FACES grant, the ADVANCE grant was renewed several times. Both programs were ultimately built into the budget of Georgia Tech and continue to this day as engines of positive change.

Recognizing our previous lack of attention to the recruitment of students from the growing Hispanic population of Georgia and the United States, we empowered a team to seek funding from the Goizueta Foundation, named for Roberto Goizueta, the former CEO of Coca-Cola. Goizueta was educated as a chemical engineer, and I came to know him as a friend. In 2001, the Goizueta Foundation began a series of gifts that totaled $6.5 million during my presidency and continued in the ensuing years. Designated for recruiting Hispanic students, providing scholarships and fellowships to Hispanic students, and endowing faculty chairs, these gifts made a significant impact. By 2005, the number of Hispanic freshmen enrolling at Georgia Tech had increased by 125 percent compared to 2001.

Women had a long history of being in the distinct minority of the Georgia Tech student body, and we realized we needed to take a larger view of their special needs. In 1994, the Women in Engineering program was created to encourage female students to stay the course and earn a degree in engineering. This initiative was followed by the creation of the Women's Resource Center in 1998 to build a supportive community of female faculty and students from across campus, regardless of discipline. Finally, the Center for the Study of Women, Science, and Technology was formed in 1998 to give our gender diversity programs an academic backbone.

By the early 2000s, we had programs in place to ensure that Georgia Tech was a welcoming institution for students from underrepresented groups. I would be wrong to say that the results in absolute terms were all I hoped for, but there were signs of progress and the groundwork was established for the future.

In all years that I was president, Georgia Tech graduated the largest number of women with engineering degrees of any institution in the nation. In 2002, *Black Issues in Engineering* recognized Georgia Tech for simultaneously graduating the most African American engineers at all three degree levels—BS, MS, and PhD—something never accomplished before or since by any other university. Thanks to the NSF-funded FACES program and the great work by Gary May and other faculty, Georgia Tech repeated its 2002 accomplishment for two more years and remained near the top of all three degree categories for my tenure as president. Then, in 2006, we learned we were named as one of the top five universities for Hispanic graduate students to study engineering. By the time I left in 2008, we were number one.

While much remained to be done, our progress on improving diversity indicated that we were doing some things right. An affirmation that our commitment to improving diversity was on the right track came from the corporate community. When asked why they came to Georgia Tech to recruit employees from among our graduates, corporations replied that in addition to being very smart and hardworking, our student body was one of the most diverse in the nation, particularly for a technologically focused university.

## INFRASTRUCTURE FOR THE
## UNDERGRADUATE EXPERIENCE

It did not take long after I arrived in 1994 to realize that little had been done to create the infrastructure needed to support a growing undergraduate student body. Serving as the Olympic Village provided a dramatic step forward in our housing infrastructure, with the construction of seven new residence halls and the renovation older dormitories. However, we still had huge gaps to address in other areas if we were to provide adequate facilities for our undergraduates. Essentially no new classrooms had been built since I was a student more than thirty years before, and little of consequence was proposed in the ten-year capital plan. Enrollment in 1994 was 50 percent higher than it had been when the student recreation center was built.

We had outlined our objectives for undergraduates in our strategic planning. Now came the hard work of incorporating those objectives into our capital plans and making them a reality. That task involved not only blending the required facilities into existing plans that were heavily tilted toward research but also sorting out how to finance them. The details of reshaping the campus are covered in chapter seven, but the process as it related to undergraduates focused on four objectives:

1. Incorporate advanced teaching and learning concepts into new classrooms and provide informal meeting spaces in large academic building projects.

2. Develop an innovative concept for the existing library and for a new building focused entirely on undergraduate education.

3. Add state-of-the-art recreation, wellness, and fitness facilities.

4. Modernize the existing student center and add food services outlets in multiple locations among the new residence halls.

The projects that addressed these objectives took the entirety of my administration and then some to complete. While each had a specific purpose, taken together they provided the physical evidence that Georgia Tech valued its undergraduates and supported their hopes for individual growth and success.

Probably the most profound was the Undergraduate Learning Commons, which took more than ten years to develop conceptually and build. Everything about it was different. It was 100 percent student-centered, and nothing like it existed anywhere before it was built. Since its completion in 2011, students, faculty, staff, and visitors have

111

passed through its doors more than 2.5 million times. I was humbled when the building was named for me, and I accepted the honor on behalf of the dozens of creative minds who had worked so long on developing the concept. A more detailed description of the development of this building is provided in chapter seven.

ENHANCING TEACHING AND LEARNING

As Joseph Pettit's presidency drew to a close in 1985, a group of faculty led by Professor Edward Loveland issued a report expressing their concerns about the state of teaching and learning at Georgia Tech. That same year, the Board of Regents mandated the use of student surveys at all institutions in the University System of Georgia. These two measures led to the formation of the Center for the Enhancement of Teaching and Learning (CETL), which was headed by Professor David McGill when I arrived on campus.

In its early days, CETL was charged with developing programs to improve faculty teaching and administering the required student surveys. Its role expanded in 1990 when the Lily Foundation awarded Georgia Tech a grant to create a "teaching fellows" program, designed to help non-tenured faculty learn what it took to be a good teacher. When the grant expired three years later, Provost Mike Thomas found university funding to keep the program going, but at a reduced level.

Thomas, with the support of President Pat Crecine, encouraged McGill to seek private funding by persuading a Georgia Tech alumni class to make a designated gift to CETL in celebration of a landmark anniversary of its graduation. He was not successful the first year, but I was fortunate to have arrived by fall 1994, when the class of 1969 celebrated its twenty-fifth anniversary by creating an endowment of more than $250,000 to support the teaching fellows program in perpetuity.

From then on, more than twenty young faculty participated in the program each year, learning how to hone their teaching skills from senior faculty, from staff who worked with them one on one, and from each other through group discussions. As an exercise in applying what they were learning, each one developed an innovative project for one or more of the courses he or she taught. During my tenure I attended every one of the "graduation" ceremonies for these teaching fellows. I never failed to come away inspired by their passion for teaching and their creative ideas to improve learning.

The success of the Class of 1969 Teaching Fellows Program led McGill and his colleagues to seek additional alumni support, and in 1997 the classes of 1957 and 1972 joined together to raise more than $500,000 in endowment funds. This gift resulted in the development of resources to help graduate teaching assistants with their teaching skills, as well as a pilot effort that extended the Teaching Fellows Program to tenured faculty.

Subsequent alumni class gifts helped create new university-wide awards to recognize faculty for outstanding teaching and student advising, and to encourage undergraduate research. The purpose of these awards was not only to recognize those who were leading the way in changing our educational culture but also to send a message that my administration was behind the effort.

Beyond soliciting financial support from alumni through reunion class gifts, we sought support for teaching and learning in our first capital campaign, which was launched in spring 1996. As the campaign got underway, Vice Provost for Undergraduate Studies and Academic Affairs Robert McMath was leading discussions regarding whether to require all entering undergraduate students to have a computer. One consideration was that if we were to expect all students to have computers, we would have to factor this cost into our financial aid packages. A few private universities had already adopted this requirement, but they had deeper pockets than we did. Of course, our size was an advantage that would enable us to reduce the cost by negotiating packages from vendors. However, cost was not the only reason we were conflicted. Not all faculty were prepared to make good use of student computers in teaching and learning.

The balance was tipped by alumnus Al West, who became chair of the Georgia Tech Advisory Board soon after the campaign was launched. West had been recognized by his peers as one of the most innovative businessmen in America, particularly in the use of advanced computing and communications tools. He wanted to help kick off the campaign with a major gift, and he wanted to discuss the possibilities with me. As we talked, it became clear that he was looking for something transformative that would help to improve teaching. Based on our conversations, he made a $2 million gift to help faculty and academic units optimize the use of student computers in the education process. His gift funded courses to help faculty learn to use new academic software, and it provided grants in support of imaginative projects that could be scaled across the university. Of course, time quickly changed how technology was used in the classroom, but Al West's gift provided the impetus that propelled us toward becoming an early leader in the use of advanced technology in teaching and learning.

In 1999, Dave McGill retired as director of CETL and was replaced by Donna Lewellyn, who served in this role for the rest of my tenure. She proved outstanding in helping us refine and expand many of the programs that were initiated earlier. In 2001, she was asked to serve on the committee that developed the then-unique concept for the new Undergraduate Learning Commons. Her participation helped ensure a prominent home there for CETL, so that its programs were visible and readily available to faculty and students.

Throughout my presidency I emphasized the importance of teaching and learning. As the final arbiter of promotion and tenure cases, I took special pleasure in advancing the cases of faculty who may not have been top researchers but were great teachers. We also implemented a "post-tenure review" process in which all tenured faculty were evaluated by their peers every five years for overall effectiveness in teaching, service, and research. If problems were identified, faculty were given time and resources to address them. In most cases this review was an effective way to help faculty who had lost momentum or whose approaches had fallen behind the times over the course of a long career.

By the time I retired from Georgia Tech, I could look back and see how the teaching and learning environment had improved. Although much work still remained, the progress we had made toward building a community of learners was satisfying. Not only had learning improved among the students and faculty, but it had been a learning process for me as well. I put some of what I had learned to work in my next job as head of the Smithsonian Institution, where education was one of my highest priorities.

It is always nice to receive awards, and I was pleasantly surprised when Dave McGill walked into my office in 1999 to tell me that Georgia Tech had been selected as the recipient of the Hesburgh Award for Faculty Development to Enhance Undergraduate Teaching and Learning. Only one such award is given each year, so it was significant to receive national recognition for our work, which was still in its early stages. Our selection was a credit to the hard work of CETL, the strong support of our alumni, and the willingness of our faculty to do the right thing, which had distinguished us from other worthy candidates. In particular, the endowments provided by alumni were evidence of a broad appreciation for the value of teaching and a long-term commitment to improving it.

McGill and I went to Washington, D.C., and on Monday, February 15, 2000, I stood before a crowd of 1,200 people to receive the Hesburgh Award. I accepted it on behalf of McGill and the CETL team, Bob McMath and his leadership, and our alumni. In a way I thought it was just a bit premature, because so many of our new initiatives were either just underway or about to be undertaken. But the award was a validation of the scope and direction of our efforts and our commitment to the task.

## WATCHING THE CULTURE SHIFT

Having been an undergraduate at Georgia Tech, I had a personal interest in improving the undergraduate education experience. As I consider the combined effect of the initiatives we undertook, I believe we shifted Georgia Tech away from a culture that expected failure to one that encouraged success. It was not accomplished by lowering academic standards but rather by emphasizing that Georgia Tech's bright undergraduate students deserved no less than our best efforts to help them learn, grow as individuals, and graduate.

Of course, Georgia Tech students themselves were an integral part of the process. In the early days, student leaders Greg Foster, Larry Stewart, Peter Stewart, Annie Anton, and Tony Chan were especially helpful, not only in providing advice but also in helping us avoid mistakes. Peter Stewart was the first to come to my office and point out that Georgia Tech needed a stronger focus on campus sustainability, beginning with a decent recycling program. This student-instigated initiative took hold, and in 2007 *The Princeton Review* named us among eighteen colleges and universities (of more than 600) on the Green Honor Roll for advancing the cause of campus sustainability. Larry Stewart helped me to understand campus racial issues and to create the Common Ground initiative, which provided a forum for people who did not agree to come together and discuss issues. Greg Foster was a leader among leaders. We lost him to the ravages of an aggressive disease, but his contributions live on.

I was proud that our efforts to improve the undergraduate education experience won a number of awards along the way, but what meant more to me than any award was the change I saw over time in our graduation rates. From 67 percent in 1994, the graduation rate by the time of my retirement reached 82 percent. As of 2020, the graduation rate had increased to more than 90 percent. Over the decades, these increases in graduation rate mean thousands more highly qualified students are earning Georgia Tech degrees and going on to make important contributions to our nation's economic and social fabric.

Nevertheless, it would be misleading to conclude this chapter by saying that all was well with the undergraduate experience when I concluded my tenure as president. Much remained to be done, and when it comes to undergraduate education, the work of making it better is never finished

## REFERENCES

Brotherton, P. "Graduate Degrees Continue Upward Trend." *Black Issues in Higher Education* 18, no 11 (2001): 45.

———. "Minority Bachelor's Degrees on Rise: Number of African American Bachelor's Degree Holders Tops 100,000." *Black Issues in Higher Education* 18, no 8 (2001): 34.

Georgia Institute of Technology. *Strengthening the Global Competence and Research Experiences of Undergraduate Students.* A Quality Enhancement Plan submitted by the Georgia Institute of Technology to the Commission on Colleges of the Southern Association of Colleges and Schools. March 2005.

*Georgia Institute of Technology Strategic Plan.* Atlanta: Georgia Institute of Technology Office of Publications, GT96-195, 1996.

"Georgia Tech Ranks #1 for Hispanic Engineering Graduate Programs." Georgia Institute of Technology press release, September 9, 2008. https://news.gatech.edu/2008/09/09/georgia-tech-ranks-1-hispanic-engineering-graduate-programs.

Kelderman, Eric. "Composers and Computers Work in Harmony at Georgia Tech's Music Center." *Chronicle of Higher Education*, January 30, 2009.

Long, William J. "Integrating Global Competence into Undergraduate Degrees in Engineering II: Foundational Curriculum." Conference paper. Madrid: Proceedings of the International Conference on Electronics and Communication Engineering, 2005.

Lux, Thomas. "The Poem Is a Bridge: Poetry@Tech." In *Blueprints: Bringing Poetry into Communities*, ed. Katharine Coles. Salt Lake City: University of Utah Press, 2011.

Marquard, Bryan. "Thomas Lux, 70, Poet Known For His Generosity as a Writer, Teacher." *Boston Globe*, February 13, 2017.

McGill, David. "Anatomy of a Hesburgh Award." *Georgia Tech Alumni Magazine* 75, no. 4 (1999): 54–58.

National Academy of Engineering. *Educating the Engineer of 2020: Adapting Engineering Education to the New Century*. Washington, D.C.: The National Academies Press, 2005.

———. *The Engineer of 2020: Visions of Engineering in the New Century*. Washington, D.C.: The National Academies Press, 2004.

Simon, Marc, ed. *The Complete Poems of Hart Crane*. New York: Liveright Publishing Company, 2001.

*The Strategic Plan of Georgia Tech: Defining the Technological Research University of the 21st Century*. Atlanta: Georgia Institute of Technology, 2002.

"Tech Boosts Opportunities for Hispanic Students," Georgia Institute of Technology press release, April 7, 2005. https://news.gatech.edu/2005/04/07/tech-boosts-opportunities-hispanic-students.

U.S. Department of Education. National Center for Education Statistics. Integrated Postsecondary Data System (IPEDS), 1995–2019, Completions.

Olympic Aquatic Center.
*Courtesy Georgia Tech Archives*

Presenting the Key to the Olympic Village for the 1996 Olympics.
Left to right: Pierre Howard, Lt. Governor; Russ Chandler,
Village Mayor; Wayne Clough, Georgia Tech President;
Bill Campbell, Atlanta Mayor; Zell Miller, Governor;
Billy Payne, ACOG CEO; and A. D. Frazier, ACOG COO.
*Courtesy Georgia Tech Archives*

Olympic Village welcomes President Bill Clinton, First Lady
Hillary Clinton, and Chelsea Clinton, Ferst Center for the Arts.

*Photograph by Stanley Leary / Courtesy Georgia Tech Archives*

Senator Sam Nunn (left) with Wayne Clough (center) and
Mayor Ivan Allen Jr. at 1996 Georgia Tech Graduation.

*Photograph by Nicole Cappello / Courtesy Georgia Tech Archives*

Senator Sam Nunn receives 2004 Ivan Allen Jr. Award
for Progress and Service, flanked by Wayne Clough
and Dean Sue Rosser.

*Photograph by Nicole Cappello / Courtesy Georgia Tech Archives*

Georgia Tech Lorraine Campus, Metz, France.
*Photograph by Constantino Shillebeeckx / Courtesy Georgia Tech Archives*

Undergraduate student Torus Washington,
Research in Materials Engineering.

*Photograph by Rob Felt / Courtesy Georgia Tech Archives*

Haile, the robotic xylophone player.

*Photograph by Brooke Novak / Courtesy Georgia Tech Archives*

Tom Lux, founding director of Poetry @ Tech.
*Photograph by Rob Felt / Courtesy Georgia Tech Archives*

The Historic District of the Georgia Tech campus.
*Photograph by James Duckworth / Courtesy AtlantaPhotos.com*

Biotechnology and Molecular Engineering Complex.
*Courtesy Georgia Tech Archives*

Manufacturing Engineering Complex and Quadrangle.
*Courtesy Georgia Tech Archives*

Campus Recreation Center.

*Photograph by Rob Felt / Courtesy Georgia Tech Archives*

Tech Green.

Photograph by John Toon / Courtesy Georgia Tech Archives

Klaus Advanced Computing Building.
*Photograph by Blakeway Worldwide Panoramas*
*Courtesy Georgia Tech Archives*

G. Wayne Clough Undergraduate Learning Commons with
Tech Green in foreground and Atlanta skyline in background.
*Courtesy Wayne Clough*

Grand Staircases, Clough Undergraduate Learning Commons.

*Photograph by Rob Felt / Courtesy Georgia Tech Archives*

Future site of Technology Square at time of land purchases.
*Courtesy Georgia Tech Archives*

Main entrance sign to Technology Square
with Scheller College of Business in background.
*Courtesy Georgia Tech Archives*

Technology Square looking east,
with Biltmore Hotel in background.

*Photograph by Rob Felt / Courtesy Georgia Tech Archives*

Fifth Street Bridge Plaza looking east from main campus,
with Tech Trolleys.

*Courtesy Georgia Tech Archives*

Georgia Tech Hotel and Conference Center.

*Courtesy Georgia Tech Archives*

Wayne Clough greeting President George W. Bush at meeting
of President's Council of Advisors for Science and Technology.

*Courtesy Wayne Clough*

Wayne Clough and Joe Hughes surveying homes destroyed by
Katrina flooding in Lakeview Neighborhood, September 2005.

*Courtesy Wayne Clough*

Duane Carver, First Promise Scholar, 2007.

*Photograph by Rob Felt / Courtesy Georgia Tech Archives*

Marquetta and Marteisha Griffin, Promise Scholars.

*Courtesy Georgia Tech Archives*

Milton James, Promise Scholar.
*Photograph by Rob Felt / Courtesy Georgia Tech Archives*

Sara Banks, Promise Scholar.
*Photograph by Rob Felt / Courtesy Georgia Tech Archives*

Steven Webber, Promise Scholar.

*Photograph by Jennifer Tyner / Courtesy Georgia Tech Archives*

*Chapter Seven*

# A CAMPUS BEFITTING GEORGIA TECH

Looking around the Georgia Tech campus when I arrived as president in 1994, I realized that one of its most salient features was an eyesore. As I searched for an explanation for the asphalt surface parking lots that blanketed the campus, I was told they helped recruit good faculty. The logic went like this: Faculty liked to drive their cars to campus and park right beside the building where their office was located. Because this arrangement was not allowed at any other campus, it was a recruiting advantage for Georgia Tech. I could see how some faculty might be glad for a nearby parking space on a rainy day, but it seemed a bit absurd to rely on parking convenience as a major factor in recruiting top faculty. It was a self-ordained prophecy for parking privileges to become a campus status symbol and for asphalt parking lots to surround every building.

When it was founded in 1885, the campus of the Georgia Institute of Technology was located at the northern boundary of Atlanta and was noted for its clean air. But the historic part of campus, which still held on to its red brick roots, had been left behind as the campus had sprawled north and west with minimal concern about architectural consistency or landscaping. By 1994, the campus had been swallowed by Atlanta's growth and was cut off from its neighbors to the east by a freeway and to the west by a commuter road. Neighborhoods to the north and south had deteriorated to the point where there were no shops or grocery stores. Asphalt parking lots were the prevailing landscape feature.

It was reasonable to ask how these conditions could have developed. From a utilitarian point of view, one could argue that it did not matter because Georgia Tech could go about its work regardless. Yet to my way of thinking, the state of the campus was a mismatch with our aspirations as well as a threat to our ability to compete for the best students and faculty. What surprised me was how few people were concerned. Some other issue always seemed more important. Parking spaces were valued over green spaces; pedestrians took second place to automobiles.

I knew something about the importance of a sense of place, having served at Duke, Stanford, Virginia Tech, and the University of Washington before coming back to Georgia Tech. While the visual appearance of each of these institutions is different, all of them are consistently listed among the fifty most beautiful college campuses in the United States. Visitors to these campuses see history reflected in the distinctive architecture, and they feel humanity and aesthetics imparted by the landscape. Asphalt parking lots are not considered an advantage.

Even for an optimist like me, it was clear we needed to think outside the box to make our cramped and unlovely campus a special place. We did not have the beautiful natural setting of Virginia Tech or the University of Washington, nor did we have the sizable endowments of Duke and Stanford or their history of maintaining a consistent architectural style. What we did have was nowhere to go but up.

## A LITTLE HISTORY

In 1888, when the first class of 85 students was enrolled at Georgia Tech, the campus consisted of two red brick buildings on nine acres of land. It was bounded on the north by Cherry Street and on the south by North Avenue, so named because at the time it ran along Atlanta's northern edge. The two structures were the Administration Building, known as the Tech Tower, and the Shop Building. The Shop Building burned down in 1892, but the Tech Tower, now named the Lettie Pate Evans Administration Building, still stands as the iconic landmark of the Georgia Tech campus.

From these first two buildings the Georgia Tech campus grew in spurts, the first coming during the tenure of its second president, Lyman Hall. Hall was appointed president in 1896 at a critical juncture when the unprofitable commercial shop program was abandoned. His goals were to expand the school's offerings beyond mechanical engineering into civil and electrical engineering and the sciences, and to offer on-campus housing. Educating these additional students required funding from the state's political leaders; Hall's personal commitment was to raise private funds to build the new buildings. It was said he died of exhaustion in 1905 from the stress of the workload.

Kenneth Matheson succeeded Hall as president in 1906 and continued the campus expansion begun by Hall. By the time Matheson retired in 1922, the campus included twelve buildings. They form what is today known as the historic district, an area added to the National Register of Historic Places in 1979. Donors to these buildings included Andrew Carnegie and John D. Rockefeller. The Carnegie Building was Georgia Tech's first library, and then it was later remodeled to serve as offices for top administrative leaders.

While the buildings of the Historic District did not conform to a consistent architectural theme, they were similar in scale and consistently used a red brick motif. The landscaping provided elegant shade trees and graceful small, open areas. However, this sensibility was lost with the campus growth that followed.

Sporadic attempts were made at master planning, with versions developed in 1912, 1948, and 1952. In 1965, a new master plan was created to accommodate a large area that was added to the northwest side of campus during the administration of Edward Harrison. In 1991, another new plan was developed, focused primarily on accommodating the new facilities that would arrive as a result of the 1996 Olympic Games. I believed the university's first fully comprehensive and forward-looking master plan was long overdue.

## A RECIPE FOR HOW NOT TO DO IT

There was no question that a new master plan was needed to guide the development of campus, but first we needed the framework of a strategic plan and a long-term facilities plan. Along the way we also had to

121

lay the groundwork for a national capital fundraising campaign to provide resources. In a perfect world, these planning exercises would have proceeded in an orderly manner, with each one building on the concepts of its predecessors, but perfect was not an option. The only part of the process that followed form was that the 1995 Georgia Institute of Technology Strategic Plan was developed first, as it should be.

The serious planning for long-term capital construction began with the 1996 facilities study, described in chapter two, which provided insights into our overall needs for the next ten to twenty years. The findings showed not only that we were in a deficit at the time of the study but also that we had to accelerate our pace of construction to prevent falling even farther behind our peers. In addition, we learned for the first time that the average age of our buildings was forty-three years, which meant that besides building new facilities, we also needed to renovate older, historic structures.

Based on these findings, we developed a tentative new ten-year capital plan, which admittedly relied on a lot of educated guesswork. For all of its flaws, this plan allowed us to undertake Georgia Tech's first formalized master planning process, one that reflected our aspirations for the future rather than primarily reacting to present circumstances.

## THE 1997 CAMPUS MASTER PLAN

Around the same time that we were in the throes of long-term capital planning, the concept of master planning became de rigueur in higher education. Campuses large and small were charged with developing "master plans," as if they could be rolled off an assembly line at the turn of a crank. However, at Georgia Tech the need for such a plan was different. The fundamental question was whether it was even possible to align the limited capabilities of our small campus with our somewhat outsized aspirations.

We clearly needed professional expertise to answer that question, and we looked for a firm that had experience with universities in urban settings like ours. Fortunately, Senior Vice President for Administration and Finance Bob Thompson was among the leaders of the National Association of College and University Business Officers, which provided an opportunity to draw on the experience of peer institutions. References from his connections led us to Wallace Roberts & Todd (WRT) of Philadelphia. We hired WRT in 1996, forming a partnership that lasted more than a decade as we addressed long-standing campus issues and took advantage of new opportunities.

The WRT approach not only assessed every nook and cranny on our campus but also explored how we could help improve neighboring communities and better connect to the City of Atlanta. The painstaking way WRT parsed the facts and arrived at their conclusions was impressive. Most importantly, they captured the conflict between where we were and where we said we hoped to go. The completed master plan was introduced in 1997. While an announcement on a university campus of such a document might easily pass below the radar, this one caught the public's attention. The goals included the following:

- Remove eighteen asphalt surface parking lots; develop options to encourage use of public transit; and construct parking decks to address the loss of surface parking.

- Create a "living campus" with a strong sense of identity and a focus on sustainability.

- Convert several streets to pedestrian use only, and add shuttle buses to transport students within campus and to relevant external destinations.

- Develop stronger links to the Midtown Alliance and the City of Atlanta.

- Create a distinctive architectural style reflecting both the history of the campus and its future.

- Cultivate a campus landscape featuring quadrangles that tie buildings into functional sectors, an expanded tree canopy, and a central signature open space.

- Enhance campus identity using gateway features at key pedestrian and vehicular entrances.

- Promote partnerships with the security forces of neighboring entities, particularly the Atlanta Police Department.

- By 2008, construct 3.25 million gross square feet of new space and renovate 1.42 million gross square feet of existing space.

- Create a Planning and Design Commission to provide advice to the administration in its efforts to implement the master plan.

The 1997 Campus Master Plan could be viewed as a "how-to" guide for Georgia Tech to reinvent its processes for campus and facilities planning and design. Personally, I saw it as once-in-a-lifetime opportunity to give Georgia Tech the campus it deserved.

The plan focused on actions for the next decade, but completing the transformation would actually take even longer. Recognizing that circumstances could change over such a long time, the plan's introduction described it as a "living document" that "must remain flexible to accommodate new and changing conditions." This approach proved prophetic, as a major new project to be known as Technology Square, the subject of chapter eight, soon appeared on the horizon.

For those on campus whose lives were tethered to their automobiles, the idea of eliminating eighteen surface parking lots was a form of heresy. The pain was reduced by building new parking decks and providing subsidies to those who could use public transit. In a show of personal commitment, some of the first parking spaces to be eliminated were those in front of the Carnegie Building, which were assigned to Georgia Tech's top administrators, myself included. Henceforth we would park in a lower lot off of North Avenue and get some exercise by climbing the steps to our offices. This change eliminated automobile traffic in this part of the Historic District, allowing for improved landscaping and benches for students and visitors. In another small but statement-making step, I mandated that everyone, including the president, had to pay for parking.

Although opposition came from some quarters, other things worked in our favor. First, we had just been through a massive construction process with the Olympics, so campus constituencies were conditioned to disruption as the cost of progress. Second, even as we were rolling out the plan, we were already making progress on some of the ideas it contained, so people could quickly see the benefits that early

124

projects provided. Third, any work beyond the existing boundaries of our campus would occur in places that were broken in body and spirit. As a result, whatever we did would represent an improvement in both appearance and safety.

## BEGINNING THE TRANSFORMATION: 1998–2003

The expression "the stars must have aligned" is used when unusual events come together for good purposes. What took place at Georgia Tech during the first five years under the new master plan fits that description, but I would argue that it was no coincidence. We were faced with addressing a host of preexisting financial problems, developing a fundamentals-based capital construction plan, creating Georgia Tech's first comprehensive master plan, and launching Tech's first national fundraising campaign all at the same time, even as we were surviving the Olympics. As a result, we learned how to multitask at a high level. We capitalized on this experience from 1998 to 2003, as we began to bring the master plan to reality on multiple fronts.

### The Planning and Design Commission

Planning and Design Commission—the name sounds suspiciously like bureaucracy in the making, but for Georgia Tech it was a necessary step. Perhaps for the first time in the university's history, a group of people was charged with keeping an eye on the big picture and providing advice on growing our campus in ways that were consistent with the context of our history, our aspirations, and the possibilities. Membership of the commission included students, faculty, staff, and a group of distinguished architects and planners from around the country. Their job was to ensure that each new project was connected to the concepts in the master plan so that our overall campus development was guided toward our goal of becoming a great university. Their advice would prove invaluable during my tenure as president.

### Building New Atlanta Partnerships

The Olympics had helped us forge relationships with the City of Atlanta, but as they were focused on a single event, they were short lived. The 1997 Campus Master Plan pointed out that long-term issues like public safety, campus expansion, water and sewer management, and sustainability called for a permanent relationship based on an understanding that we were joined at the hip. Building this relationship called for us to take the initiative, because in our past we had done so little.

Senior Vice President for Administration and Finance Bob Thompson took the lead in working with the Midtown Alliance, a nonprofit funded by the business community of Midtown, our neighbor across the Downtown Connector, as the I-75/I-85 interstate corridor was called. Because the alliance was active in planning improvements to landscaping, transit, and sustainable development, this relationship proved to be invaluable to our own efforts. I took responsibility for working with the Metro Atlanta Chamber of Commerce, which focused on regional issues related to water, infrastructure, homelessness, and crime abatement. Other members of the executive team and faculty joined the two of us when their talents and expertise were a good fit with the issue at hand.

At the more granular level of outreach, we created an Office of Community Relations to help us connect with our neighbors, including local schools and churches. This office helped align our student volunteer efforts with schools and food banks and connected us with African American churches and Neighborhood Planning Units, which were citizen groups that provided input to City Hall. In time, all of these mechanisms for partnerships paid dividends by establishing lines of communication, helping us shape our plans in ways that took our neighbors into account, and creating good will.

*Case in Point: Clean Water Atlanta*

Even before the bloom was off her election as mayor of Atlanta in November 2001, Shirley Franklin knew she was in a catch-22 bind regarding water. The city's water treatment systems had been neglected for decades and no longer met federal and state standards. As a result, Atlanta was paying burdensome fines and facing lawsuits from the federal Environmental Protection Agency, the state Environmental Protection Division, and the Chattahoochee River Keeper. The catch-22 was in the solution. Any reasonable approach called for billions of dollars in new construction—monies the city would have to borrow through the issuance of bonds. However, the bonds could not be issued unless funds to repay them had been identified, which meant asking the citizens of Atlanta to consent to a special local tax increase. Given the public's lack of trust in the city and its engineers, it seemed unlikely that voters would approve a new tax. The mayor knew she had a problem, and in early spring 2002 she had an idea. It involved Georgia Tech and me.

Mayor Franklin met with me and said she hoped I would agree to create and chair a panel to review the options proposed to address the city's water and sewer problems, and then recommend the best one. And by the way, the solution should be cost effective. In addition, she asked that we proceed in a way that would help to develop credibility for the plan, so it would be possible to pass a tax increase to pay for the improvements. The mayor also noted that we should hold public hearings after each of the panel's meetings to keep the public informed and allow citizens to express their concerns.

I must admit that my first thought was to say no, because this whole thing was obviously a can of worms. Then the mayor played her hole card—she told me she had talked to my wife, who had said I would do it. I was now definitely committed. Besides, this effort would be a chance of a lifetime for Georgia Tech to stand front and center in solving a problem of generational importance to Atlanta.

From the outset it was clear that even though the technical issues were significant, the larger problem was building credibility. Critics abounded on all sides. Citizens were aghast at the costs of the proposed solutions and distrusted the city's engineering consultants, whom they felt were focused on solutions that would give themselves a piece of a very costly pie. Local engineers poured gas on the fire by offering technical criticisms and suggestions that sounded good but were not practical. Environmental groups, frustrated by more than twenty years of inaction, were suspicious of any plan that did not deal with the regular sewerage overflows from the combined sewers that served downtown Atlanta.

These problems were compounded by the fact that the city's water system served much of the Atlanta region, while the city itself made up only 12 percent of the metro area. Further, large numbers of commuters

127

and tourists poured into the city's businesses and attractions each day, using the water system but not paying for it. The one positive was that Atlanta had hired a respected national engineering firm to conduct a carefully thought-out study to evaluate the major options available.

I told Mayor Franklin I would form a panel of the best engineers and ecologists in the nation and require two things of each of them: all of their work on the panel would be pro bono, and they would agree not to seek work on this project in the future. The goal was to remove any hint of a conflict of interest in the findings of the panel. In return, I asked the mayor to support our findings, no matter how difficult they might seem. She looked at me and said, "You and your panel tell me what needs to be done, no matter what, and I will take care of the politics." And she did.

Nothing about the process that followed was simple, especially the public hearings in which we spent most of our time trying to help people understand the issues and appreciate the options available to solve them. Many viewpoints emerged, not only from those primarily interested in costs and technical matters but also from residents of African American neighborhoods who were concerned that they would bear the brunt of the construction or become the dumping ground for facilities that handled waste disposal. We held many conversations with particular interest groups, and it helped that those of us on the panel had prior experience with difficult public hearings. Mayor Franklin, true to her word, also worked to allay the understandable fears of various constituencies and neighborhoods.

Along the way we reached out to the organizations that had filed lawsuits against the city, keeping them informed about how the deliberations were going. It was also important to keep the mayor informed, especially as we reached the critical decision-making stage. Our goal was no surprises for anyone as we entered the home stretch and prepared for the final announcement of our findings.

By August 2002, the panel had come to unanimous agreement on what we felt was the best approach, which was to separate the wastewater and sewer systems in the suburbs but require a new large-scale tunnel and treatment system for central Atlanta. The cost was more than $3 billion, but in addition to addressing specific problems, the new infrastructure would replace aging and leaking pipes and pumping stations. As a bonus, we proposed creating more greenspace through the design of the project, adding monitoring devices to track water quality, and using the project as an educational resource. Our concluding statement was, "Seizing the opportunity now to bring its infrastructure up to standard will go a long way in helping Atlanta achieve its aspirations of becoming one of the great cities of the world."

When we presented our proposal to the mayor, we were worried that it was a big ask. But she smiled and thanked us, saying she was determined not only to address what was necessary but also to make Atlanta known globally for its commitment to livability and environmental sustainability. I could not think of a better way to conclude our efforts.

The postscript to this story has three parts. First, Mayor Franklin's announcement of her conclusions from our recommendations drew a standing-room-only crowd. Sitting on the front row with me as the mayor spoke were representatives of the three parties that had sued the city, all there to support her plan. We watched proudly as she announced the rollout of a project called Clean Water Atlanta that would change Atlanta's future. Second, with the help of concerted efforts by the local news media and the Metro Atlanta Chamber of Commerce, the bond referendum subsequently passed, allowing work to proceed. And third, over time the city would continue to advance its efforts toward livability and sustainability, efforts that would be mirrored by Georgia Tech in its own search for a new campus ethic.

In 2006, I received an inconspicuous package in the mail from the mayor's office. My first impression was that it was heavy. Removing the wrapping, I found a rock core, one of the last made to ensure that the alignment was right for the eight-mile-long Nancy Creek Tunnel. This tunnel was key to eliminating sanitary sewerage overflows from the Atlanta sewer system and meeting the requirements of the federal consent decree. I have many plaques, certificates, and awards that I could have displayed in my Georgia Tech office, but the Nancy Creek rock core was the one I truly enjoyed seeing each time I arrived. Shirley Franklin rightfully went on to be named one of our nation's most outstanding mayors.

## A NEW ERA FOR ACADEMIC FACILITIES

Even a casual observer could tell new building construction on campus was proceeding at a rapid pace, but something subtler was also happening. Four new academic buildings were completed from 1998 to 2003, and they were much needed, but taken together they represented the first step toward fulfilling the concepts of the 1997 Campus Master Plan. While each had a separate identity, they were linked architecturally through the use of brick cladding that mimicked the motif of the historic district. Even the first of the new parking decks built during this time brought its own distinction with a design that looked just like a building, right up to its brick cladding.

The new academic buildings were deliberately grouped in "research neighborhoods" clustered around open landscaped quadrangles. To encourage interdisciplinary research, the buildings housed faculty from different disciplines but with related backgrounds and research thrusts. Shade trees and outdoor seating in the quadrangles encouraged casual interactions among students and faculty.

Three of the new academic buildings were located on the site opened by the removal of the old Highway Materials Building, as described in chapter four. A fourth building was added later in my administration to complete the biotechnology and molecular engineering quadrangle. The first two of these buildings—the Petit Biotechnology Building and the U. A. Whitaker Biomedical Engineering Building— formed the base for our new initiatives in biotechnology and biomedicine. The third building of the cluster, and the largest of the three with 292,144 gross square feet, was the Ford Environmental Science and Technology (ES&T) Building, which was partially funded by a gift from the Ford Motor Company. It brought together faculty from environmental sciences and from chemical and biological engineering.

Each of these three buildings had an innovative feature in its design. Occupants of the faculty offices in the Petit Biotechnology Building alternated between scientists and engineers to promote collaboration. The Whitaker Biomedical Engineering Building encouraged students to write on the walls of their laboratories and classrooms as part of the problem-based learning approach. And the Ford ES&T Building contained space for an active business start-up incubator.

The fourth major academic building completed in the 1998–2003 timeframe was the J. Erskine Love Manufacturing Building to house the Woodruff School of Mechanical Engineering and the School of Materials Science and Engineering. Its site was chosen to create a second academic quadrangle, which connected the Love Building with the Fuller E. Callaway Manufacturing Research Center and the Manufacturing Related Disciplines Complex.

These four new academic buildings were the first to bring to life the ideas found in the 1995 Strategic Plan and the 1997 Campus Master Plan. Together they made a statement about what was to come in the future—a new day for the Georgia Tech campus.

When it came to the Price Gilbert Memorial Library, I was reminded of Mark Twain's twist on a well-known quote: "Necessity is the mother of taking chances." About the time I arrived as president, the Association of College and Research Libraries informed us that our library accreditation was at risk because of a lack of investment in the collections. In addition, in-person visits to the library were in steep decline. Students increasingly used computers for remote access to the library's digitized collections and saw little reason to go there. The result had been a reduction in the hours the library was open.

Things changed in 2000 when Richard Meyer, an expert on the use of libraries in a digital age, arrived as the new dean of libraries. While his appearance might lead the casual observer to expect a traditional librarian who stamped books and shushed patrons, he proved to be a risk-taker and an innovator. He quickly became a leader in helping us redefine the purpose of our library facilities.

Soon after he arrived, Meyer and his colleagues presented us with an intriguing proposal to use part of the first floor of the Price Gilbert Memorial Library to explore innovative concepts regarding how a library building might be used in the future. In the process, it had the potential to increase student use of the facility. What became known as Library West Commons was a unique joint effort between the library and the Office of Information Technology (OIT). It began with furniture and surroundings that were actually comfortable and attractive, but, knowing the nature of Georgia Tech students, it was also chock full of high-end computer information and presentation development tools. Beyond furniture and computer equipment, the space was staffed by experts from both the library reference desk and OIT—a completely new concept. West Commons offered a unique combination of facilities and staffing that students could find nowhere else on campus. After it opened in 2002, student use of the library jumped by 65 percent almost overnight.

Not content to rest on their laurels, the library staff began planning for a second phase of the commons idea in 2003. This time students were actively engaged in the planning, and two companies—the office supply firm Steelcase Corporation and the furniture designers from Herman Miller—joined in designing the layout. This project, called Library East Commons, was even more innovative than the first phase.

In East Commons, drop-down cable access to high-speed computers could be had anywhere. The furniture was on wheels and wall dividers were movable so that groups of any size could configure the space as needed to work together. There was a stage to test presentations, and a coffee shop was added. The results surprised even us. Between East and West Commons, visits to the library doubled, and the library went from reduced hours to a twenty-four-hour schedule.

East and West Commons not only proved to be a success for Tech students but also garnered national attention. In 2007, we learned that Georgia Tech would receive the Excellence in Academic Libraries Award from the Association of College and Research Libraries. On the day the award was made, I was proud to be on the steps of the Price Gilbert Memorial Library to accept it on behalf of Georgia Tech and my colleagues. As I listened to the comments by Rich Meyer and others, I quietly reflected on how far we had come, remembering that in 1994 our library was threatened by loss of accreditation by the same organization that was now recognizing us with its award for excellence.

## ENHANCING STUDENT LIFE

Students' needs are often forgotten as research universities rush to build new academic and research facilities. But we were determined not to make this mistake. The first step would be to complete a job left to us by the Olympics—converting the Aquatic Center into a state-of-the-art Campus Recreation Center (CRC). In addition, the 1997 Campus

Master Plan recommended that two more new components be colocated with the CRC: a large, multiple-use, turf-grass field and a new student health center.

## THE CAMPUS RECREATION AND FITNESS CENTER

There was no question that we needed a new campus recreation and fitness center. The old Student Athletic Center was built in 1977 to serve a student population of about 10,000. Twenty-three years later it was in poor condition, and our enrollment had increased by 50 percent. To replace it, we faced the special challenge of converting the open-air Olympic Aquatic Center into a year-round facility to serve a university campus. The design would be complicated, and no money had been identified to pay for it. It was time to put on our thinking caps and come up with answers not only for ourselves but also for the University System's Board of Regents, whom I would have to convince that our plan was a good idea.

The road before us traveled down two parallel tracks with no margin for error in either one. The first track involved lining up the money—more than $60 million. We would have to secure bond funding and have a reliable stream of revenue to pay off the bonds. Because this multiuse facility would serve the needs of students, faculty, and staff, we believed user fees would be a workable payback source. But there was a fly in the ointment—our students would have to vote to adopt the user fee required to support the payback. What was more, the fee would go into effect two years before the facility would open, meaning juniors and seniors would pay fees for a facility they would never use. The precedent for this arrangement had been set back in the 1970s when the old Student Athletic Center was built. Tech students had faced the same situation then, and they had stepped up to the bar. The task of championing this not-so-pleasant argument with our students fell on the broad shoulders of Tyler Brown, the president of the Student Government Association in 2000. I was fortunate to know him personally and was impressed by his maturity and integrity. In addition, he knew something about this problem. His father, Tech alumnus Carey Brown, had done the same thing when he was president of the Student Government Association in the 1970s. To Tyler Brown's

133

enduring credit, he succeeded in getting student approval for the fee, securing our financial plan.

Brown subsequently graduated from Georgia Tech and joined the Army Rangers as a lieutenant in an infantry unit. He was killed in Iraq in a small arms skirmish. As we searched for a way to honor him, we knew it would come back to student fitness. Knowing he had loved to run every morning on a 3.1-mile route he had charted through campus, we created the Tyler Brown Pi Mile Trail. Everyone who runs this course learns about his legacy of outstanding leadership.

The second track to project completion was bringing together a team that could do it on time and on budget, while providing an appealing architectural concept for a state-of-the-art facility. We decided to use the "design-build" process and solicited proposals from firms around the nation that were willing to come together as partners with each other and with us. After reviewing dozens of proposals from some of the nation's premier firms, we selected the team of Hastings+Chivetta (architecture and design) and Skanska (construction). It proved to be a good choice. The Campus Recreation Center (CRC) was designed and built over the period of 2001 to 2003 and was completed on time and on budget.

The concept turned out to be a bold one, creating a facility that provided more than 300,000 square feet of usable space. At its core were the Olympic pool and diving well, which were modified not only for use by our campus community but also to accommodate high-level competitions at the collegiate, national, and international levels. Above the pools, massive steel beams supported a reinforced concrete floor that provided space for six basketball courts and multiple special-purpose rooms. When it was built, it was the largest single-span concrete floor in the world. High under the eaves, an indoor track ringed the upper levels of the building, providing views of our surrounding neighborhoods and the Atlanta skyline. A large exercise room, outfitted with an array of training equipment along with a rock-climbing wall, was located near the entry to the building. Finally, an indoor recreational pool was built along the side for those who were not lap swimmers.

We knew we had done something special when the CRC opened in August 2004 to rave reviews from our students, faculty, and staff.

For the remainder of my tenure, the CRC averaged 200,000 visits annually. The early reviews were confirmed when the awards began to roll in. They included Outstanding Sports Facility by the National Intramural and Recreation Sports Association, the Gold Medal Award of *Building Design + Construction* magazine, and the National Award of Excellence from the Design-Build Institute. College Ranker named it the number one Collegiate Competition Swimming Pool—a distinction it still holds. Perhaps most satisfying of all was that after panning us for years, *The Princeton Review* gave the CRC its top Athletic Facility Award for all universities and colleges.

## FINISHING TOUCHES FOR STUDENT LIFE FACILITIES

The completion of the CRC, an adjacent multipurpose turf field named for alumnus Roe Stamps, and a new student health center signaled our commitment to the health and well-being of our students. However, the task of enhancing student life was not complete. Next, we directed our attention to the center of campus, where we intended to create a core of support for student activities and academics. The Wenn Student Center, the Ferst Center for the Arts, and the Price Gilbert Memorial Library were already located there.

The student center was more than twenty-five years old and in need of renovation. The construction of Technology Square, which included a large, full-service bookstore, paved the way for an elegant upgrade to the student center, funded with a gift from alumnus Roe Stamps and his family. Closing the old bookstore in the student center provided space to expand student dining options, open an optical shop to serve students' vision needs, and offer student groups much-needed office space.

## CREATING THE TECH GREEN

The heart of any campus is its commons—a large, landscaped open area surrounded by distinctive buildings that serves as a gathering place for students, faculty, staff, and visitors alike. When Georgia Tech was founded in 1885, the lawn in front of the Administration Building served this purpose. However, it was left behind on the fringe as the campus sprawled to the west and north in the following years. It was my belief—an idea supported by the 1997 Campus Master Plan—that we needed to create a new commons. The logical location was between the Wenn Student Center and the Price Gilbert Memorial Library, a natural nexus. The only problem was that the northern end of the site was occupied by the Hightower Textile Engineering Building.

The Hightower Building had opened in 1949, when textile engineering was in its heyday. The 1940s and 1950s had seen a flourishing of this discipline, and the building was a state-of-the-art facility at the time. It was designed in the International Style by Paul Heffernan, a distinguished architect who was the director of Tech's School of Architecture. Built on what was then an open area of campus, it was named for a family prominent in the textile business with more than a few sons who were Georgia Tech alumni. However, by the late 1990s, student interest in textile engineering was in steep decline, and the Hightower Building, which had been overtaken by campus expansion, had become our biggest maintenance problem. Change was inevitable, and it began when the School of Textile Engineering itself decided to change its nature. A new identity as the School of Materials Science and Engineering and new quarters in the Erskine Love Building, part of the manufacturing disciplines quadrangle, gave it a chance for a revitalized future.

Once the Hightower Building had been vacated, it was time to demolish it and let the site serve a new purpose. I knew and respected Neil Hightower, who had been a student at Georgia Tech at the same time as I and was president and CEO of Thomaston Mills. So it fell to me to inform the Hightower family of the need to remove the building. Out of respect for the family, we decided to propose a display in the Erskine Love Building honoring their commitment and the history of the Hightower Building. I called on Neil Hightower at his home in Thomaston, Georgia, and explained the need to remove the building and the plan to honor his family in the Love Building. He was obviously sad that the Hightower Building had to be removed, but he was gracious in his understanding of what Georgia Tech needed for its future. I will be forever grateful to the Hightowers for all they did for Georgia Tech, including their support for removing the Hightower

Building to enable the creation of a new commons.

The way was now clear for an open space of more than three acres that would be called the Tech Green. It was bounded on the south end by a grove of old-growth trees, on the north by the Van Leer Building, on the west by the Ferst Center for the Arts and the Wenn Student Center, and on the east by an asphalt parking lot. Needless to say, that parking lot was on our list as slated to disappear, and we were already planning for a new building to occupy its space—one like nothing ever built before at Georgia Tech.

When it was completed in 2003, the Tech Green welcomed visitors to a grassy expanse offering a sense of respite and play in the midst of a busy campus. Used by students as a place to throw frisbees, lounge in the sun, host band concerts, and gather in groups to exchange ideas, the Tech Green passed all of its tests.

## BUILDING ON SUCCESS: 2004–2008

Then we encountered a good problem. We were caught off guard by the success of our efforts in the first round of reshaping campus, but there was no time for reflection. Even as we had been building positive momentum, circumstances for higher education had been changing. State funding was tightening; dire reductions in federal funding for research were predicted; futurists declared brick-and-mortar institutions obsolete; and research universities were under fire from both left- and right-wing quarters.

I remained optimistic, because I believed we had invested in the right things—faculty, students, and facilities. We also had maintained the expectation that our students should be challenged, no matter how bright they might be. All of that was well and good, but it was time to rethink what was possible.

The first step was to develop a new strategic plan to replace the 1995 version. Completed in 2002, the new plan was more coherent and detailed than the 1995 plan, because the Olympics were behind us and we were now more confident in our capabilities and resources. It also had broader input, with Kenneth Knoespel, associate dean of the Ivan Allen College, and Sandra Bramblett, director of institute research and planning, conducting personal interviews with some 200 faculty about the future of Georgia Tech. Surprisingly, many of the earlier themes still were echoed, but the goals of the new plan were more explicit and ambitious. It emphasized ideas like sustainability, multidisciplinary research, teaching, and international scope.

What was different in the new strategic plan was the sense that we were ready to increase our impact on national policy decisions and play a leadership role in setting new directions for cutting-edge research. It was Provost Jean-Lou Chameau who captured these thoughts in the tagline and overriding goal of the plan: "Georgia Tech will define the technological university of the twenty-first century."

The 2002 strategic plan was used as the philosophical basis to revise the 1997 master plan. The 2004 Campus Master Plan Update recognized that Georgia Tech had made significant progress in transitioning from a "traditional campus" to a "knowledge-based community" and in building new facilities more rapidly than anticipated in 1997. While the updated plan continued the same basic themes, it highlighted the need for improved mobility and better access for those with disabilities, and it increased our focus on campus sustainability.

We became more intentional about applying sustainability to the design of both new buildings and landscaping, including the management of runoff water from rainfall. We began to think of our campus as an "eco-commons"—a performance landscape designed to slow runoff and collect it to reuse as gray water. On the north side of campus, we planned to collect runoff water in a rock-filled water course that followed what once was a natural streambed, connecting scenic open spaces along the way. In other areas of campus, we planned rain gardens along with a system of underground cisterns to hold the collected water for reuse.

It was not only a neat concept in its own right but also had the side benefit of strengthening our connection to the city and the ambitious goals of its Clean Water Atlanta project. Retaining and reusing much of our surface runoff water slowed and reduced the water flow from our campus into the city's combined sewer system at the very time when the system was struggling to avoid untreated overflows into the Chattahoochee River.

## NEW BUILDINGS: 2004–2008

The years between 2004 and 2008 represented the final stage of my tenure as president of Georgia Tech. While we had added infrastructure at a frantic pace during the prior ten years, we still had more facilities to build. Most of them completed the concepts and filled in the gaps of what we had already begun. The first was the Molecular Science and Engineering Building, which was the fourth and final piece of the biotechnology and molecular engineering quadrangle. At 292,828 gross square feet, it was the largest of the four buildings, bringing the total for all four buildings to 905,094 gross square feet.

Next was the Christopher W. Klaus Advanced Computing Building, which provided much-needed space for the rapidly growing College of Computing and also included our first underground parking deck. The Klaus Building topped 417,000 gross square feet of space, including the parking deck. It was named for Georgia Tech alumnus Chris Klaus, who had made a multi-million-dollar contribution to its construction when he was only twenty-five years old. A remarkable young man, he had developed one of the first cyber-security systems and created a successful start-up with fellow alumnus Tom Noonan to market it. They sold the company to IBM for more than a billion dollars. Both Klaus and Noonan went on to create other successful enterprises and continued to help Georgia Tech and other nonprofits through their philanthropy.

The last of the new academic buildings of this era expanded our capacity in nanotechnology, which was becoming a force in a wide range of fields, including new materials, computing technology, medicine, and biological sciences. The Marcus Nanotechnology Research Building, one of our most sophisticated laboratory buildings, was named for philanthropist Bernie Marcus, co-founder of The Home Depot. His life story is an American classic of self-made success, and he had long had an interest in helping to provide the medical profession with tools to tackle some of the most difficult diseases humans face. His gift for this building was motivated by the possibilities that were emerging from nanomedicine, some of them from the Coulter School at Georgia Tech. The capabilities of the Marcus Building provided a boost to Georgia Tech's emergence as a power in the fields of medicine and wellness.

## TECHNOLOGY ENTERPRISE PARK

There was an eighteen-acre parcel of land, located on North Avenue just west of the twenty-five-story Coca-Cola headquarters building, and it was unloved even by its owners. On its north side we were developing our North Avenue Research Area, with specialized new laboratory buildings for the School of Aerospace Engineering, the School of Civil and Environmental Engineering, and the Georgia Tech Research Institute. But otherwise it was surrounded by a nest of railroad tracks to the east, rundown neighborhoods to the west, and a decrepit public housing project to the south. No one but Georgia Tech saw this place as an opportunity.

Growing an urban campus like Georgia Tech's can be challenging. The 1997 master plan envisioned purchasing land to the southwest of the campus and eventually linking the parcels together to accommodate future expansion. So throughout my presidency we were on the lookout for properties to buy in this area, and this ugly duckling offered an immediate opportunity.

The early successes of our programs in bioscience and biotechnology had spurred rapid growth, with more than one hundred talented new faculty in the Institute for Bioengineering and Bioscience and the Coulter School of Biomedical Engineering. New buildings provided them with specialized research facilities matched only by a few other universities. Building on our partnership with Emory's School of Medicine, we won grants for four federally funded national centers of excellence between 1999 and 2006, strengthening an already robust research enterprise. It did not take long to realize that our success had created a challenge of another sort. At first the new ideas and inventions trickled out slowly, but the flow soon became more substantial. The question was, where could we find a place to convert these intellectual properties into products useful to society?

Of course, Georgia Tech was home to the Advanced Technology Development Center (ATDC), Georgia's business incubator for technology-based industry. Relocated to Technology Square, it had become an icon for Atlanta's high-tech community. However, its strong suit was digital and electronic technologies. Bioscience and biotechnology start-ups were different. They called for patient venture investments

140

that allowed time for government approvals, and they needed wet labs and specialized clean rooms to develop products for the commercial market. The unloved eighteen acres, then owned by the Coca-Cola Company and the Georgia Power Company, were destined for a new future. In 2006, with the financial help of The University Financing Foundation (TUFF), we negotiated deals to purchase both parcels.

To the surprise of just about everyone, we announced our intent to create Technology Enterprise Park (TEP) on this site. It would be dedicated to the commercialization of creative ideas developed by the inventive minds of our bioscience and biotechnology faculty. Unlike the development of Technology Square in Midtown, which had caught the imagination of the media, the announcement of TEP fell largely on deaf ears. Still we moved ahead and opened our first innovation center, TEP1, in 2007—a building with a forward-looking architectural presence that housed wet labs and clean rooms. TEP1 by itself could not fulfill all of our aspirations, but it was a start.

It took time for the larger world to appreciate the strength of Georgia Tech's research in bioscience and biotechnology, but eventually it took root and began to grow. Even as I was writing this book in 2020, Georgia Tech announced a $750 million expansion of TEP to create a world-class site for commercialization of advances in bioscience and biotechnology.

## ACQUISITIONS

Two acquisitions between 2003 and 2008 were readily adaptable to our goals and helped to enhance our campus plans. The larger was the Georgia State University Village, built adjacent to our campus to house Olympic athletes. The surge in new housing from the Olympics had been larger than Georgia Tech could accommodate in one fell swoop, so Georgia State University (GSU) had taken ownership of this housing complex for its students. The GSU Village, 958,772 gross square feet in size, was located on North Avenue across the street from our campus, bounded on the east by the Downtown Connector and on the west by Centennial Olympic Park Drive. At the time, GSU was in great need of student housing, but this complex was a less-than-desirable solution. The heart of the campus was downtown, requiring students to be bused to classes. Over time, GSU began to develop new housing much closer to its campus. Word leaked out in 2007 that they were willing to give or sell the North Avenue complex to Georgia Tech if a deal could be struck. We were interested because, over the decade since the Olympics, our own student body had outgrown our housing capacity. However, this complex would not come cheaply, even as a gift. It carried a substantial bond debt and was in need of renovation after ten years of use.

Fortunately, this story had a happy ending. After an initial set of give-and-take negotiations, the state of Georgia and the University System of Georgia stepped in to limit the pain and make the exchange workable for all parties. In 2007, the newly named North Avenue Apartments became Georgia Tech housing, giving us space for 2,000 more students. Beyond adding capacity, this complex allowed us to form three housing neighborhoods around the campus: one to serve freshmen, another for sophomores, and the third for upperclassmen. The North Avenue Apartments realized their full potential with a renovation that provided dining and recreation services and meeting spaces, giving students a full-service residential menu.

The second, smaller acquisition was the Institute of Paper Science and Technology (IPST). In 1989, with the American pulp and paper industry in full bloom, T. Marshall Hahn, CEO of Georgia Pacific and former president of Virginia Tech, had convinced his fellow industry executives to move the industry's stand-alone research arm from Appleton, Wisconsin, to Atlanta. The goal was to be close to the strong research and graduate programs of Georgia Tech. After about a decade, however, the industry had begun to consolidate; the technology of papermaking had begun to change radically; and production had begun to move offshore.

In the early 2000s, we were approached about the possibility of merging the IPST into Georgia Tech. We were interested because there were research overlaps with our School of Chemical and Biomolecular Engineering. In addition, the growth of our campus had literally brought us to the doorstep of the IPST, and the building and its site made sense as a campus addition. Finally, from my perspective, the small paper science museum of the IPST was first rate and would represent our first step toward a campus-based museum. After the merger, the lines of research were shifted toward sustainable technology, and the IPST was subsequently renamed the Renewable Bioproducts Institute.

## THE UNDERGRADUATE LEARNING COMMONS

On a university campus, the purpose of a chemistry building, a mechanical engineering building, or an architecture building is obvious. The name is a giveaway, and it tells you that the university values what is inside. Such buildings not only house the faculty of their designated disciplines but are also "homes" for the upper-level students who have selected these majors. The concept of particular buildings to house particular disciplines is an organizational tradition that has governed university campus design for hundreds of years. Its flaw is that it leaves out half of the undergraduate student body, namely freshmen and sophomores. At Georgia Tech, we knew these lower-level students were the most likely to struggle with academics, choices about majors, and learning to fit in. Why not have a building that was "home" for them? It was a nice idea, but it proved difficult to make a reality.

Not long after the Olympics, we began to think about a new building that fit our aspirations for undergraduate students. I had a few ideas in mind:

- Make a statement about the importance of entry-level students to Georgia Tech.

- Provide services for those who were uncertain about majors or in need of academic tutoring.

- Offer assistance to students and faculty alike to improve teaching and learning.

- Give students access to collaborative workspaces.

- Have a link to the library.

- Be located at the center of campus and open twenty-four hours a day.

My list was a start, but it was not enough. There were deeper questions: What would draw entry-level students there on a daily basis? Why would faculty ever come there? What would be its programmatic

143

connection to the library? What would make it distinctive as a building? It turned out there were no easy answers.

Because the building would not belong to a particular academic unit, a diverse group of people was required to develop its concept. So in 2000 we asked Bob McMath, vice provost for undergraduate studies and academic affairs, to chair a planning committee that included members from the office of facilities planning and the library, plus interested faculty and students. I charged the committee to answer a simple question: Did any other university campus have an existing facility like the one we were thinking of? Members of the committee went on a nationwide search to find the answer, which was no, not really. However, the committee discovered good ideas here and there that we could incorporate.

During the early years following the creation of this committee, our ideas were still in a state of flux and not certain enough for us to request state funding for the new building. However, things gradually began to fall into place. In addition to the concepts the committee brought from other campuses, our own experiments with Library West and East Commons provided ideas. The 2002 strategic plan and the 2004 Campus Master Plan Update helped to determine the site for the building, which was an asphalt parking lot along the east side of the new Tech Green.

It was a group from the College of Sciences, including Dean Gary Schuster and Associate Dean Anderson Smith, that came up with the key to giving the building an academic core and a Georgia Tech flavor. "I was in my office with my assistant deans talking about this project," Schuster recalled, "when we came up with the idea of teaching all of the introductory science labs in the new building. It just seemed like the right idea at the right time." It was indeed. At any given time, all Georgia Tech freshmen and most sophomores are taking required entry-level laboratory science courses. Teaching these courses in the new building would guarantee that these students would come there almost every day. The science faculty who taught the labs would also be there, giving the building an academic anchor. As a side benefit, moving entry-level lab courses to the new building would free up space in the science buildings for other purposes.

The idea was so compelling that all those who learned of it agreed with it, including me. It had just one caveat. The design of the new science labs should be consistent with the philosophy of the new building, meaning they had to be adaptable and able to change in the future as the science itself changed. Soon everyone was on board with no debate. After Bob McMath left for the University of Arkansas in 2005, Andy Smith became vice provost for undergraduate studies and academic affairs, and he brought much-needed continuity and a special passion to this project.

The last philosophical decision about the building centered on sustainability. Given the importance of the building to our campus and our students, it was clear to me that this facility needed to make a statement about sustainability. We had made a commitment to build sustainable facilities, and we had received our first LEED Gold certificate from the U.S. Green Building Council for the Klaus Advanced Computing Building. Now we had an opportunity to shoot even higher—a LEED Platinum designation. Reaching this level was not easy. It required us to consider not merely how the building was outfitted but how it was built from the ground up. We agreed that it was worth the effort, and we were convinced that any additional initial cost would be offset by savings in energy and water usage over the life of the building. Fortunately, Harold Wertheimer arrived in 2006 to take over Georgia Tech's capital planning and space management operations. He was a committed advocate for sustainability and successfully championed the effort to achieve LEED Platinum certification.

In 2007, the Board of Regents of the University System of Georgia approved the construction of the building. It would cost $85 million, with the state providing $60 million and private contributions covering the remainder. Principal contributors included Georgia Tech alumni Al West and Michael Tennebaum, and the Robert Woodruff Foundation.

The pieces were now in place to begin formal programming and design. After a national competition, the firm of Bohlin Cywinski Jackson was chosen as the architects and Turner Construction Company as the contractor. We were fortunate that Bernard Cywinski himself became the principal architect. It turned out to be his last major project, and he passed away before the building was opened. Groundbreaking for the building took place on April 5, 2010, and the dedication occurred on September 24, 2011.

The concept for the building was unique. It climbed the hillside of its site using a series of internal grand staircases and connected to the library on two levels at the top. The staircases were made intentionally wide so that students could sit there between classes. The west side, which faces the Tech Green, was clad with glass siding to admit light, and internal controls adjusted the use of artificial lighting according to the amount of natural light that was available. In addition to forty-one classrooms, the aforementioned science laboratories, and two 300-seat auditoriums, the building included offices for tutoring, writing assistance, and academic advising. The rooftop gardens soon became a favorite place for students, faculty, and visitors alike, offering a peaceful setting with spectacular views of the campus and the Atlanta skyline. Open twenty-four hours a day, the building is filled to the brim with students.

The facility won awards for its architecture and building concepts. Its commitment to sustainability, including a 1.4-million-gallon cistern under Tech Green that collects rainwater and runoff, resulted in its LEED Platinum certification in 2013. At the time it was the largest building on a college campus to receive that designation. Even Hollywood got in the game when the building was chosen in 2013 as the set for the movie *The Internship*.

Before I left Georgia Tech in 2008, I was more than a little surprised to learn that the Georgia Tech Foundation and Georgia Tech itself had joined forces to request permission from the University System's Board of Regents to name the building the G. Wayne Clough Undergraduate Learning Commons. It was humbling, especially since so many people had contributed to its creation. At the dedication I accepted this recognition on behalf of all of them and all future generations of undergraduate students who would use the building.

Ultimately the greatest reward was watching the building live up to and even exceed its promise. Records show that more than 2.5 million visits by students, faculty, staff, and visitors are made annually. As one student put it, "I can't imagine not having access to this [building].... Clough is how I define Tech; it's the keystone of Tech."

## THE SUM OF THE PARTS

When I arrived at Georgia Tech in 1994, the campus building inventory amounted to about 6.5 million gross square feet. When I left in 2008, the inventory totaled more than 14 million gross square feet. Because Tech had been so far behind in developing its campus, more than doubling the building space inventory during my tenure was gratifying. Equally important, we had accomplished most of this rapid growth within the guidelines of our master planning process, which changed the look and feel of the campus and allowed for a new approach to teaching, learning, and knowledge discovery.

I never expected that our efforts would land Georgia Tech on the lists of the most beautiful campuses in the United States, but it was affirming when the campus was cited among *The Princeton Review*'s top fifty "Green Colleges" and named one of the top ten "Cool Schools" by the Sierra Club's magazine. Just as important were the comments from visitors who consistently mentioned being surprised by the beauty of the campus.

Then there were those who saw something more. When director Shawn Levy was on campus for the filming of *The Internship*, he said, "Georgia Tech is one of the most unique and dynamic campuses I have ever seen." The word "dynamic" resonated with me. It was reinforced when a visitor from Emory University commented to me, "Emory's campus has that classic university look because of its marble buildings, but when I come on Tech's campus I feel an energy." I knew we had come a long way from the days of contemplating the removal of eighteen asphalt parking lots.

## REFERENCES

"ACRL Excellence in Academic Libraries Winners Announced." American Library Association press release, January 30, 2007.

Fox, Robert, and Crit Stuart. "Creating Learning Spaces through Collaboration: How One Library Refined Its Approach." *Educause Review* (Louisville), March 26, 2009. https://er.educause.edu/articles/2009/3/creating-learning-spaces-through-collaboration-how-one-library-refined-its-approach.

"Mayor Appoints Independent Panel of Experts to Provide Advice on One Part of Atlanta's Overall Clean Water Plan—Georgia Tech President and Panel Members to Review Court Ordered CSO Plan." Clean Water Atlanta press release, June 28, 2002.

"Mayor Franklin Pledges Clean Water for All Atlanta Citizens as CSO Plan Is Unveiled." City of Atlanta press release, October 18, 2002.

The Mayor's Clean Water Advisory Panel. *Final Report to The Honorable Shirley Franklin, Mayor of Atlanta*, October 2002.

McMath, Robert C., Jr.; Ronald H. Bayor; James E. Brittain; Lawrence Foster; August W. Giebelhaus; and Germaine M. Reed. *Engineering the New South: Georgia Tech, 1885–1985*. Athens: University of Georgia Press, 1985.

Sierra Club. "Cool Schools: Top 100," 2010. https://vault.sierraclub.org/sierra/201009/coolschools/top100.aspx.

Wallace Roberts & Todd. *Georgia Institute of Technology Campus Master Plan*, March 1998.

*Chapter Eight*

# TECHNOLOGY SQUARE

I still enjoy watching the flow of human activity at Technology Square, even though it has been more than fifteen years since its dedication. Students walk through the Fifth Street Plaza; diners chat over their meals in the sidewalk cafes; customers browse in the Barnes & Noble bookstore. People enjoy drinks in the lobby of the Georgia Tech Hotel or discuss issues in the common areas of the Global Learning Center. Then there are the young folks strolling by from start-up companies in the Georgia Tech business incubator or from the advanced laboratories of the Technology Square Research Building. As I watch the flow, I reflect from time to time that what I see today almost did not happen. An incredibly diverse team faced with adversity had to come together and beat the odds to make it a reality.

All told, the creation of Technology Square spanned a decade, from 1996 to 2006, concluding with the construction of the Fifth Street Plaza across the Downtown Connector during the last three years. During this time, Georgia Tech saw its enrollment increase by more than 5,000 students and its faculty by 150 professors. The university developed two successive strategic plans and a campus master plan and also conducted its first national capital fundraising campaign. Those ten years spanned the service of three governors (Zell Miller, Roy Barnes, and Sonny Perdue), two University System chancellors

(Stephen Portch and Tom Meredith), and five chairs of the Georgia Tech Foundation (Charlie Brown, Julian LeCraw, John Staton, Henry "Buck" Stith, and A. J. Land). It took a playbill to keep track of all the comings and goings on that stage.

Technology Square was not even a name we used until 2001. I proposed it after tiring of calling our dream the "Fifth Street Project." Everyone agreed that this name was an improvement.

## THE BEGINNING

It was spring 1996, and the Olympic Games were approaching. With the Georgia Tech campus increasingly locked down behind Olympic Village security fences, I was forced to use a new route to reach my office from the President's House. The drive could not be characterized as scenic. Heading east on Tenth Street, I crossed the expanse of the Downtown Connector, as I-75/I-85 is called, then turned south on Spring Street. At Fifth Street I turned west to the aptly named Fifth Street Bridge, once again passing over the noisy sea of cars and trucks on the interstate.

That trip brought me face to face with the reality that the area just to the east of our campus had become a wasteland. Graffiti covered exposed wall surfaces, and the few businesses that remained hid behind high chain-link fences. The once grand Biltmore Hotel was a hulk with broken windows, its only occupants homeless people looking for a roof over their heads. Prostitutes stood on street corners strewn with used needles.

The decline of what was once a thriving part of the Midtown neighborhood began in the 1950s. Two north-south interstate highways, I-75 and I-85, were slated to cross in Atlanta, and the city embraced the idea of funneling them together through the heart of downtown in a massive trench. The original Downtown Connector had three lanes of traffic in each direction, but a major reconstruction in the 1980s widened it significantly. Today it has seven lanes in each direction at its busiest point, which is just where it passes through the Georgia Tech campus. The Downtown Connector did link thousands of commuters from the suburbs with their places of work, but its construction carved up Atlanta neighborhoods all along the way.

150

I was a freshman at Georgia Tech, living in Harrison Dormitory on the eastern edge of campus, when the first iteration of the Downtown Connector was completed in 1960. The view from Harrison was of the interstate, and at night we were lulled to sleep by the white noise of its traffic.

Upon my return as president, I realized that the blighted landscape created by the Downtown Connector in Midtown not only posed a safety hazard for our students, faculty, and staff but also dimmed forever any hopes we had for a campus worthy of our aspirations. Mulling over this reality as I drove to my office in the days before the Olympics, I noticed "for sale" signs on many of the lots and buildings. It dawned on me that what these signs actually said for Georgia Tech and by extension for Atlanta was "opportunity." How that might happen was not obvious at the time, but I thought this area just might be the place to develop a new kind of technology hub—a place that was closely linked to Georgia Tech and its campus and had the potential to brand Atlanta as an innovation center in the way Silicon Valley had for the Bay Area and Kendall Square had for Boston.

## 1997: ACQUIRING LAND

Early in 1997, Senior Vice President for Administration and Finance Bob Thompson and I met with the board of trustees of the Georgia Tech Foundation and broached the idea of buying land along Fifth Street. We were talking about acquiring a small acreage in what was an undesirable part of Atlanta. Even so, millions of dollars would be required. Fortunately, we had two things in our favor. First, the foundation had learned how important it was to help us acquire land, although until that time the purchases had principally involved small tracts on the west side of campus. Second, the volunteer leadership of the foundation in 1997 included Charlie Brown, Kim King, and Julian LeCraw, all commercial real estate developers. Although some trustees questioned the wisdom of buying land on Fifth Street, Brown, King, and LeCraw understood why it was important to the future of Georgia Tech.

The foundation's first official action came at its June 1997 board meeting, when Charlie Brown, then chair of the board, sought and received support for $12 million to begin purchasing land along Fifth Street in the two-block stretch between the Downtown Connector and West Peachtree Street. Another $1 million was added later, bringing the total to $13 million.

## 1998: THE PIECES BEGIN TO FALL INTO PLACE

In 1998, events began to pick up speed. In January, the Novare Group, headed by Georgia Tech alumnus Jim Borders, bought the Biltmore Hotel, located on West Peachtree at the end of Fifth Street. Their plan was to renovate it for office space and restore the old ballroom area as rental space for events. While we had given thought to buying the Biltmore ourselves, Novare's plans were not inconsistent with ours and allowed us to focus our limited resources on other objectives. Beyond that, the willingness of Borders and Novare to buy a dilapidated hotel in a rundown part of Midtown was a signal to other developers that the area might have potential.

Now that we were acquiring land, it was time to sort out what the highest and best uses of the property should be. Practically speaking, the two obvious candidates were a continuing/executive education center and a hotel/conference center. Demand for such facilities was growing, and to meet it Georgia Tech was renting space on a catch-as-catch-can basis in the general vicinity of the campus. Because the facilities we could find were often ill-suited for our purposes, we felt that to some extent the rental fees were wasted cash.

The remaining question was what else to add to the mix. My bet was on Georgia Tech's award-winning business incubator, the Advanced Technology Development Center (ATDC), which had a strong track record of creating new start-up companies. Moving ATDC to Fifth Street would give this project a technology heartbeat and provide a natural place for young entrepreneurs to congregate, making them more visible to angel and venture investors.

While this pot was simmering, Bob Thompson received an invitation from Herman Bulls of Jones Lang LaSalle (JLL) to visit the University of Pennsylvania in Philadelphia, where JLL was working on a new project. Like Georgia Tech, the University of Pennsylvania had deteriorating areas on its fringe, and President Judith Rodin and her leadership team had decided to do something about it. Their plan focused on a struggling neighborhood adjacent to campus where they intended to build a $120 million mixed-use project that included a hotel, retail, apartments for students, and the university bookstore. They hoped their investment would catalyze private-sector redevelopment of the surrounding area. Begun in 1997, the Commons was slated to open in 1999. Thompson's visit in 1998 was perfectly timed, and on his return he said, "Our plan needs to do something like this." We liked the concept of convenience retail, a need waiting to be filled for students, faculty, and staff alike. The bookstore was a different matter, but it had potential to add vitality to the mix if our development were to attract more than just Georgia Tech traffic.

The year 1998 ended on a positive note. Late in the year, the Georgia Tech Foundation hired the Atlanta office of JLL to conduct a feasibility study of our emerging plans for Fifth Street. The scope of their study encompassed roles for continuing education, a hotel/conference center, the Georgia Tech bookstore, convenience retail, parking, offices, and an ATDC component. They were charged with reviewing the history of comparable projects around the country, considering the business and financial potential of our project, and soliciting views from a suite of stakeholders about each of the proposed components.

Broader events late in the year also boded well for what would eventually become Technology Square. After months of deliberations, both the Georgia Tech Faculty Senate and the Board of Regents of the University System of Georgia voted to support an academic restructuring that removed the School of Industrial Management from the Ivan Allen College and elevated it to a college in its own right. This change signaled an opportunity for the new College of Management to step up its game and establish its reputation as a business school with a difference—a strong focus on technology. It also instigated the idea of finding a new physical home for the college, whose building was buried deep in the campus—a home that would provide greater visibility and easy reach to the Atlanta business community.

During 1998, I was spending more of my time on an airplane. Raising money for our capital campaign meant meeting Tech alumni where they lived, which was generally wherever a technology or financial hub was to be found. Surprisingly Tech alumni welcomed me, even though I had my hand out. By the end of 1998, fundraising was ahead of schedule, and at its December meeting the foundation voted to raise the capital campaign goal from $400 million to $500 million.

Also on the rise were the total assets of the Georgia Tech Foundation, which increased from $419 million in 1996 to $607 million in 1998, partly as a result of a strong stock market and partly because of gifts coming in from the campaign. Rising assets always improved the mood of the foundation trustees—a nice way to enter the new year.

At the state level, Roy Barnes was elected governor of Georgia in November, riding a tide of good economic news for the state. Barnes, an activist, immediately began formulating initiatives that would distinguish himself from his successful predecessor, Zell Miller. We had some insight into his plans since Kim King, Georgia Tech alumnus and trustee of the Georgia Tech Foundation, had served as the treasurer for Barnes's campaign. High on the list was the idea of helping Georgia compete in the growing fields of telecommunications, broadband, and computing, which resonated with the strengths of Georgia Tech.

Nationally the economy was strong, having expanded steadily since the recession of 1991. Among the drivers were the growing impact of the public internet and the greater availability of home computers. Surging along with this trend was the emergence of the "dot-com" sector, composed largely of new companies that raised large sums of venture capital but were not making a profit. At the time, few questioned the logic of this unbalanced equation; instead there was a sense of the inevitability of a rising tide.

### 1999: THE FIFTH STREET PROJECT TAKES ON TWO PERSONALITIES

Wasting no time, Governor Roy Barnes kicked off his administration early in the year with the announcement of the Yamacraw project. Named for the bluff where General James Edward Oglethorpe founded the colony of Georgia in 1733, it was intended to help Georgia become a leader in the broadband, chip manufacturing, telecommunications, and computing industries. Eight universities in the state were to be involved, but only one, Georgia Tech, had an engineering program. Over the course of five years, $100 million was to be invested to support targeted research, hire eighty-five faculty, and create a venture investment fund. The initiative also established the Yamacraw Design Center, whose intent was to link twenty-two companies working in the areas targeted by the initiative with each other and with the new faculty. The creation of the Yamacraw Design Center called for a new building to serve as its home, whose location and scope would be decided later. Professor Jim Foley of Georgia Tech's College of Computing was designated the director of the Design Center on the strength of his career in both industry and academia.

Barnes's announcement set off jockeying among the eight universities, each one looking to get as large a share of the resources as possible. Georgia Tech was the only player among the contenders to be recognized nationally for competence in the Yamacraw target areas, but this competition was a political game. As such, I looked to play what cards we held. It helped that I was asked to serve on the Yamacraw steering committee that provided oversight of the project.

As is the wont of such multi-institution initiatives, the resources were spread to some extent across all eight universities. However, in recognition of its strengths in the core areas of Yamacraw, Georgia Tech eventually received forty-five new faculty, upwards of half of the positions. These new hires would provide a remarkable boost for years to come.

Although the Yamacraw Design Center had no building as yet, Foley moved forward quickly on the expectations set out by Governor Barnes. He began recruiting companies to participate in the center, giving them access to the new faculty who were coming on board.

Midway through 1999, Kim King created a stir by announcing his intent to acquire land for a development on the north side of Fifth Street. To avoid a conflict of interest, he resigned from the board of the Georgia Tech Foundation. Although King would be a friendly developer, we worried about how he would work with us and how his choices would align with our vision.

King's plan depended on purchasing two adjacent parcels of land between the Downtown Connector and Spring Street—one a large tract owned by the Coca-Cola Company and the other a lot recently purchased by the Georgia Tech Foundation. He was able to build beachhead by obtaining an option on the Coca-Cola tract. The foundation then agreed to sell him their property if he could close the Coca-Cola deal, shifting Georgia Tech's efforts to the south side of the street. Suddenly the Fifth Street Project, which had begun as a straightforward concept, had the potential to develop a split personality, with different purposes on either side of the street. It had never occurred to me that the north side of Fifth Street might turn out to be a developer's idea of what would make a profit but possibly have little to do with Georgia Tech. The question was how to corral these components into one framework—a framework that centered on Georgia Tech and Atlanta. There was no answer for the moment.

With the concept of the Fifth Street Project and the potential King development beginning to evolve, the Georgia Tech Foundation created an oversight committee with a new trustee, Tom Gossage, as its chair. The committee included Bob Thompson, senior vice president for administration and finance, representing the Tech administration. Gossage, who had been a lineman in Bobby Dodd's football program in his student days at Tech, was a chemical engineering graduate and had gone on to a highly successful career. He had recently retired from serving as the CEO of the Hercules Corporation and had decided to make Atlanta his home. He was a physically imposing man, and his executive experience lent an equally large view of the world to his role as chair of the committee.

As the clock ticked down on 1999, Jones Lang LaSalle was scheduled to present the findings of their study regarding the potential of the Fifth Street Project at the October meeting of the Georgia Tech Foundation. Their overall conclusion warmed my heart: "The development of the site will create a significant gateway to campus and provide a centralized facility in the heart of the emerging technology community within Midtown."

The report was favorable regarding the prospects for each of the potential components JLL had been asked to review: the continuing education center, the hotel/conference center, convenience retail, office space, ATDC, and a bookstore. Equally important, the report showed that almost all of the units would have income streams that could be used to pay back loans that financed the construction of the buildings. The only pushback came in their interviews about moving the bookstore from the Wenn Student Center at the heart of campus to Fifth Street. Some of those interviewed opposed the idea; others were confused about it. I knew it was up to me to overcome the resistance because it was a matter that involved faculty, students, and staff.

With a positive report in hand, the foundation asked JLL to proceed with the next phase of preliminary study, which focused on issues related to who would own the various proposed units and on refining their analyses about income streams. In concert with this phase of the study, the foundation created a new subcommittee, chaired by Marcus Dash, a former Goldman Sachs executive. The subcommittee had two charges: (1) engage the consulting firm Paine Webber to explore using bonds to fund construction, with foundation assets as collateral, and (2) begin the process of creating a memorandum of understanding between the foundation and Georgia Tech regarding ownership and financial issues.

As 1999 drew to a close, the south side of Fifth Street, where the Georgia Tech Foundation had acquired eight acres of land, was coming into focus. However, the north side—the area most likely to deviate from our vision—was struggling. Kim King was not any closer to purchasing the Coca-Cola property he needed. Thus, he was also unable to acquire the adjacent tract owned by the Georgia Tech Foundation because that deal was contingent on the other one. To boost his credibility and resources under these circumstances, King decided to partner with Cousins Properties. Tom Cousins was a well-known and respected commercial property developer in Atlanta and had an outstanding track record for completing major projects. I was of two minds about the King/Cousins partnership. On the one hand, the involvement of Cousins Properties would bring stability to the area if the venture succeeded. On the other hand, bringing in yet another commercial entity with goals of its own could shift the objectives for the north side of Fifth Street farther away from our objectives. If the opposite sides of the street were at odds with each other, then the area's potential to develop into a major technology hub would be curtailed.

## 2000: THE FIFTH STREET PROJECT
## BECOMES TECHNOLOGY SQUARE

Sometimes when you get deeply involved in the details of a project, it becomes difficult to step back and ask whether something might be missing from the big picture. When it came to the Fifth Street Project, the "something missing" was students. We had nothing in our plans that would attract students to Fifth Street on a daily basis. Once we recognized the problem, the solution was almost immediate. If this deficiency were a round hole, the obvious round peg to fit it perfectly was emerging before our eyes: our recently elevated College of Management. Dean Terry Blum had made her case for a new building, and it was convincing. But her proposal had assumed state funding, which inevitably would be years in coming. Including a new building for the College of Management in the Fifth Street Project would not only solve our student problem but would also give the college a visible location on the edge of the rapidly expanding Midtown business community and bring it into proximity with ATDC, our business incubator. To cap it off, the college would get its new building within a few years, not the decade or more it would take to percolate up the state-funding list. The idea was just too good to turn down; after all, the only issue was the money to build it.

The plan to move the College of Management to the Fifth Street site was announced at the February meeting of the Georgia Tech Foundation. The trustees, particularly those who were management graduates, were supportive of the concept. While I did not yet know exactly how much it would cost or whether management alumni would be willing to contribute to its construction, I told the trustees that I believed Georgia Tech could retire the debt in seventeen to eighteen years. I was grateful that no one questioned my statement, but our recent fundraising success provided good reason to think it was possible.

Meanwhile, things on the north side of Fifth Street were heading south. The February meeting of the foundation was in full swing when news arrived that the King/Cousins deal was falling apart. Not only were the two parties unable to reach terms for moving forward, but the requirement for a $1 million deposit to maintain the option on the Coca-Cola tract had not been met. If the development of the north side of Fifth Street fell through, our endeavors on the south side of the street would be impacted as well. We could not simply stand aside. We needed to take our best shot at saving the north side in order to preserve our own interests on the south side.

I had a quick discussion with Bob Thompson, and then he quietly asked Tom Hall to step out of the foundation meeting for a conversation. In addition to being a trustee on the Georgia Tech Foundation board, Hall was a founder and officer of The University Financing Foundation (TUFF), an organization whose history was closely linked with Georgia Tech. That history had begun in 1982, when President Joseph Pettit was seeking the means to build the Centennial Research Building. With no chance of getting state funds, TUFF was created as a nonprofit entity with borrowing capacity that could procure the construction bonds. Then Georgia Tech repaid TUFF through a lease arrangement using indirect costs from research activities in the building. As a nonprofit, TUFF could also offer Tech lease rates that were lower than market values. The idea worked, and TUFF subsequently expanded its reach to include other universities in Georgia and beyond.

Thompson's request to Hall was simple: Would TUFF loan us $1 million to take over the option on the Coca-Cola property? Hall's answer was yes, and his board supported him. This decision marked a seminal point in support of what would become Technology Square, and it was surely one of the debts of gratitude Georgia Tech owed to those who believed in us. TUFF not only made it possible for us to acquire the Coca-Cola property but also doubled down on its support, becoming the financial backer for the entirety of the north side of Fifth Street. We could not have been happier. Kim King continued to be involved in the development of the north side, but TUFF brought in Gateway Ventures, a real estate management firm, to work with him. Most importantly for Georgia Tech, the north side of the street now had a financial backer that supported our vision rather than pursuing interests of its own.

TUFF's involvement also gave us a unique advantage in making our case for the Yamacraw Design Center building to be located on the north side of Fifth Street. State law specified that neither the state nor Georgia Tech, as a state university, could sign a lease for more than one

159

year. However, TUFF, as a nonprofit with a long track record, could offer a lease with multiple one-year extensions. As a result, TUFF could borrow the money and build the building, and the state could rent it from TUFF through a series of one-year leases. It was a much more appealing alternative than asking the state to appropriate full funding for construction.

TUFF and its partners could now begin developing a conceptual plan for the north side of Fifth Street. The plan hinged on two projects: the Yamacraw Design Center building and a building to house Georgia Tech's ATDC, plus space for private tenants to generate an external income stream.

As for Georgia Tech, keeping all the balls in the air in this ongoing juggling act caused pulse rates to increase. But at least we now had two reliable financial backers—the Georgia Tech Foundation for the south side of Fifth Street and The University Financing Foundation for the north side.

*The Bookstore*

In 1995, an enterprising young man in Seattle created a start-up business selling books online out of his garage. His name was Jeff Bezos, and his company was Amazon. By the time we were discussing moving our campus bookstore to Fifth Street in 1999, Amazon was already transforming the way books, including textbooks, were sold. Its success meant Georgia Tech's campus bookstore closed at 5:00 p.m. on weekdays and remained closed on weekends because of lack of clientele. Although selling Georgia Tech sweatshirts and mugs helped the bottom line, it was clear that the bookstore's business model would have to change, move or no move.

Initially there was some resistance to the idea of moving the bookstore from the student center to the Fifth Street Project. However, in discussions with faculty and students I asked how many of them had actually gone to the bookstore to buy a book during the prior year. Few raised their hands. Most students used the bookstore principally to purchase the sundries that were sold there, and the faculty sent in their textbook orders by email.

In the end, selling the idea of moving the bookstore turned out to be easier than I expected. After getting past the initial emotional responses, I pointed out four advantages: (1) the new location would allow us to serve a larger community, improving the bottom line; (2) an expanded clientele meant the bookstore would be open for extended hours and on weekends; (3) moving the bookstore would open a significant space in the student center, which would be renovated to expand our convenience food service and provide much-needed space for student groups; and (4) although the Fifth Street Project was on the edge of campus, once it opened an expanded Georgia Tech transit system would provide ride service from all parts of campus.

The icing on the cake came when we selected Barnes & Noble to operate the bookstore. They were excited by the concept of the Fifth Street Project and told us they wanted to build a flagship bookstore that would demonstrate to other universities what could be done. There were no more objections after that.

*Going Public*

With the agreement of the Georgia Tech Foundation, we proceeded with a public announcement of the Fifth Street Project in early June. (It was still not known as Technology Square.) Our announcement was limited to plans for the south side of Fifth Street, but it did include the decision to locate a new building for the College of Management there. The news was lauded by Susan Mendheim, president of the Midtown Alliance, who said, "The two plans [Blueprint Midtown and the Fifth Street Project] are really mirror images of each other, because they are both focused on creating a vibrant live-work-play environment."

Hidden deep in the announcement was a sentence that foreshadowed a new day for the shabby Fifth Street Bridge over the Downtown Connector, which linked this new project to our campus: "Plans call for the bridge to be widened to add broader sidewalks and green space, creating an enhanced gateway to the campus and a pedestrian friendly route between central campus and the Midtown business district." This goal would take time to accomplish, but we put the idea out there from the start.

Georgia Tech was now committed to the Fifth Street Project, and the June meeting of the Georgia Tech Foundation would be a key to solidifying their support. We came into the meeting bearing good news. Based on the findings of a study by Brookwood Planning & Design, Governor Barnes had concluded that the new building to house the Yamacraw Design Center should be located on the north side of Fifth Street. Finally, both sides of the street had coordinated, positive momentum.

Sea Island was a lovely place to have a foundation meeting with its well-appointed facilities, tennis courts, and golf course. But there was also business to attend to and a vote on the Fifth Street Project. As chair of the Fifth Street Project Development Committee, Gossage presented the committee's report, bringing everyone up to date and setting up a vote. He concluded with a list of reasons why the project was important and said, "The train is leaving the station. You either vote to stop it, or if not, get out of the way." The vote was positive.

It was a sprint to the end of 2000. With the last phase of our national campaign winding down, I was in travel overdrive, and whenever I was in town, one aspect or another of the Fifth Street Project demanded my attention. Sometimes the two overlapped, as in the case of needing to raise $45 million for the College of Management building.

The south side of Fifth Street had come into clear focus. Between the Downtown Connector and Spring Street, a complex of buildings would include a hotel/conference center, a continuing education center, offices for the Georgia Tech Foundation and other Georgia Tech administrative units, and a parking deck. Facilities for the College of Management and the bookstore would be located between Spring and West Peachtree streets.

For the north side of Fifth Street, the next critical step was closing the deal on the Coca-Cola property that had eluded King for more than a year. I made several phone calls to Coca-Cola executives to explain how far the Fifth Street Project had come since they had last heard about it and to emphasize how critical their tract of land was to the effort. Then Tom Hall and I met with their executive team at the Coca-Cola headquarters on North Avenue, close to our campus. We were prepared to pay a fair price but still had some qualms. They did not need to sell the property at this time, and our plans to develop the south side of the street meant they could likely command a higher price by waiting. Fortunately for us, they recognized the positive effect our plan for the property would have on our shared neighborhood in the long term, and their community spirit prevailed. The purchase of the Coca-Cola tract put TUFF in a position to acquire the adjacent lot owned by the Georgia Tech Foundation, neatly tying up the land needed to develop the north side of the street.

Although loose ends remained about the details of the financing, everyone understood that nothing was to be gained by waiting. In September, I gave my first formal, public presentation to the Board of Regents of the University System of Georgia about the Fifth Street Project. No objections were made to our proceeding.

During autumn 2000, the Georgia Tech Foundation pressed ahead, lining up the design and construction team for the south side of Fifth Street. It included a who's who of the best firms in Atlanta as well as the JLL Atlanta team, whose deep knowledge of the project would be helpful. The architectural design was led by Tom Ventulett of Thompson Ventulett Stainback & Associates, a Georgia Tech alumnus who brought broad experience in designing major conference centers around the world. Construction would be a joint venture between Holder Construction Company and Hardin Construction Company, a team that boasted projects in every business sector. On the north side of Fifth Street, TUFF, Gateway, and King lined up the highly respected Atlanta-based firm of Smallwood, Reynolds, Stewart, Stewart & Associates to design and construct their two buildings.

The year 2000 had been a rush of events, including bringing our capital campaign to a close after raising $712 million, more than double the original $300 million goal. Of course, most of these funds were dedicated for scholarships, faculty chairs, athletics, and other good causes, but the success of the campaign created a sense of optimism. The campaign itself concluded too early to have much impact on raising the $45 million required for the College of Management building. That effort would have to stand on its own two feet.

But there was one thing I did not want to defer any longer—finding a real name for what we had been calling "The Fifth Street Project." With the prospect of exciting project renderings on the horizon, we needed a name that fit, flowed off the tongue, and had a little hipness to it. I objected to anything with "silicon" in it, because it would look like a knockoff of Silicon Valley. "Technology" seemed a logical choice, but what went with it? One night as I was looking at a plan view of our project, I realized its shape was beginning to resemble a square. This word was also apt in the sense of "town square," a gathering place for a community. I thought "Technology Square" would be a name that brought the new and the old together to make something unique. I began trying it out on Tech folks. I was never quite sure whether it was because they had gotten tired of hearing me propose it, or because it seemed right, but it stuck. At the December 2000 meeting of the Georgia Tech Foundation board, we introduced the name Technology Square. The board's acceptance was reflected in the minutes, which referred to "the Fifth Street Development Project, now called Technology Square."

## 2001: PREVAILING IN THE FACE OF ADVERSITY

In Chinese astrology, 2001 was the Year of the Snake, and I had been born in 1941, an earlier Year of the Snake. The snake symbol is seen as a combination of both potential malevolence and good works, a blend that signals uncertainty. On the one hand, 2001 began with a sense of optimism for Technology Square. Plans for both the north and the south sides of Fifth Street were moving forward, and our architects and designers could finally begin to give life to something that until that point had been abstract. On the other hand, we faced the grind of hashing out the details of who would own what, and where responsibility would fall if something went wrong. These issues threatened to bring us down. Bob Thompson realized he needed some help, and we got lucky.

Scott Levitan was a bright young man who had grown up in New Orleans and graduated from Harvard University. After a series of jobs in real estate development, he went to work for his alma mater at a critical juncture. Harvard's historic campus in Cambridge was straining at the seams, and the university was quietly acquiring land across the Charles River for an expansion. Levitan was hired to develop the real estate plan for what would become the Allston Campus. At the same time, nearby MIT, cloistered within a neighborhood that was languishing for lack of new enterprises, developed the concept of what is today Kendall Square, a mix of MIT facilities and high-tech businesses. As Levitan worked on the Harvard Allston Campus, he watched closely as MIT invested in Kendall Square. He knew how difficult such projects could be, and he learned their ins and outs.

At the very time we were looking for someone to help us, Scott Levitan felt it was time for him to move on. He had two job offers, one from the Research Triangle and one from Georgia Tech. However, he and his wife had a unique requirement for a new place to work. They had a son with special needs, and Atlanta offered the resources they were looking for. So Levitan chose us, and his skill set played a major role in addressing the issues we faced in 2001. His title was executive director of real estate development, but Technology Square would take his responsibilities beyond real estate.

By the time Levitan arrived, the south side of Fifth Street was embroiled in a personality clash between two strong-willed people—my team leader, the tenacious Bob Thompson, and John Staton, chair of the Georgia Tech Foundation, who had made a successful legal career out of being pugnacious and unbending. Staton and the trustees who supported him wanted documentation for every last detail of the financials along with guarantees about how Georgia Tech would compensate the foundation for any missed financial expectations. I understood and appreciated the fiduciary responsibilities of the foundation trustees, which required them to guard against the excessive ambitions of any Georgia Tech administration. However, I also needed them to lift their eyes above the minutia of financial details and see the vision of Technology Square's future, believe in its possibilities, and grasp the reality that delay could doom our prospects. Yes, the foundation held the private assets of Georgia Tech, but those assets were growing during my administration and the university itself was a thriving billion-dollar enterprise. From my point of view, if a problem should arise, it could be worked out.

The logjam was eventually broken with the help of Levitan, who brought his experience to bear, and those foundation trustees who took the larger view. Feelings remained bruised for a long time, but by midyear almost everyone was ready to move forward.

While the financial details were being hammered out for the south side of Fifth Street, the north side was experiencing its own difficulties. By the conclusion of the 2001 session of the Georgia General Assembly in March, the location and the funding mechanism for the Yamacraw Design Center building were a done deal. TUFF would put up $76 million in bonds to build the 200,000 gross-square-foot building, and the state of Georgia would cover the debt service through lease payments. The key question was how much the state would pay per square foot for the lease. In the end, this problem was sorted out through tough but friendly negotiations among myself, Tom Hall, Kim King, and Governor Roy Barnes.

The new building would accommodate the Yamacraw Design Center and its industry members, plus a group of Georgia Tech's highest-flying technology centers, including the Electronic Design Center; the Graphics, Visualization, and Usability Center; the Research Network Operations Center; and the Interactive Media Technology Center. In addition, the building would house faculty from both the College of Computing and the School of Electrical and Computer Engineering who were working in broadband and chip manufacturing. All told, more than 300 faculty and graduate students would have offices and laboratories there. In short, the Yamacraw Design Center building would be home to a powerhouse of faculty, students, centers, and industry affiliates, fulfilling the vision Governor Barnes had expressed when he had announced it back in January 1999.

The second building on the north side of Fifth Street was a different can of worms. Dubbed Centergy One, it was expected to house ATDC plus private entities. In essence the building would have two owners: TUFF for the ATDC portion and King/Gateway for the commercial part. Rental income from tenants would enable both owners to pay off the bonds that had financed the purchase of the land and construction of the building. However, as the financials took shape, we faced a conundrum. As a state-supported entity with a mission to serve start-up companies, ATDC could only afford rental payments at the low end of the market. Midtown was rapidly transforming into a high-end real estate market. To enable ATDC to locate at Technology Square, we had to find a way to subsidize its share of the land and construction costs, reducing the amount its rental payments had to cover.

It was time to play a hole card. Over the years the Woodruff Foundation had come to our aid when we faced a financial need at a critical stage in a project of importance to Georgia Tech and the City of Atlanta. We knew this door was open to us for Technology Square should we have no other option, and now was the time. Pete McTier, president of the Woodruff Foundation, and the foundation board agreed to hear our case and decided to provide a $5 million grant. Applying these funds to ATDC's share of the land and construction costs enabled TUFF to reduce their rental payments to an affordable level. It was a little-appreciated decision at the time, but it was another seminal moment in the development of Fifth Street. Without ATDC, Technology Square would have lost its entrepreneurial keystone.

The Centergy One building was configured in a "L" shape. One wing of the building was five floors high, and the other was thirteen floors. The first five floors in both segments were to house ATDC, and the remaining eight floors in the taller wing were for private clients. This "condominium" model, developed by King/Gateway, proved to be a winner for all parties.

With regards to the south side of Fifth Street, the results of the hard negotiations of the spring unfolded at the June 2001 meeting of the Georgia Tech Foundation. Thompson and I were asked to make presentations to bring all trustees up to speed on where we stood and what came next.

My job was to show not only what Technology Square would be but also what it would do for Georgia Tech at large and how it tied into other new projects on campus. I used the preliminary renderings Tom Ventulett made for the project, which showed impressive buildings as well as street scenes of sidewalk cafes filled with people. I used this occasion to introduce the term "Global Learning Center" to refer to the continuing education component of Technology Square. This new moniker made a statement that the center was truly state-of-the-art, allowing classes to be projected to and received from anywhere in the world. In closing, I emphasized the critical importance of completing all the work by August 2003. Meeting this deadline would allow us to begin a new academic year with faculty in their new offices, class-rooms prepared for our students, and paying activities at the ready in the Global Learning Center. And it would open the hotel/conference center in time for football season.

Thompson went through financial models for each building, explaining the planned use floor by floor. He concluded with the bottom line, which was a request for $192 million in bonds—$173 million for design and construction and the remainder for carrying costs and interest. After questions, motions were made to continue funding for each of the various pieces of the south side of Technology Square. One by one each was approved.

After the foundation's June meeting, everything on both the north and south sides of Fifth Street seemed to be headed in the right direction. Plans were made for groundbreaking ceremonies for both sides: September 6 for the south side and November 13 for the north side. The September 6 date was chosen to coincide with the September 7 meeting of the Georgia Tech Foundation. The only cloud on the horizon seemed to be the impending collapse of the dot-com business sector, which would dim the glow that had developed around a large group of technology stocks.

September 6, 2001, was a hot day in Midtown Atlanta but a joyous one for the 300 people who joined us for the groundbreaking ceremony for the south side of Technology Square. The event had been a long time coming, and I welcomed it. Speakers included Midtown Alliance president Susan Mendheim, Georgia lieutenant governor Mark Taylor, Atlanta mayor Bill Campbell, Georgia Tech Foundation chair Buck Stith, and on behalf of the University System of Georgia, Board of Regents chair Hilton Howell. All remarks were well received, but perhaps the best insight was provided by someone who was not there in person—Governor Roy Barnes. He sent a written statement in which he said, "Technology Square has the potential to become the nerve center, the very center of the technology universe of Georgia." As it turned out, he was right on target.

After the excitement of the groundbreaking, the foundation board meeting the next day seemed almost an afterthought, but it included several significant moments. One was the announcement that Crestline had been chosen to operate the hotel/conference center. Although a dark horse at the beginning of the selection process, they had become my favorite because they had long experience in operating university-based hotel/conference centers. They also were willing to accept a share of the risk if things took time to get started, and they did not want their name on the building. So the facility would be branded as the Georgia Tech Hotel and Conference Center.

The rest of the business at the foundation meeting involved wrapping up lease agreements and ownership details. Before the gavel fell to end the meeting, Marc Dash, who had worked out the arrangements with the bond agencies for the loans, asked the trustees to approve the issuance of up to $200 million in bonds for Technology Square. The motion passed.

A few days later, shortly before Foundation Chairman Buck Stith was scheduled to leave for New York City to close on the bonds, the Year of the Snake displayed its menacing side. At 8:46 a.m. on September 11, while I was holding a cabinet meeting in the Carnegie Building, terrorists crashed a plane into the North Tower of the World Trade Center in New York. A second plane hit the South Tower at 9:03 a.m. In Washington, D.C., a third plane crashed into the Pentagon at 9:37 a.m. In the space of an hour our lives changed forever. The nation was stunned and angered. Banner headlines in large type blazed across the front pages of newspapers around the country. "U.S. Attacked," declared *The New York Times*. "Outrage," shouted the *Atlanta Journal-Constitution*. "War at Home," proclaimed *The Dallas Morning News*. "Nightmare," cried the *San Francisco Chronicle*.

On campus we reached out to students who were from New York to give them support. A few days later we held a memorial service with 20,000 people in attendance to honor Americans who had died in the attacks and to voice our commitment to protecting our Muslim students, some of whom were being threatened. One of the most moving speakers was a Muslim student who said that no one who had committed such heinous acts could be considered a Muslim.

But even as emotions subsided, the unexpected dominoes from the terrorist attacks continued to fall, and among them were the prospects for Technology Square. We wondered whether people would be willing to travel on airplanes again. Would they use hotels? Would it be better to stop work on Technology Square now and restart sometime in the future? The Georgia Tech Foundation put everything on hold for the south side of Fifth Street so that due diligence could be done to see what made sense.

With the state's commitment in hand for the Yamacraw Design Center building, TUFF was in a better position than the foundation to move ahead. The groundbreaking ceremony was held as scheduled on November 13, and this one was immediately followed by design and the beginning of construction. It was a reassuring step in the midst of uncertain times.

The foundation placed the decision about the future of the south side of Technology Square in the hands of its Executive Committee, which met prior to the December board meeting for a deep-dive re-consideration of the project. Participants reported that the discussion was less than unanimous, and the vote was unusually close. But in the end the Executive Committee decided to allow the September vote of support by the full board to stand. A few tweaks were made to the agreements and goals, but overall everything remained as before. At the December meeting, Chairman Stith announced to the trustees that the committee had decided to proceed. Somehow, in spite of it all, the positive side of the Year of the Snake had won out.

## 2002: JACK BE NIMBLE, JACK BE QUICK

The way forward looked clear, but then it had looked clear in 2001. As 2002 unfolded, we watched as the dot-com bubble burst, and the telecommunications sector began a spectacular meltdown. In January, Global Crossing filed for bankruptcy, followed soon afterward by WorldCom. Plummeting stocks destroyed fortunes, including those of some Georgia Tech alumni. Nortel Networks, which had recently opened a new facility in Alpharetta to great fanfare, saw its market capitalization drop from $398 billion to $5 billion. Even the "Baby Bells," including BellSouth, began to struggle.

I was a little uneasy that this meltdown might throw a wrench into our plans for Technology Square. However, strong consumer demand kept the economy going, and the shift from "portable" to "mobile" in

170

communications and computing devices created entirely new lines of business. Apple celebrated 2002 with a new concept called iTunes, and Amazon expanded beyond books to change the way we purchase almost everything. I am sure that early in the year Governor Barnes must have wondered for at least a moment or two about his bet on the Yamacraw project, but emerging new technologies made its underlying concepts more relevant than ever. It turned out to be the right investment for the future—just not the future we had expected at the time.

The September 11 terrorist attacks and the telecom meltdown were worrisome to me for a different reason. In my experience, large construction projects were always better served by proceeding with all due speed. Allowing time to elapse offered opportunities for inflation to eat away at budgets; for material shortages to create delays; for politics to change; for unforeseen events to cripple progress; for critics to gather steam; and for a university president in the state of Georgia on a one-year contract with no tenure to be fired. Fortunately, in the case of Technology Square, we had assembled great teams on both sides of Fifth Street, and in a way, they were competing. Nobody wanted to be the one who let their team down. We also had a deadline—August 2003—and nobody wanted to be the one who caused it to be missed. Everyone was working in high gear to get the job done.

In spite of the pressure to meet the deadline, the first half of 2002 turned out to be a joy, especially watching Tom Ventulett create images in his sketchbook. In an interview for this book, I asked him what inspired him about Technology Square. He said without hesitation, "You rarely get a chance to design a project that is so comprehensive, so end to end. This was the opportunity of a lifetime to make a difference in Atlanta and for my alma mater, Georgia Tech."

Georgia Tech had a chance to work with Ventulett on the characteristics that would underlie the design for Technology Square: on the outside, a pedestrian-friendly environment with tree-lined streets that had wide sidewalks, no overhead wires, and street-level retail; on the inside, colorful and open interiors. We also knew we wanted ample lighting for evening visitors, and Ventulett came up with the idea of incorporating large glass "lanterns" into the building corners to provide soft lighting from above rather than relying on streetlamps alone. He used his creative genius to make all the details work together. Brick cladding connected the look of the buildings with the Georgia Tech campus on one side and the adjacent historic Biltmore Hotel on the other. Their elegant design respected the Biltmore and was enhanced by interior courtyards. The end result was a testament to the experience and talent of one of Georgia Tech's most famous architecture alumni.

For all of us, sustainability was a bedrock principle, including efficient, low-energy utilities, ambient lighting in daytime, and white rooftops to reflect summer's heat back into the atmosphere. Then there was the Tech Trolley. We wanted a signature transportation system that would serve both our campus community and the visitors who arrived on MARTA, Atlanta's transportation system. The idea of a trolley seemed a bit funky and old-fashioned in a good way, and it would be free. Students, faculty, and staff could use the Tech Trolley to get to Technology Square from campus. Anyone who landed at the airport and traveled to Midtown on a rapid rail MARTA train would find the trolley waiting to whisk them to the Georgia Tech Hotel or the campus. I still use it myself, and you cannot beat it.

The almost daily run of new ideas and the responsiveness of the teams to those ideas were exhilarating. Nothing intervened in our progress, and no more negotiations or votes were needed. The only change grew out of the changing focus of what had been the Yamacraw Design Center. The name "Yamacraw" went by the wayside, and the building became known as the Technology Square Research Building.

During 2002, my personal commitment to helping Georgia Tech become a player in Washington, D.C., policy circles was taking more of my time, but my growing respect for the teams developing Technology Square gave me confidence to leave the day-to-day operations to them. I had been appointed by President George W. Bush to the President's Council of Advisors on Science and Technology, which provided visibility and impact for Georgia Tech. This activity coincided with growth in our research funding from sources like the National Science Foundation, the Department of Defense, and NASA. When I returned from my trips to Washington, the reports on Technology Square affirmed the decisions we had made and reflected progress on all fronts.

## 2003: THE SPRINT TO THE FINISH

The national news of 2003 was dominated by such dramatic events as the completion of the Human Genome Project, the U.S. invasion of Iraq, and the *Columbia* space shuttle disaster. All of these went down in the history books, but for my money the truly big news was the dedication and formal opening of Technology Square on October 23 and 24. Our speakers included the assistant secretary of the U.S. Department of Commerce, the president of the U.S. Council on Competitiveness, the CEO of BellSouth, the governor of Georgia, and the mayor of Atlanta. Panels of international experts and Georgia Tech faculty discussed "innovation neighborhoods" such as Technology Square and their role in powering the local and national economy. Free goodies and ice cream were provided for the students, faculty, and staff, and the Georgia Tech Marching Band along with our mascot, Buzz, performed for the crowds. All in all, it was a notable celebration. It was also a time to reflect.

It had started with a detour. My drive to the Tech campus before the Olympic Games in 1996 had taken me though a desolate landscape filled with for-sale signs. Then the Georgia Tech Foundation rose to the challenge, initiating the process by purchasing land. Teams from Georgia Tech, the Georgia Tech Foundation, the University Financing Foundation, Kim King Associates, Gateway Ventures, architects, and contractors, all working together, created the concept, provided the financing, designed the buildings, and built what became Technology Square.

North and south of Fifth Street, it added up to a total of 1.6 million gross square feet of building space, created at a cost of $320 million. Remarkably, the entirety of the money had come in the form of loans. Who in their right mind back in 1997 and 1998 would have imagined that we would borrow $320 million? Who would have believed we would come up with schemes to pay it all back in twenty years or so and own the land and the buildings? Our success speaks to the power of an idea. It brings to mind the words of architect and city planner Daniel Burnham: "Make no little plans; they have no magic to stir men's blood."

The north side of Fifth Street got started well behind the south side, and the two sides were bankrolled by different entities and built by different construction teams. Nevertheless, both sides finished on time in August 2003. On the north side the project came in on budget; on the south side it actually came in under budget. Someone told me that bringing the two sides to completion at the same time was a miracle. I could not have agreed more.

It was not long before the awards began to roll in: Award of Excellence from the Atlanta Urban Design Commission; Development of Excellence from the Atlanta Regional Commission and Regional Business Coalition; Best Overall of the Best in Atlanta Real Estate Awards from the *Atlanta Business Chronicle*; Silver LEED designation for the College of Management building; Golden Shoe Award from PEDS for pedestrian awareness; and Project of the Year Award from the Atlanta District Council of the Urban Land Institute.

Then in 2004 we received the news that the Urban Land Institute had chosen Technology Square as one of ten winners of its Global Award of Excellence. I went to New York City to accept that award on behalf of all those who had worked on the project. It was humbling to think that Technology Square was counted among the best of the best in a worldwide competition that honored some of the most historic and innovative projects. I did allow myself a moment of pride when I noticed that the University Park at MIT was one of the winners. The surprise was not that they won but that Technology Square and Georgia Tech showed up alongside them. The award notation from the Urban Land Institute was noteworthy:

> In a previously blighted and vacant three-block area of Midtown Atlanta where security was a constant concern and pedestrian activity was nonexistent, Georgia Institute of Technology has overcome physical and psychological barriers to reconnect the university with the Midtown neighborhood by developing a vibrant 24/7 urban campus for students and community members alike. In Technology Square at Georgia Tech students, faculty, Midtown residents, businesspeople, and visitors meet and interact, attracted by wide, tree-lined sidewalks with benches and bicycle lanes, shops and restaurants, a hotel, on-street and garage parking, and access to public transportation....Technology Square was the first develop-

ment to implement Blueprint Midtown, a set of guidelines adopted by the Atlanta City Council as a special zoning district, and the project has set the standard by which future development in the area will be judged.

## 2004–2006: A NEW ENTRANCE TO CAMPUS

A standard-issue, drab, steel-plate-girder structure, the Fifth Street Bridge had been built by the Georgia Department of Transportation when the Downtown Connector was widened in the mid-1980s. Its purpose was to carry four lanes of traffic over the Downtown Connector, but by the 1990s it was little used because there were few reasons to travel between the Georgia Tech campus and Midtown. The bridge had sidewalks, but they were barely wide enough for two people to pass each other. High chain-link fences along the outside edges of the bridge protected the cars and trucks passing below from anyone who might think about dropping something on them. It was about to get a much-needed extreme makeover.

The idea of replacing the bridge was there from the start and was mentioned in the first public announcement of Technology Square in June 2000. Our goal was that pedestrians walking over the Downtown Connector to Technology Square would not have the impression that they had left the campus behind but rather would feel that they were passing along a continuum to another part of it. This illusion could be maintained only if the design of the new bridge made it seem to a pedestrian that there was no Downtown Connector. It was a great idea. The problem was that it was not our bridge. Although the Fifth Street Bridge was now in the midst of Georgia Tech property, it belonged to the Georgia Department of Transportation (GDOT) and was governed by the policies of the Federal Highway Administration (FHA).

In an ideal world, the target would not have been a replacement bridge. It would have been an expansion of the eastern edge of the campus using a cover that extended over the Downtown Connector between Tenth Street to the north and North Avenue to the south. To help us imagine a creative, people-sensitive version of such a cover, we invited our architecture students to participate in a design competition. They showed what was possible—a park-like greenway with periodic openings allowing people above to view the traffic passing below. I liked this idea because it posed a contrast between the frantic world below, where frustrated drivers passed the time encased in their vehicles, and a serene world above, where people strolled through a landscaped park relaxing, chatting, and perhaps tossing a frisbee to each other. Unfortunately, the real world offered neither money nor time for this vision to materialize. Instead, we had to compromise.

What was possible would be determined in discussions with GDOT, and to their credit they were open to working with us. The result was what was referred to as a "bridge/plaza." Its dimensions were controlled by parameters only an engineer could love. The length had to be longer than the existing Fifth Street Bridge to accommodate the possibility of adding express lanes to the Connector in the future. The width was limited to the maximum that could be built before large-scale ventilators would be required in case traffic backed up below. In the end, it became 256 feet and 6 inches long by 233 feet and 3 inches wide. We were pleased that its width was enough to include 25-foot-wide sidewalks, matching those of Technology Square, with room between the sidewalks and the outside edges for large planters with shrubs and trees on the south side and a large greenspace on the north side.

GDOT agreed to fund the basic structure, which was a significant concession because the heavy planters required large structural components to support them. Georgia Tech was responsible for adding the shrubs, trees, and greenspace, and maintaining them in the future.

To accelerate the project, GDOT chose to use design-build, which meant that teams of engineers and contractors would work together to get the job done. The architects were Smallwood, Reynolds, Stewart, Stewart & Associates, the same firm TUFF had used for the buildings on the north side of Fifth Street. The engineering was done by Arcadis U.S. Inc., and the contractor was Sunbelt Structures Inc. The contract was awarded in July 2004, and the project was completed in December 2006.

The Fifth Street Plaza was an immediate hit. I remember the first day it opened. Students were throwing frisbees in the green space and visitors were walking around in amazement that chain-link fences had been replaced by shrubs and trees. But what was immediately striking

176

was the silence. Not only had the fourteen lanes of traffic below disappeared from view, but their roar had diminished to a faint hum as if at a far distance. The illusion was complete.

Of all the people who were there marveling at the new Fifth Street Plaza, I was the only one who remembered an article written a year before in the *Technique*, the student newspaper, criticizing me for wasting Georgia Tech's money on a fancy bridge that served no purpose other than to satisfy my ego. I thought about looking up the student who had written it and inviting him to join me for a walk through the plaza, but I decided against it.

## POWERING GEORGIA'S HIGH-TECH ECONOMY

By the time I left Georgia Tech in 2008, Technology Square was running on all cylinders. Even I was surprised to see that everything we planned was working as we had hoped. During the ensuing years, my successor G. P. "Bud" Peterson made Technology Square a priority, and it continued to thrive and grow. Phase II of its development produced Coda—a 750,000 gross-square-foot high-performance computing center of which Georgia Tech is the anchor tenant. Phase III, which is on the drawing board as I write, will add two towers—one for Georgia Tech's Ernest Scheller Jr. College of Business and the other for Tech's H. Milton Stewart School of Industrial and Systems Engineering and related programs.

Of course, the combination of Georgia Tech research labs and ATDC's successful mentoring of entrepreneurs made start-ups a key component of Technology Square right from the start. Georgia Tech has subsequently partnered with metro Atlanta corporations and in some cases the city itself on incubators, accelerators, venture capital funds, and support systems to help start-ups thrive. These efforts include specialty programs for manufacturing, financial technology, healthcare, information security, and neuroscience. As I write this book, the number of start-ups at Technology Square is approaching one hundred.

Major corporations also have a significant presence. In today's rapidly moving economy, many companies utilize technologies from outside their own labs, and virtually all corporations need to understand a broader range of innovations that will impact their product lines. The general concept behind the Yamacraw Design Center—to bring a group of related industries together with each other and with Georgia Tech's experts and research labs—made Technology Square a magnet for the innovation centers of well-established corporations. As I write this chapter, some thirty-five corporate innovation, design, technology development, and research centers from a wide range of companies are located in and around Technology Square. NCR even went a step farther, building a twenty-story tower a block to the north to house its worldwide headquarters.

Such a flurry of activity attracted attention beyond Atlanta. On March 1, 2016, the online edition of *Harvard Business Review* posted an article, written by Brookings Institution scholars Scott Andes and Bruce Katz, that began, "Something is happening in Midtown Atlanta. Georgia Tech's city-centered campus has become one of the nation's leading destinations for corporate research centers."

Today the footprint of the area that Atlanta refers to as Technology Square has grown from its original three blocks to span ten blocks. It boasts the highest density of start-up companies, corporate innovation centers, and academic researchers anywhere in the Southeast. It also takes sustainability a step into the future, with its energy needs supplied by an innovative microgrid in collaboration with the Georgia Power Company, offering an opportunity to explore how smart energy management systems can interact with the larger power grid.

Through it all, Technology Square has continued to maintain its streetscape appeal. On a recent visit to the Technology Square Research Building, a faculty member working there summed it up for me. Having lived in European cities, he told me Technology Square reminded him of what it was like there—people walking tree-lined streets with wide sidewalks, eating in sidewalk cafes, riding by in trolleys, and talking to each other. He said he had not seen this scene anywhere else in the United States but New York City. I thought his comments were the ultimate accolade for the work and effort we put into Technology Square.

# REFERENCES

Aitken, Jim, Mike Clements, and Tim Schmitz. "Fifth Street Pedestrian Plaza Bridge." *Aspire Bridge Magazine*, Winter 2008, pp. 23–24.

Andes, Scott, and Bruce J. Katz. "Why Today's Corporate Research Centers Need to Be in Cities." *Harvard Business Review*, March 1, 2016. https://hbr.org/2016/03/why-todays-corporate-research-centers-need-to-be-in-cities.

"Barnes Unveils Yamacraw Initiative as Blueprint for State's Economy: Georgia Tech Among Eight Universities Participating." *The Whistle* 23, no. 3 (January 18, 1999). Georgia Institute of Technology Archives.

"Board of Regents Hears Yamacraw Mission on Track." University System of Georgia press release, May 9, 2000. https://www.usg.edu/news/release/board_of_regents_hears_yamacraw_mission_on_track.

Brooke, Bob. "Penn to invest $120M in retail, hotel complex." *Philadelphia Business Journal*, July 14, 1997.

"Fifth Street Project Pushes Campus Limits Across Connector." *The Whistle* 24, no. 21 (June 12, 2000). Georgia Institute of Technology Archives.

"Georgia Tech Reconnects, Renews Section of Atlanta Business District with Technology Square." Georgia Tech News Center press release, October 20, 2003. http://www.news.gatech.edu/2003/10/20/georgia-tech-reconnects-renews-section-atlanta-business-district-technology-square.

Highnite, Karla. "Georgia Tech Squared." *NACUBO Business Officer*, January 2003, pp. 27–33.

Jones Lang LaSalle. *5th Street Feasibility Study for Georgia Tech Foundation, Inc.* Atlanta: Jones Lang LaSalle, July 1, 1999.

"Midtown 'Like No Other Market' as More Companies Expand, New Towers Soar." *Atlanta Business Journal*, January 14, 2020.

Oesterle, Dale A. "Year 2002: The Year of the Telecom Meltdown." *Journal on Telecommunications and High Technology Law* 2 (2003): 413.

"Tech Square Wins Urban Land Institute Award." Georgia Institute of Technology press release, November 9, 2004. http://www.news.gatech.edu/2004/11/09/tech-square-wins-urban-land-institute-award.

"Terrorists Hijack 4 Airliners, Destroy World Trade Center, Hit Pentagon,

Hundreds Dead." *The Washington Post*, September 12, 2001.

"U.S. Attacked, Hijacked Jets Destroy Twin Towers and Hit Pentagon in Day of Terror." *The New York Times*, September 12, 2001.

*Chapter Nine*

# PUTTING A POLICY STAKE IN THE GROUND

It was a tipping point—the moment back in the late 1980s when the dollar amount of externally sponsored research at Georgia Tech surpassed the amount of its state appropriation. The difference has continued to grow ever since. This comparison does not denigrate the value of the support provided by the state, which has a very different purpose than research funding acquired in competition with other universities. Rather it is a reflection of Georgia Tech's growth into a research powerhouse.

Because of the growing importance of research funded by the federal government, Georgia Tech maintained two offices in Washington, D.C. One was a small government relations office located downtown; the other was a large suite of offices in Arlington, Virginia. The former focused mainly on research funding agencies such as the National Science Foundation (NSF) and NASA and on congressional committees that influenced higher education. The latter centered on the work of the Georgia Tech Research Institute with the Department of Defense and the Pentagon. These two offices in the Washington area gave us a dual presence most other universities did not have.

In 1997, with the hoopla of the Olympics behind us, I sensed that we might be able to parlay our growing volume of federally funded research into an opportunity to participate more fully in the policy arena.

Various agencies had begun to seek our advice, but we had no seat at the table where the decisions were made that set the science and technology research agenda. I believed Georgia Tech had expertise to contribute, and we could bring a perspective from the Southeast, a region that was often underrepresented in policy discussions.

Washington, D.C., is home to a jungle of lobbying firms, government agencies, nonprofit groups seeking to advise the government, and dozens of congressional committees important to higher education and to research and development. The task of guiding me through this maze fell to Patricia Bartlett, the director of our federal government relations office. She knew the ropes, was respected by her peers from other research universities, and worked well with people.

## OPPORTUNITIES PRESENT THEMSELVES

As the new boy on the block, the question for me was where to begin. I was an elected member of the National Academy of Engineering (NAE), an organization that provided advice to the federal government. I already served on several committees, and I sought to become more active there.

Besides the NAE, I cast my lot with the U.S. Council on Competitiveness, an organization formed in the 1970s to help the United States respond to the growing challenges from countries such Japan who were seeking to overtake our lead in manufacturing and technological development. It was unique in its breadth and diversity, drawing its membership from labor unions, industry, universities, and state and federal governments. And it had a history of providing nonpartisan advice without lobbying. My friend, Charles "Chuck" Vest, president of MIT, had already blazed the trail for university presidential leadership at the council by serving as its vice chair, the highest position to which a university member could aspire. The chair was reserved for a prominent industry CEO.

My decision to work with the council in 1997 was one of the best of my life because its mission and style of operation fit me to a T. It was fortuitous that Duane Ackerman, CEO of BellSouth whose office was near Technology Square, was active as well. Duane and Wayne became the "Atlanta team" for the council. During our tenure, we were fortunate to work with Deborah Wince-Smith, the president of the council. She was not only talented but also came with years of experience working in the policy world.

In 1998, the council began working with Michael Porter of Harvard Business School to frame regional economies in terms of his "cluster" theory. A cluster was defined as a group of businesses that made each other successful because, taken together, they provided all of the elements needed to serve the supply, production, and distribution chain of a particular industry. The argument was that the presence and interactions of a cluster enhanced the innovative potential of a regional economy. An example was the wine cluster in the Napa Valley of California. This area contained not only dozens of independent wineries but also the support system they needed to thrive. Located in their midst were the viticulture research engine of the University of California, Davis; suppliers of oak barrels; specialized aging facilities; and logistics agents to deliver the wines to customers.

The Council on Competitiveness formalized this work under the rubric of the Clusters of Innovation Study. Ackerman agreed to co-chair the initiative with Porter, and I served on the national and regional committees. It was no surprise that Atlanta was chosen as one of five areas to be studied, with Columbus added in to provide a larger regional perspective.

The Clusters of Innovation report was published in 2001, providing unique insights into the workings of the five regional economies and making suggestions for clusters in each one that showed potential for the future. Strengths for Atlanta were identified as higher education, strong state government/university collaboration, transportation/logistics, information technology, and quality of living. The financial services sector was identified as a smaller cluster that could become an economic growth factor in the future. The surprise was that tourism, long seen as a bastion of the Atlanta economy, was not identified as a cluster because of lack of growth potential and relatively low wages.

Looking back, the report got many things right, especially the potential for financial services, now known as "fintech," which has grown into a trademark of the Atlanta economy. What was overlooked was healthcare and biotechnology. The study took place too early to anticipate the impact of the growth of Emory Healthcare and Children's Hospital of Atlanta, the Georgia Research Alliance's investments in bioscience, and the success of the Emory/Georgia Tech biomedical engineering collaboration.

By 2001, my policy dance card was filling up, but I received two more invitations that I could not turn down. First, George W. Bush asked me to serve on the President's Council of Advisors on Science and Technology (PCAST). Composed of leaders from higher education and the corporate sector, PCAST provided advice directly to the president on matters related to science and technology. To his credit, President Bush took this council seriously. We worked with the President's science advisor, and following most of our meetings we met with the President himself to review the findings of our studies and discuss the recommendations we had decided to make. I considered it an honor to be the first Georgia Tech president to serve on PCAST.

Second, the National Academy of Engineering began a first-of-its-kind initiative to create a future-looking agenda. Called the Engineer of 2020, its goal was to lay an aspirational foundation for the future of the engineering profession and engineering education. It was an ambitious agenda, and I was asked to chair the Engineer of 2020 committee. I was enthusiastic because engineering was historically retrospective—changing only after events had forced its hand. The Engineer of 2020 would attempt to predict where engineering needed to be in the future and recommend changes to prepare for it. The committee consisted of a stellar group of younger and older engineering leaders.

Our early committee discussions were frustrating because we realized that any attempt to predict the future in a time of great change was unlikely to succeed. Eventually I suggested that while we could not say with certainty what the future would be like, we might well agree on what we hoped engineering would become as a profession and on our hopes for the future of engineering education. Once we shifted our focus to our aspirations, we found common ground. We settled in, dividing our efforts into two parts: one focused on engineering writ large and the other on engineering education. Our goal was to finish our work in 2004, allowing sixteen years for implementing the changes we hoped would be made by 2020.

Then in 2003 the Council on Competitiveness decided to launch the National Innovation Initiative (NII) to establish an agenda for innovation that could be adopted at federal and state levels. Building on the Porter cluster concept, it involved more than 500 state and federal leaders to broaden its findings. I was honored to be asked to serve as co-chair with Sam Palmisano, the CEO of IBM. Our goal was to complete the work by the end of 2004, at which time a summit would be held in Washington, D.C., to announce the results. This project proved to be a great ride and a great opportunity to broaden Georgia Tech's role in national policy activities and its recognition as a player at the national level.

## MY CUP RUNNETH OVER

Like most nonprofit organizations, the Council on Competitiveness had guidelines that called for a regular rotation of its voluntary leadership. In 2004, BellSouth CEO Duane Ackerman was named the chair, and I replaced MIT President Chuck Vest as the vice chair. Never before had these two positions been filled simultaneously either by two individuals from the South or by two individuals from the same city. It was a coup for Atlanta.

The year 2004 held one more surprise. President Bush asked me to serve on the National Science Board (NSB) as one of his personal appointees. The NSB is the governing board for the National Science Foundation (NSF) and consists of leaders from industry and universities who work with the director of NSF to make the operational decisions for the foundation. Because I was the only person who served on both PCAST and the NSB, my role was to help the leadership of the two organizations to coordinate their activities. You could say that my policy cup was now overflowing.

Fortunately, by 2004, the NAE Engineer of 2020 initiative was wrapping up its work. We produced two reports: *The Engineer of 2020: Visions of Engineering in the New Century* and *The Engineer of 2020: Adapting Engineering Education to the New Century*. The first laid out the aspirations for the engineering profession in 2020, including becoming more representative of the nation's growing diversity, more engaged in the public debate on technical issues, and more open to innovation. It was rewarding to see many of the professional engineering societies undertake their own "2020" initiatives and emphasize issues such as what a sustainable future would look like and what would be required to make it possible.

The second report laid out a roadmap to prepare engineering graduates for the world they would face in 2020. In many ways the recommendations reflected the ideas we were working to incorporate into the engineering education experience at Georgia Tech. I was pleasantly surprised to see many deans of engineering schools around the country take the report to heart and begin planning changes in the way their students were educated. The issuance of the report for engineering education led to a host of invitations to speak at other universities about its findings and recommendations. I was glad to accept them, not just because I felt obligated but also because they provided opportunities to make a difference. As I visit universities today, it is rewarding to see that many of the recommendations of the Engineer of 2020 report have had an impact. The real beneficiaries have been the students who now receive a more holistic education that encourages them to be better stewards of our planet and the people on it.

In December 2004, the summit to announce the findings of the National Innovation Initiative was held in Washington, D.C. It was one of the earliest large meetings to be streamed on the internet. The summit was the culmination of two years of hard work and laid out a national agenda to capitalize on the nation's innovation potential. Afterward the findings were shared through a series of regional meetings emphasizing that "innovation is local" and is based on creating the right environment to capitalize on clusters of excellence.

Over the next three years, the Council on Competitiveness and its members worked with members of Congress and their staffs to create a bipartisan legislative package called the "America Competes Act" that embraced the recommendations of the NII report. Several times I was called to testify before Congress on the proposed legislation, which required a degree of dexterity to avoid being pulled into partisan debates when leading questions were asked by members on both sides of the aisle. The act was passed and signed into law in 2007, and it still serves as an aid to innovation today.

Along the way, the National Governors' Association (NGA) undertook a companion effort to the NII at the state level. I was one of four university presidents asked to provide advice to the NGA over a two-year period. Helping to spread the recommendations of the NII across the country was a great way to bring my work on this project to a close.

## HURRICANE KATRINA

I had no intention of taking on additional policy obligations beyond those I already had, but in 2005 nature and the National Academy of Engineering intervened. As that summer was winding down, meteorologists saw a monster storm brewing in the Gulf of Mexico. Hurricane Katrina struck New Orleans on August 29. The combination of the power of the storm, the accompanying collapse of the hurricane protection system, and the ineptitude of the local and federal responders led to one of the greatest natural disasters in our history. More than 1,800 people perished in New Orleans as a result of the hurricane.

Shortly after the storm I went to New Orleans with Joe Hughes, then chair of Georgia Tech's School of Civil and Environmental Engineering, to view the damage Hurricane Katrina had wrought. Our tour was arranged by the Army Corps of Engineers, which was still reeling from the damage to the hurricane protection system. We drove through New Orleans and flew by helicopter over areas where the levees had been breached in Plaquemine Parish south of the city. This flight gave us a bird's-eye view of the 350-mile system of levees and floodwalls intended to protect New Orleans and Plaquemine Parish from hurricanes and Mississippi River floods. The system, built over the course of sixty years, had multiple owners, including the City of New Orleans, several semi-independent levee districts, and private entities such as petroleum companies. Most of the system had been designed and built by the Corps of Engineers, and they were charged with annual inspections.

On our tour, the scenes of devastation were both awe-inspiring and dispiriting. In the now empty Lakeview and Lower Ninth Ward neighborhoods, the walls of houses were marked with high-water lines up to nine feet above the ground. If a house had been inspected and marked with a red "X," as most were, it would be demolished. Kitchen tables were still covered with breakfast dishes and the morning newspaper, evidence of how residents had to drop everything to flee the rising waters. Along the Seventeenth Street and New London canals, massive sheet-pile walls intended to hold back floodwater had been split apart as if by a giant hand. As we flew over Plaquemine Parish below the city, we could see that entire sections of the levees had been washed away by massive twenty-five-foot waves, caused by surges that had built up as the winds of Katrina roared across the surface of Lake Borgne.

The devastation brought back vivid memories of my first job as a civil engineer. I was working for the Mississippi River Commission in the 1960s, designing flood control projects. One of them involved raising the flood walls that protected Morgan City, Louisiana, from the waters of the Atchafalaya River. Morgan City was an important operations base for oil rigs in the Gulf of Mexico. In summer 1965, I was in charge of field tests for new pile systems to reinforce the foundations of the floodwalls. The weather was hot, but the work was exciting. As the test results accumulated, I began to ask myself, "How safe is safe?" If we used one less pile per group to save money, could the floodwalls still be considered safe?

My question was answered in September, when Hurricane Betsy, armed with 155 mph winds, swirled up out of the Gulf of Mexico. I told my colleagues we should delay our departure to observe what happened. We watched as waves of helicopters brought in workers from oil rigs in the Gulf, and then as cars loaded with people, pets, and luggage evacuated the city. You could sense the fear that was driving those who chose to leave. Others chose to stay, especially those responsible for life safety. As the outbound traffic dwindled to a trickle, workers began to position the "stop logs" that filled the gaps where roads cut through the floodwall. When the storm surge from Betsy charged up the Atchafalaya River, Morgan City would become an island. The only protection for the city and its remaining residents would be the floodwall. If it failed or shifted too much to maintain its integrity, floodwater would rush in, and that would be the end.

By the time we finally left Morgan City just ahead of Betsy, the normally placid waters of the Atchafalaya River were covered with white caps. When the hurricane hit, the winds gusted to 130 mph. This experience taught me that one extra pile per group was well worth the cost. It would provide a clear margin of safety for a system that was critical to preserving life and property in a location where it was not possible to anticipate the full extent of what might happen. Witnessing firsthand what it meant to depend solely on a floodwall for protection was an experience I never forgot.

Hurricane Katrina left New Orleans void of protection, with its economy nonexistent. As the weight of the disaster seeped in, the Army Corps of Engineers was asked to begin the process of rebuilding the hurricane protection system. In October 2005, I received a call from Jeffrey Jacobs of the National Research Council (NRC), the policy arm of the National Academy of Engineering and the National Academy of Sciences. He explained that Assistant Secretary of the Army Civil Works John Paul Woodley had asked the NRC to establish a commit-tee to provide independent advice about the New Orleans hurricane protection system—examining both its failure and the design to replace it. Because the Corps of Engineers reported to the Department of the Army, the Army felt that an outside advisory committee with no ties to the corps could play a check-and-balance role. Jacobs's question was whether I was willing to chair the committee. He told me that with luck the work of the committee on the New Orleans Regional Hurri-cane Project would be complete in not much more than a year. I did not hesitate to say yes, but I suspected this task would bring unexpected complications.

The Corps of Engineers had a two-part plan to restore the hurri-cane protection system. First, a group of external experts and engineers from the U.S. Army Waterways Experiment Station would be charged with explaining why the old hurricane protection system had failed and using the lessons learned to make recommendations regarding a new system. This group was called the Interagency Performance Task Group, or IPET, and our committee would primarily interact with it. Second, based on the recommendations from IPET, a new system would be designed and built by the Corps of Engineers and a host of private consultants and contractors it would employ.

As IPET geared up to do its job, the landscape quickly filled with other groups competing to tell the story of why the system failed. Some were self-empowered; others were supported by state and federal agencies. Then there were the news reporters following the story. They included Mark Schleifstein of *The Times-Picayune* of New Orleans and John Schwartz of *The New York Times*, both well-informed and excellent writers.

My committee members were chosen for their expertise in areas related to hurricanes, hurricane and flood protection systems, and evacuation strategies. All had agreed to work pro bono. We were informed that in accordance with NRC practice, our committee meetings would be private, but we were to save an hour at the end of the day's meeting for the public at large to make statements. Hearings would be open to the public. Given the charged nature of the process, periodic tensions between our committee and IPET were to be expected. Still, we had our job to do, and that included being critical when necessary.

When I arrived in New Orleans in December for our first committee meeting, the scene reinforced the devastating impact of Hurricane Katrina. The airport was empty; only a small handful of hotels and restaurants were open; and there was no traffic. New Orleans had lost more than half of its population, and to this day the city has not regained the numbers it had before the hurricane.

Going into the meeting our immediate tasks seemed clear: First, ask IPET to present their findings to date and explain how they intended to proceed. Next, allow the citizens of New Orleans to testify about their experiences. Finally, develop a report for Secretary Woodley by the end of February 2006. However, nothing about this operation would turn out to be straightforward.

I already had concerns before the meeting. As I read the advance materials, my Morgan City experience immediately came to mind. Elements of the design criteria used for the old pre-Katrina floodwall and levee systems had relied on unusually low safety factors. How could this negligence have been possible? As I read, I also realized that the lawyers for the Corps of Engineers were not focusing on what the corps had done in the past that contributed to the system's failure but rather were attempting to blame Mother Nature and the levee boards. There was obviously plenty of blame to go around, but if the future designs of the corps were to have credibility, the group's members needed to admit the mistakes they had made the first time around.

While the IPET presentations at the first meeting were made in earnest, my committee members had numerous questions that could not be answered without further study. Then came the public testimony. Citizens told stories about being homeless, lacking job prospects, and feeling hopeless. By the end of the first day, we realized this project was going to take more than one year.

For the next three years, we held additional hearings and heard witnesses not only from IPET but also from organizations that contested their findings. We had no intention of continuing the hearings ad infinitum or broadening our mission, but different points of view had to be considered if we were to provide advice that would sharpen the work of the Corps of Engineers. Several additional issues also arose. For example, we devoted a number of sessions to considering future sea-level rise due to climate change. It began when I asked a simple question: "What is the intended design life of the new hurricane protection system?" The response was, "One hundred years." To which I replied, "Over the next one hundred years sea level is predicted to rise two to five feet. Please explain how your design recommendations will accommodate rising seas." The room was silent for a few moments as everyone took in the import of my question. Eventually the answer was, no, sea-level rise had not been considered in the recommendations. Everyone knew then that IPET had to go back to the drawing board, and to their credit, they did. But it added more time to the process.

Throughout the hearings, I was impressed by the thoughtful questions offered by my committee members. I was also pleased that the IPET team, led by Ed Link of the University of Maryland, was willing to take our recommendations into account. It made our work much easier. In the end their report, more than 7,000 pages long, served as a guide for the design of the New Orleans hurricane protection system and for other projects as well.

I was also reassured by meetings with Secretary Woodley and his team. I was consistently instructed to rely on the best judgement of my committee, particularly regarding the safety of the public. I was grateful for their support. Finally, I appreciated the excellent coverage by the reporters from *The Times-Picayune* and *The New York Times*, with whom I spoke a number of times. Between their work and a greater effort on the part of the Corps of Engineers, communications with the public improved dramatically.

As we were rounding the final turn into the homestretch of the project, one of the last, and most important, decisions for IPET and the corps was what flood recurrence level to use to control the design of the new system. For example, a "one in one-hundred-year event" level would mean assuming a one percent chance of the event happening in any one year of the hundred-year span. My committee included experts in the design of systems to protect against flood events. They knew the future posed hurricane dangers for New Orleans that required design for a one in five-hundred-year event. This higher-level standard is used to design dams and major flood protection systems where life safety is involved. It also would protect against another Katrina-like hurricane, which was considered a one in three-hundred-year event.

At this very moment, just as we were moving toward a plan that was consistent with the gravity of the circumstances and considered the long-term effects of climate change, a wild card appeared. The Federal Emergency Management Agency (FEMA) declared without much explanation that the design control should be a one in one-hundred-year event. Their decision was apparently based on a desire to speed up approvals for flood insurance so that building permits could be issued. Suddenly we faced the prospect of a new $15 billion system that could be overtopped by another Katrina-like event. To the credit of the Corps of Engineers, the new system did include allowances to prevent collapse in the event of overtopping. Nevertheless, it was frustrating and ironic to see the end result become a system that was vulnerable, even as politicians were claiming that the city was safe at last.

In 2010, five years after our committee began its work, the National Research Council issued our final report. In it we pointed out that FEMA's decision was inconsistent with proper consideration of long-term public safety issues. In recognition of the reduced safety level of the new system, we encouraged public officials in New Orleans to place renewed emphasis on evacuation plans. We also emphasized that they consider working with homeowners in the Lakeview and Lower Ninth Ward neighborhoods to relocate them to safer sites. We knew this recommendation was politically fraught, and it was basically ignored as these neighborhoods were rebuilt.

Looking back, I believe our committee helped to improve the design of the hurricane protection system by asking questions others would have preferred to ignore. Were you honest in accepting responsibility for inadequate designs in the original system? If not, how do you expect to gain credibility for the future? Did you consider sea level rise in the design? Why not? Explain clearly, for us and the public, how you are building resiliency into your designs for the new system, given that it will be overtopped if another Katrina-scale event occurs.

As for the longer-term impact, the decision by FEMA to downgrade the capability of the system continued to reverberate. On February 24, 2018, *The New York Times* published an article titled "Fortified but Still in Peril, New Orleans Braces for Its Future" and written by John Schwartz and Mark Schleifstein—the same two reporters with whom I had interacted during the work of our committee. The article spoke to the need to revisit FEMA's decision, noting that the Army Corps of Engineers admitted that New Orleans could be inundated again like it was during Hurricane Katrina.

The work of the committee on the New Orleans Regional Hurricane Project extended into 2010, beyond my tenure as president of Georgia Tech. It represented the culmination of my efforts in response to the decision to engage Georgia Tech in the policy world of Washington, D.C. At the outset I had hoped to raise Tech's national profile and make a contribution, at least in a small way. Along the way I was fortunate to be offered leadership opportunities by the National Academy of Engineering, the U.S. Council of Competitiveness, the National Science Board, and the President's Council of Advisors on Science and Technology. Multi-year projects like the Clusters of Innovation Study, the Engineer of 2020, the National Innovation Initiative, and the Committee on the New Orleans Regional Hurricane Project allowed me to contribute to meeting a specific and timely need, and they were great learning experiences. The opportunity to serve on the National Science Board, PCAST, and the Council of Competitiveness allowed me to contribute perspectives from the Southeast and from a prominent technological university.

The bottom line was a new level of visibility for Georgia Tech and the state of Georgia. No longer relegated to being an afterthought, Georgia Tech had come to be recognized as a valuable source of input on national policy decisions that involved technology.

## REFERENCES

"Council on Competitiveness Hosts Innovation Summit." Georgia Institute of Technology press release, December 13, 2004.

*Innovate America: Thriving in a World of Challenge and Change.* Washington, D.C.: U.S. Council on Competitiveness National Innovation Initiative Summit and Report, 2005.

National Academy of Engineering. *The Engineer of 2020: Visions of Engineering in the New Century.* Washington, D.C.: The National Academies Press, 2004.

National Academy of Engineering. *Educating the Engineer of 2020: Adapting Engineering Education to the New Century.* Washington, D.C.: The National Academies Press, 2005.

National Hurricane Center. "Preliminary Report on Hurricane Betsy." *U.S. National Oceanic and Atmospheric Administration Tropical Cyclone Report*, September 15, 1965.

*The New Orleans Hurricane Protection System: Assessing Pre-Katrina Vulnerability and Improving Mitigation and Preparedness.* Washington, D.C.: The National Academies Press, 2009.

Porter, Michael E. *Clusters of Innovation: Regional Foundations of U.S. Competitiveness.* Washington, D.C.: U.S. Council of Competitiveness, October 2001.

Schleifstein, Mark, and John McQuaid. *The Path of Destruction: The Devastation of New Orleans and the Coming Age of Superstorms.* New York: Little Brown and Company, Hachette Book Group, 2006.

Schwartz, John. "Full Flood Safety in New Orleans Could Take Billions and Decades." *The New York Times*, November 29, 2005.

Schwartz, John, and Mark Schleistein. "Fortified but Still in Peril, New Orleans Braces for Its Future." *The New York Times*, February 24, 2018.

*Chapter Ten*

# STEPS TO MATURITY

Although the Georgia Institute of Technology was more than one hundred years old when I became its president, it was still a youngster in the world of universities, which stretches back many centuries. Its efforts to become a research university had only begun in the 1970s, and it had yet to attempt its first national fundraising campaign. However, this challenge also posed an opportunity to leapfrog parts of the time-worn path to institutional respectability. We expressed this prospect in the vision statement for our 2002 strategic plan: "Georgia Tech will define the technological research university of the twenty-first century."

While some thought it was braggadocious, I liked it. It was an aspiration without reference to being ranked first, fifth, or tenth. Instead, it said we would chart our own course, take calculated risks, and in the end arrive at a place of excellence that was right for us. As we said in the strategic plan, "We want to lead in a fashion that is distinctly Georgia Tech." I was pleased to find leaders on campus who got the message. They were encouraged to be creative and tackle big issues, and they rose to the challenge. We also worked deliberately at fundraising to provide the resources required for excellence. As for rankings, I believed they would follow good ideas—ideas that were designed to help us define the technological research university of the future.

Our reason to believe this approach could work was that it already had. Beginning in 1994, at a time when Georgia Tech was barely on anyone's radar for bioengineering and bioscience, we took a different approach to becoming a leader in these fields. We formed a unique collaboration with a private partner, Emory University, and blended engineering, science, and computer science to capitalize on emerging fields like biotechnology, nanotechnology, and bioinformatics. Something surprising happened as a result. By 2002, the Emory/Georgia Tech biomedical engineering program was ranked in the top three in the nation, and we were home to the National Science Foundation-funded National Engineering Research Center for the Engineering of Living Tissues. By 2008, the Georgia Tech/Emory collaboration had added three National Institutes of Health centers of excellence in nanomedicine. In the blink of an eye on the timeline of the university world, we stole a march on the competition because, together with our collaborators, we chose a different route and offered a new way to make a difference. It happened because a small group of people believed in what was possible.

## PRIMING THE PUMP

Unless a university has massive endowments like those of Harvard or Stanford, there is never enough money to go around. Georgia Tech was no exception. When I arrived in 1994, our endowment was $228 million, annual giving topped out at $40 million, and our allocation from the state was $130 million—numbers that were small compared to those of any other major university. Until we had more resources, we would be slogging through sand in the race to compete with our aspirational peers.

Before I arrived, Georgia Tech had decided to undertake its first ever national fundraising campaign with the expectation that its public launch would coincide with the 1996 Olympic Games. However, the public demise of the Crecine presidency put a crimp in the plans. Academic units were told to halt fundraising activities. Only the Athletic Association was given permission to proceed, because funds were needed for the renovation of the basketball arena in preparation for the Olympics. This decision made the college deans and school chairs unhappy; they believed the Athletic Association would use its fundraising advantage to poach donors. In other words, the state of the campaign when I arrived as president could be described as a little pregnant.

## THE CAMPAIGN FOR GEORGIA TECH, 1996–2000

By late 1995, with the process of righting the ship well underway, pressure grew to return to the original plan of launching the capital campaign in tandem with the Olympics. In spite of my reservations, we made plans to announce the Campaign for Georgia Tech in spring 1996. Given the circumstances, we set the initial campaign goal at a modest $300 million. University fundraising campaigns generally begin with a quiet period during which a quarter or more of the goal is raised before the public announcement of the campaign. Although what might be called the quiet phase of this campaign had been disjointed and interrupted, we found to our surprise that we had $120 million in gifts and commitments in hand by spring 1996. So, in a moment of unbridled optimism, we upped the goal to $400 million for the public announcement.

We now had liftoff in principle but not so much in practice. We did not have campaign case statements ready. We had no campaign consultant. Our campaign director, Barrett Carson, did not arrive until the end of the year. Because capital planning was still in progress, fundraising goals for important new facilities would not become available until 1997.

In our favor was the strong group of alumni we had lined up to lead the campaign: Pete Silas, CEO of Phillips Petroleum, as chair; Larry Gellerstadt, former CEO of Beers Construction Company, as vice chair; Tom Gossage, former CEO of Hercules Corporation, heading up corporate gifts; and Henry "Buck" Stith, CEO of Stith Equipment, as chair of major gifts. These men and their families would all become major donors to the campaign. We also had momentum from a strategic plan calling for a different future for Georgia Tech, and we had the loyalty of Georgia Tech alumni behind us. The rest we would have to make up on the fly.

The campaign proved good for two things beyond fundraising. First was my Delta Airlines frequent flyer account. Because of the nature of the Georgia Tech alumni base, my trips took me to technology and finance hubs all across the country. Chicago, New York, Austin, San Francisco, Los Angeles, and Seattle were obvious places to begin. In the two years before the Olympics, I made fifteen extended trips out of state, along with dozens more within the state. This first round of visits was focused on meeting people and getting to know them and their families, not on asking for money. Then, after the campaign had been announced, Carson and his staff staged rollout events in forty-four different cities to make sure alumni everywhere realized we were actually doing a campaign. As I crisscrossed the country with Carson in tow, I lost track at times of whether I was in Dallas or Denver. The process of asking for and then closing on gifts kept the travel merry-go-round spinning.

The second benefit of the campaign travel was meeting alumni outside of Atlanta who had not had a real connection to Georgia Tech for years. More than a few had earned MBA, law, or medical degrees at prestigious universities after leaving Georgia Tech. Their post-graduate universities had been cultivating them for years, appointing them to advisory boards whose members were expected to make large donations as a matter of course. I learned that when it came to our most accomplished alumni, we were often competing with Harvard, MIT, Stanford, and UPenn's Wharton Business School for gifts. As a Johnny-come-lately making his first visit to see them, I found that my pitch often fell on skeptical ears. After all, my predecessor had lasted only six years, and they were not sure I would stick around to implement the changes I was proposing. It was frustrating, but it was not the time to give up. I saw it as an opportunity to make the connection and lay the groundwork for a later time when Georgia Tech would prove more worthy of their trust and support.

Nothing was easy. The dream of some distant but loving alumnus dropping $100 million on us was just that—a dream. But we gradually found our footing, and fixing the problems back on campus gave us good news to share. As a result, something else began to happen. We started to find alumni who had begun to believe that Georgia Tech was finally moving in the right direction, and they came on board in larger numbers than we thought possible. As a result, we raised our campaign goal several times by $100 million increments. In 2000, with the stated end date for the campaign approaching, we set the final goal at $600 million—double the original goal.

There is no question in my mind that if we had extended the length of the campaign, we could have raised $1 billion. But this was Georgia Tech, and because we had said the campaign would last five years, that would be it. I suspect there was also a bit of a fatigue factor in this decision. We had just survived the Olympics; the campaign had been launched on a wing and prayer; and we were about to borrow a record sum of money to construct Technology Square.

Final accounting showed that the Campaign for Georgia Tech had raised $712 million, and the funding it provided could not have been better timed. To thank our donors, we held celebration events in twelve cities across the country in 2001 and 2002. As the lead-in to my remarks at these celebrations, I asked the audience to remember these numbers: 712, 54, 233, 11, 46,000, and 57. The 712 was obvious—the total dollars raised—but the rest were not so easy to discern. Fifty-four new endowed faculty positions had been created—double the twenty-six that had existed before the campaign. Two hundred thirty-three new endowments for scholarships and fellowships were funded. Eleven new buildings had received support. Forty-six thousand donors had participated, and they lived in fifty-seven countries, illustrating the growing global reach of Georgia Tech.

## MEMORABLE MOMENTS

The campaign produced many memories, including a cab ride to an event at the Chicago Zoo, during which our driver, who seemed hopelessly lost but happy, informed us he had just arrived in the United States from Ethiopia the day before. Then there was a white-knuckle flight on a small plane in bad weather on the way to an event in Philadelphia. On boarding, we learned that the plane was mainly used to surveil marijuana fields. Given the heavy cloud cover, the pilot informed us that the only way we were going to get to Philadelphia was by flying VFR (visual flight rules). I had no idea what he meant, but it turned out that he flew below the low clouds, guided by what he could see on the ground, while checking for oncoming flights on his radio. I kissed the ground when we landed. As for the forty-four campaign rollout events, most are a foggy memory with the exception of the last one in New Orleans. At this one, the alumni consumed all the hard liquor first and then made do with the wine and beer.

Other memories stand out because they were unexpected. One of these began with a visit to a philanthropic foundation that liked to work behind the scenes and make anonymous gifts. In preparation I was told to keep my expectations modest, because Georgia Tech had little history with this foundation. Our goal was to test their level of interest in making a grant toward the construction of the Environmental Science and Engineering Building—one of three buildings then planned for what became our biotechnology and molecular engineering quadrangle. However, in the course of our visit, I let my enthusiasm get away from me. In addition to describing the building for which we were seeking funds, I diverged into a discourse about the collaborative potential of all three buildings. I explained that our approach was different from academic tradition in which each new building was a stand-alone entity. Our complex would bring together scientists and engineers from different disciplines whose expertise and research interests could be combined in different ways to tackle large interdisciplinary problems. Our goal was to make Georgia Tech a national player in areas that would define the future—bioengineering, biosciences, nanotechnology, molecular sciences, and material design. If we succeeded, we could expand our joint interests with Emory University and put Atlanta in a position to compete with cities such as Boston, San Francisco, and Seattle. Although I was feeling good during my presentation, afterward I had to wonder whether going off message had ruined our chances to get a grant for the one building that was immediately in front of us.

Weeks later we were invited to submit a proposal, which we did in July 1998. Feeling optimistic, we asked for $2 million to help build the Environmental Science and Engineering Building. Six months later, in January 1999, I received a phone call from the president of the foundation asking if I would host him and his program director for a breakfast at the President's House. This request set off a round of speculation among campaign staff. No one believed we would be given our full request, but the consensus was that it was promising. On the appointed day, as I gamely welcomed my guests, I noticed that the president of the foundation was wearing a Georgia Tech tie. I took it as a good omen.

After a longish chat about current events over breakfast, the president of the foundation said he wanted to come to the point. His board had been impressed by our concept for the complex, and they wanted to give us $10 million to be used as we thought best to get all three buildings built. They also wanted us to use their funds in a matching challenge to encourage others to join in. I was not sure I had heard him correctly, but I do remember saying "yes."

This gift was transformational. Instead of focusing just on "the next building," we could think broadly about a larger concept. By August 2000, we not only had gifts coming in for the match but we were now planning a fourth building in the complex. Barrett Carson had been bullish enough to promise the foundation that we would match their gift by two to one. By April 2002, we had met those terms and the full $10 million grant was committed for our building complex.

The lesson I learned from this experience was that context matters. Aspirations matter. Yes, the needs of universities and other charitable organizations are specific, but donors want to understand how the pieces fit together to make a whole. And time proved that the collaborative, interdisciplinary vision we had for our complex brought enormous benefits. It was a lesson I carried with me for years to come.

Another campaign memory that spoke to the heart of the matter began with a call from an estate lawyer who told me an older Georgia Tech alumnus had decided to make a gift. The alumnus in question had never been in the president's box for a football game or attended a dinner at the President's House, nor had he been identified in our donor research. Not a rich man, he had lived prudently and seen his estate grow over time. He had outlived all of his friends and had no heirs. As I talked with the lawyer, I realized that the alumnus lived in a retirement home on Peachtree Street in Atlanta, not far from my personal home in Buckhead. The estate lawyer said he would enjoy meeting me, and I said, "Of course."

His name was Alton Costley, and he was ninety-six years old at the time of my visit in 1998. I had been told ahead of time that he was bedridden but that his mind was still sharp. When I entered his room and told him who I was, he reached up to grab a bar hanging over his bed and pulled himself up. He explained to me that he used the bar to exercise every day and demonstrated by doing five pull-ups. He may have been ninety-six, but he was spry and had a great sense of humor. We talked for more than an hour. At one point he told me that for many years he had had season tickets to Georgia Tech football games, and the memory of it inspired him to sing Tech's famous "Ramblin' Wreck" fight song. He got the first verse right, but farther along he blended in snippets from other songs he remembered. Somehow it worked. When he finished, we laughed, but I had to brush away my tears at seeing his delight. I visited him a few more times before he passed away in 2000.

During my visits with Alton Costley, neither of us ever mentioned money. So it came as a surprise when we learned that he had left Georgia Tech more than $3 million, most of it in his will. It was to be split between a scholarship and a faculty chair in the College of Management, where he had earned his degree. It was an honor to have gotten to know him and see what love for an institution really meant.

## FUNDRAISING POST-2000

Even though Georgia Tech's first national capital campaign had been a great success, the end of the campaign in 2000 did not mean that fundraising was over. In fact, ongoing fundraising became part of Georgia Tech's "new normal" as we retained our fundraising staff and continued our outreach efforts. Commensurate with a shift toward ongoing fundraising, we increased our efforts to steward our major donors. We hired Elizabeth Gallant to lead this effort, and she created the "Hill Society" to recognize donors of a million dollars or more. Before the campaign we had only a small handful of million-dollar donors, but at the inaugural Hill Society dinner at the newly renovated Biltmore Hotel in March 2001, we recognized 160 donors. As we thanked them, I knew we had reached a new level. Instead of a few dozen, we now had a few hundred people who needed our close attention, and that was a good thing.

In 2000, the final year of the capital campaign, annual giving set a new record of nearly $100 million. It tapered off for a few years as the campaign excitement diminished. However, during this time fundraising was focused on major gifts that fueled significant undertakings. The rise of our biomedical engineering program was made possible by $50 million total from the Coulter and Whitaker foundations. Ford Motor Company, with an interest in supporting sustainable technology, made the key gift of $15 million that allowed us to proceed with the construction of the Environmental Science and Technology Building in the new quadrangle for biotechnology and molecular engineering. A new building named for Erskine Love, made possible by a large commitment from his family, completed the sustainable manufacturing quadrangle. Love, a great Georgia Tech alumnus, was a successful entrepreneur and a leader in the first campaign before he died tragically of a heart attack.

In 2001, two gifts totaling $4.25 million for recruiting Hispanic students, supporting scholarships and fellowships of Hispanic students, and endowing faculty chairs came from the Goizueta Foundation. Roberto Goizueta had been born in Cuba and had a degree in chemical engineering from Yale. He had worked his way up through the ranks of the Coca-Cola Company and served as CEO during its international expansion. He and his wife Olguita had created their foundation in 1992.

Goizueta was a remarkable person, and I came to know him because he reached out to me. As CEO of the Coca-Cola Company, his office was in the Coca-Cola Tower on North Avenue, which overlooked our campus. In my time at Georgia Tech, Coca-Cola had more than a few CEOs, but only one, Roberto Goizueta, invited me to have lunch with him in his office, and not just once but every year until his death in 1997. I was always impressed that during our lunch together he never looked at his watch, even though I was clearly not important to his business. He listened carefully and made me feel as if I were the most important person in the world. I still do not know why he invited me to lunch. Yes, we were fellow engineers, but I think he did it because we were neighbors, and he wanted to be a good neighbor. He was that kind of person.

The Goizueta Foundation provided another $2.3 million in 2004. The cumulative impact of these gifts was to increase the number of

Hispanic students attending Georgia Tech. By the end of my presidency, *Hispanic Business* magazine had named Georgia Tech the top university for Hispanic graduate students to study engineering.

I was proud that we were making progress between campaigns in bringing in major gifts that helped to lift Georgia Tech to a new level in targeted areas.

COLLEGE OF MANAGEMENT BUILDING

One of the biggest tasks remaining after the campaign was raising the money required for the new College of Management building at Technology Square. Unlike other Technology Square components, this building would not generate a revenue stream to repay the cost of its construction. At the February 2000 meeting of the Georgia Tech Foundation, I had stated that if we borrowed the money to build the building, we could repay it in seventeen or eighteen years—a promise based entirely on the prospect of philanthropy and a dose of hope. By the time the cost for the building had been established at $45 million, the national capital campaign was drawing to a close and I felt a bit like the proverbial man out on a limb.

At the time, the site of the future College of Management building was a vacant lot surrounded by a chain-link fence located in a desolate part of Atlanta. We were in desperate need of a few early donors to help convince others to get on the bandwagon. However, all we could do was walk prospective donors around the fence and ask them to imagine a beautiful new building filled with students and faculty that would make all the difference to the future of the college.

The first gift, $5 million, came in October 2000 from Larry and Nancy Huang. Larry Huang, a management graduate, was one of the Georgia Tech alumni who founded Ciena, a networking and systems company. He was the sales guy and knew about taking risks. In addition to his day job, he competed in sports car races on the side. After the Huangs announced their gift, Dean Terry Blum and her staff made a video of Larry walking around the chain-link fence, talking about how exciting the new building would be. I thought, only Larry Huang could have done that because he was such an optimist.

The Huang commitment was soon followed by three more seven-

figure gifts from alumni who understood how delicate our circumstances were. In November, Julian and Joanne LeCraw made the first
of the three. Julian LeCraw had been chair of the Georgia Tech Foundation in 1997, and he had led the charge to buy the land that was to
become the heart of Technology Square. The other two gifts arrived in
December. One was from Charlie Brady, the CEO of Invesco, an international investment firm he had built from the ground up. Although
he could have moved the firm to any of the great financial capitals of
the world, he kept it in Atlanta, where it still is today. Brady was quiet
but had a great sense of humor. He and I shared a sense of curiosity
about the world, and I bonded with him on family trips and hunting
and skiing trips. He was a man who understood the big picture. Then,
just after Christmas, James "Polly" and Dot Poole, an old-line, elegant
Atlanta couple who loved Georgia Tech, made a seven-figure commitment. Poole had a distinguished career in life insurance and estate planning, and he was a founder of Georgia Tech Charitable Life Inc. We
now had four major gifts to launch the building campaign, all from
people who represented the best of our alumni.

The remainder of the fundraising took time and was not complete
until 2006. When we finally declared victory, we had gifts and commitments for more than $48 million. I will be forever grateful to eve-
ryone who stepped up and made me an honest man.

### CAMPAIGN GEORGIA TECH, 2004–2008

Even as we continued raising funds from 2001 through 2003, we were
also preparing for the next campaign, and we began the quiet phase in
2004. This campaign was very different from the first one. This time
there were no calls without a full research report on the donor; no need
to explain why Georgia Tech seemed unable to get a clean financial
audit; and no flights on tiny prop-planes otherwise used for marijuana
surveillance. We now had an experienced and talented fundraising
staff; our regional networks were established; our alumni had a better
understanding of why we were raising funds; and a well of trust had
developed based on our keeping our promises and making significant
improvements.

Perhaps the best news was that alumnus Al West agreed to chair the campaign's quiet phase. One of the smartest people I knew, West was a hands-on chair. In addition to leading through his own gifts, he participated in fundraising trips, inviting us to join him on the flights he scheduled through his NetJet account. He even gave us two weekends a year to entertain donors at San Rafael, Rancho de la Particion, a 22,000-acre South Texas spread he had acquired for ranching and hunting (and business purposes on the side). No one ever turned down an invitation for a weekend adventure at San Rafael, and they all decided to become donors before they left.

Giving totals per year quickly moved to levels never achieved before. Major gifts included $20 million from Carolyn and Milton Stewart to endow and name the School of Industrial and Systems Engineering. A $5 million gift from Brook Byers endowed the Brook Byers Institute for Sustainable Systems, reflecting his passion for conserving the environment. Another $5 million gift from Steve Denning created an undergraduate interdisciplinary minor that brought together students from the College of Management and the College of Engineering to learn from each other while working on hands-on projects. Both Byers and Denning provided additional funding as the programs created by their initial gifts flourished. Gifts totaling more than $80 million established more than seventy new endowed faculty chairs and professorships.

Capital projects were a significant part of the portfolio for the quiet phase of the second campaign, and we were fortunate to have alumni and friends who stepped up to make this part of the campaign a success. The list included $15 million from Bernie Marcus, co-founder of The Home Depot, for the Marcus Nanotechnology Research Center and multiple gifts for the G. Wayne Clough Undergraduate Learning Commons.

Student scholarships were another priority for many donors. In 2006, Penny and Roe Stamps made a $5 million gift to endow the Stamps Scholars Program for students who exhibited interest and ability in leadership. This program proved so popular that they provided additional funding over time, and the program was replicated at more than forty other universities.

As the quiet phase of the campaign continued, tuition increases became necessary to offset cuts in the funding that Georgia Tech received from the state, and we began to think seriously about need-based scholarships. One of the most important of these initiatives was the Georgia Tech Promise Program, which was created to provide financial support for Georgia students from low-income families and is described in chapter eleven.

The first four years of the quiet phase of the second campaign coincided with my last four years at Georgia Tech, and it was a productive time despite the fact that the campaign had not yet been publicly launched. More than $615 million in gifts and commitments were made. It was up to my successor, G. P. "Bud" Peterson, to complete the job, which he did in style. The public announcement of the second campaign occurred in 2010, and it concluded in 2017, having raised a total of $1.8 billon.

After leaving Georgia Tech, I looked back at these efforts and took pleasure in having helped to establish a culture in which fundraising was accepted as meaningful and necessary. More than $1.5 billion was raised while I was president thanks to the efforts of a great development team and my academic colleagues. These funds contributed to the well-being of our students and gave them the educational opportunities they needed to grow as human beings. They provided our faculty with the infrastructure and tools they needed to teach and conduct research at the highest levels. They gave Georgia Tech the fuel it needed to lift its game to a new level of competition, not just nationally but also globally.

## MAKING WAVES OF THE BEST KIND

I often said, half-jokingly, that Georgia Tech needed a faculty as good as our students. After all, our students came with some of the highest test scores in the nation, and I believed we needed a first-rate faculty to match. We made progress toward this goal during my tenure, as new positions and turnover enabled us to hire more than 400 faculty. The timing of this surge in hiring could not have been better. Our capital campaigns, combined with initiatives like Yamacraw and the Georgia Research Alliance, provided resources and fueled our ambitions. It was a buyer's market, and our growing prominence made us a desirable place for some of the nation's best to work. The top five institutions from which our new hires obtained their PhD degrees were, in order, MIT; the University of California, Berkeley; the University of Illinois Champaign-Urbana; Stanford University; and the University of Michigan, Ann Arbor—all among the best in the nation.

Each year my wife Anne and I held a reception for new faculty at the President's House, giving me a chance to talk with many of them. I always asked why they chose Georgia Tech when they could have gone anywhere. The most common reply was that while a lot of universities talked about encouraging interdisciplinary teaching and research, we were known for actually doing it. They wanted to work at a university that encouraged creativity and collaborative thinking, and we were that place. Now I had tangible evidence that our decision to create a new culture was working and had become self-reinforcing.

We also deliberately engaged faculty in decision-making. They served on panels that designed our buildings and in groups that made decisions about large-scale investments in future research initiatives. I personally chaired each Faculty Senate meeting and answered questions, which I like to think provided a sense of transparency and a willingness to discuss controversial topics. It was also a means of avoiding surprises, because it brought faculty into a dialog about controversial matters before they could become rancorous. In addition, the provosts and the faculty members who served as my executive assistants participated in our weekly administrative cabinet meetings at which they were free to introduce faculty concerns. Keeping the faculty engaged in discussions and decisions over the long haul was never easy, especially when we faced the prospect of budget cuts and salary freezes later in my tenure. I will be forever grateful to Provost Jean-Lou Chameau and to Gary Schuster, who succeeded him in 2006, for creating a vibrant academic enterprise based on respect for the faculty and the work they did.

As we worked to elevate the quality of our faculty, we paid careful attention to the announcements of CAREER Award winners by the National Science Foundation. This recognition, which came with five years of research support, was given to young faculty considered to be at the top of their class with the highest potential for the future. It was a matter of pride that Georgia Tech ranked consistently among the top five universities in the nation by number of award winners. By the end of my tenure, 120 Georgia Tech faculty had won CAREER Awards, the second highest total for any university in the nation.

But it was not just the young faculty who were impressive. We also hired many senior faculty who brought leadership skills and research portfolios with them. Our efforts to recruit faculty stars were enhanced by more than one hundred new endowed faculty positions and numerous state-of-the-art facilities made possible by our capital campaigns. These established professors steadily increased the number of faculty who were members of the National Academy of Engineering from six when I arrived in 1994 to twenty-nine when I left in 2008, putting us in the top ten nationally.

The combination of new talent and sophisticated new laboratory facilities lifted Georgia Tech's game in the competition for national centers of excellence. These centers were sponsored by major research funding organizations as a way to give universities a chance to take risks in new areas and form collaborations with multiple like-minded institutions in the process. Georgia Tech faculty have always been entrepreneurial, but encouraging them to compete for national centers of excellence was like throwing Brer Rabbit into the briar patch. Over a decade or so, Georgia Tech was part of winning teams for ten national centers of excellence funded by the National Science Foundation, the National Institutes of Health, the National Oceanic and Atmospheric Administration, NASA, and the European Union. The centers were funded for multiple years and were catalysts for initiatives in aerospace engineering, nanotechnology, biosciences, predictive medicine, bioinformatics, sustainable manufacturing, photonics, international affairs, and discovering the foundations for the origins of life. They led to partnerships with the best universities in the country and allowed us to push outward to the edges of knowledge.

In addition to centers of excellence funded by external agencies, our capital campaigns generated gifts from alumni that led to the formation of forward-looking interdisciplinary centers such as the Brook Byers Institute for Sustainable Systems and the Arbutus Center for the Integration of Research and Education.

I often pointed out to my colleagues that outstanding faculty hires, awards, academy memberships, and centers of excellence had "ripple effects." The waves from them washed over distant shores and created a new level of awareness of Georgia Tech as an institution on the rise. The impact was also felt in the growing volume of externally sponsored research conducted at Georgia Tech. In fiscal year 1995, which coincided roughly with my first year as president, the university conducted $212 million worth of sponsored research. By the time of my departure at the end of fiscal year 2008, Tech's annual sponsored research expenditures had more than doubled, standing at $522 million. Ten years later in fiscal year 2018, that figure totaled nearly $900 million. Among universities with no medical school, Georgia Tech ranks second only to MIT in the value of its sponsored research expenditures.

## RANKINGS—THE ONES THAT COUNT

Once there were no university rankings. Then the National Research Council initiated the idea when it began to survey faculty every ten years or so on the perceived quality of particular PhD programs at the nation's universities. But the rankings game was really ignited in 1983, when *U.S. News and World Report* (*USNWR*) stumbled on the magazine sales potential of annual university rankings. Today an assortment of rankings ranges from regional to global. Much as a university president might like to ignore the rankings, it is not possible, because alumni, donors, and potential students and their parents follow them.

Personally, I had three rules about rankings. First, because no two ranking systems are the same, it is important understand the rules that drive them. Only a very few are based solely on the level of excellence in academics. Most incorporate other factors as well, and these additional factors bias the results—some in favor of your university and its programs, others not so much. Understanding the rules is essential to explaining the results to your constituencies. Second, rankings use parameters that actually can be helpful in benchmarking studies for your university. But make sure you trust them. Finally, do what is right for your university, its students, its faculty, and its alumni regardless of the rankings, and the rankings will take care of themselves.

*University Rankings*

When *U.S. News and World Report* did its first ranking of colleges and universities in 1983, neither the internet nor social media existed. The top-ranked TV shows were *Dallas*, *The A-Team*, and *Magnum, P.I.* On the big screen the hits were *The Big Chill*, *National Lampoon's Vacation*, and *Risky Business*. *Risky Business* was Tom Cruise's first big hit, and it was every adult's guilty pleasure. We all wished we had been as cool as his character when we were in high school.

In their infancy, the *USNWR* rankings were pristine, focused almost entirely on academic reputation. Then the magazine realized that adding other criteria to the equation could broaden the commercial appeal of the rankings. In 1983, *USNWR* ranked the University of California, Berkeley—my PhD alma mater—fifth in the nation, based exclusively on academic reputation. By 1989, its ranking had fallen to twenty-fourth. What had happened at Berkeley to cause its reputation to collapse in just six years? The answer: nothing. The drop was entirely the result of changes in how *USNWR* determined the rankings. Parameters were added to the calculation that favored private universities with large endowments, causing them to leap ahead of public universities like Berkeley. Today, *USNWR* uses forty-one criteria to rank universities, many of which intertwine to create a bias that favors private universities. Does it make sense that the top twenty universities in the United States are all private? No. Does it make sense to assume that just because a university is private, it offers a better education? No. Does it make sense that public universities that serve thousands more students than private universities are not rewarded for it in the parameters? I think not. But as they say, it is what it is.

Georgia Tech finally graced the *USNWR* top fifty rankings in the mid-1990s, but just barely. In 1997, we ranked forty-eighth overall and thirteenth among public universities. From that time on, Georgia Tech steadily improved its ranking as our investments began to pay off. By the end of my tenure in 2008, Georgia Tech ranked thirty-fifth overall and seventh among public universities. While this improvement was rewarding to me personally, I was particularly proud for our faculty, staff, students, and alumni. In 2020 rankings, Georgia Tech broke into the top thirty universities for the first time and was ranked fifth among public universities. It was a long journey from 1997 when Tech barely had squeezed into the top fifty.

*The College of Engineering: The Bell Cow*

At Georgia Tech, doing well in the rankings began with engineering. Of the six colleges on campus, it was by far the largest, and it consistently graduated the largest number of engineers in the nation. When I arrived as president in 1994, Tech's strength in engineering was clearly real, but the 1995 *U.S. News and World Report* rankings put our College of Engineering at eleventh—outside the top ten. Just four of Tech's eleven engineering disciplines were ranked among the top ten in their field. John White was the dean of the College of Engineering at the time, and he and I had collaborated when I served as dean of engineering at Virginia Tech. His tenure as a dean at Georgia Tech had been frustrated by the issues that dogged President Pat Crecine's administration, and when his alma mater, the University of Arkansas, invited him to become its chancellor in 1997, he accepted.

White was replaced by a man I knew well. Jean-Lou Chameau had been my PhD student at Stanford University and was Georgia Tech's vice provost for research and graduate studies. The timing of his move to become dean of engineering was right because his energy and ideas about facilities and interdisciplinary research paralleled my own. He also worked well with Dean Gary Schuster of the College of Sciences, and together they formed a dynamic team.

By the time of the 2000 *USNWR* rankings, the College of Engineering had moved into the nation's top five, and seven of its programs were ranked in the top ten. In 2002, Mike Thomas stepped down as provost, and Chameau replaced him. Don Giddens, who had successfully launched our biomedical engineering partnership with Emory University, became the new dean of the College of Engineering. Under his leadership, the schools of engineering continued to rise in the rankings of their fields. By the time my tenure ended, only chemical engineering was outside of the top ten, and it was ranked eleventh.

The march up through the rankings continued after my departure. As I write this book, USNWR's 2020 rankings have placed all programs in the College of Engineering among the top five in the nation in their fields. No other university comes close. What does it mean? Rankings are temporal shiny things, so I tend not to put too much weight on them, but there is now no question that Georgia Tech's College of Engineering and its programs are as good as any anywhere in the world.

*The College of Computing: In a League of Its Own*

One of President Crecine's achievements was to reorganize the academic structure of Georgia Tech into six colleges, one of which was the College of Computing. He brought this idea with him from Carnegie Mellon University, where he had been the provost before coming to Georgia Tech. I felt it was a good decision because it helped to balance the dominance of the College of Engineering and better positioned the College of Computing to collaborate with other colleges at a time when computing was coming into broad use in many fields. However, at the time it was an unusual model. The norm was for computer science programs to be housed within another college—either engineering or arts and sciences. Adding to the confusion, "computer engineering" programs had evolved, a specialty that Georgia Tech had wrapped into its School of Electrical Engineering. As a result, when it came to rankings, our College of Computing seemed to be neither fish nor fowl. During much of my tenure, the College of Computing was ranked as a computer science program and did not crack the top ten, while the School of Electrical and Computer Engineering, with its computer engineering program, easily made it into the top ten in the rankings of engineering fields.

In the early to mid-2000s, computer science went through a period of soul searching, caused by the combination of the dot-com collapse and the discipline's growing reputation as a captive of the gaming industry. This predicament was not good news for anyone who was thinking about majoring in computer science, especially women. Why would any woman want to be associated with a gaming industry in which a bunch of geeks objectified women? Not surprisingly, the number of women enrolled in computer science programs nationwide dropped precipitously.

About this time, Peter Freeman, the founding dean of Georgia

Tech's College of Computing, stepped down. We had benefitted from his service, but we were fortunate to hire Richard DeMillo to replace him. DeMillo came from industry and brought new ideas about how to turn the perceptions of computer science around, as well as a new approach to the undergraduate curriculum. He created "Threads," an approach in which students could concentrate in computing while also fulfilling their broader interests in humanities and other areas. I applauded this concept, not only because it was immediately popular and encouraged women to major in computer science but also because it fit well with our mantra to define the technological research university of the twenty-first century.

The payoff was almost immediate. In 2008, the number of women in the College of Computing rebounded, and the college itself moved into the top ten of the *USNWR* rankings for computer science. The college also gained recognition for its programs in artificial intelligence, theory, systems, and programming languages. Today it is ranked among the best in the world.

### The College of Business: A Long Story That Ends Well

In 1913, Georgia Tech created a School of Commerce with two tracks, one offering evening classes to the business community of downtown Atlanta and the second offering day classes to undergraduates on campus. Both proved successful. However, in 1932 during the throes of the Great Depression, the Board of Regents of the newly created University System of Georgia decided to save costs by reducing duplication in the system. They resolved to eliminate Georgia Tech's School of Commerce, reasoning that the University of Georgia had a well-established business school—"only 68 miles away," as the regents said. Not unexpectedly, no one was happy about this decision except administrators at the University of Georgia.

When the Atlanta business community objected to losing their access to business education, the Board of Regents compromised, taking over the evening program and renaming it the University System of Georgia Evening School. It eventually became what is today Georgia State University. Students in the day program of the School of Commerce were incensed that the only option left to them was to travel to the University of Georgia to get their degrees. Their protests were led by a student named Ivan Allen, Jr., the future mayor of Atlanta, and they were so effective that the regents relented. They allowed Georgia Tech to continue its program on campus but stipulated that its name not include either "business" or "commerce." As a result, the School of Commerce reemerged in 1935 as the School of Industrial Management, a program in which I took a few courses as an undergraduate student.

When Crecine reorganized Georgia Tech's academic structure in 1990, the School of Industrial Management was lodged with liberal arts in the new Ivan Allen College, an arrangement I found odd. It took some time, and there were bumps along the way, but in 1997 I was able to get the school removed from the Ivan Allen College and elevated to a college in its own right—the DuPree College of Management.

It was named for alumnus Tom DuPree, a successful entrepreneur who in 1996 had pledged $25 million to create an endowment for it. He had contributed $2 million at the time; the rest was promissory. As we were making the decision to move the college to Technology Square, DuPree informed us that his businesses were facing trouble. By 2004, he admitted he could not meet the expectations of his pledge, and we removed his name from the college. It was a painful decision because DuPree was an upstanding person with the best of intentions. To his credit, his original $2 million gift remained in place and continued to provide deserving students with scholarship funding.

The DuPree episode put a dent in our hopes for elevating the status of the College of Management, but its leadership proved resilient. The prospect of a new home in Technology Square kept the wind in our sails, and Dean Terry Blum led the way in reshaping the mission of the college to take advantage of the technological strengths of Georgia Tech and the proximity of our business incubator, the Advanced Technology Development Center, now also located at Technology Square. In addition, the Board of Regents, with a bit of arm twisting on my part, gave us permission in 2005 to change the name to the College of Business, finally correcting a wrong perpetrated back in the 1930s.

Competing against the nation's top business schools was no small matter. Our College of Business was small, had little in the way of an endowment, and taught a large cohort of undergraduates. Most prestigious business schools did not even deign to have an undergraduate program, focusing entirely on the MBA and PhD levels. In the competition to win respect, our College of Business was like David going up against Goliath.

We needed special leaders who knew how to use a slingshot. Terry Blum, who served as dean from 1999 to 2006, and Steve Salbu, who served from 2006 to 2014, were up to the task. It helped that we were able to add faculty to expand the graduate and professional programs. By 2008, the college had broken into the ranks of the top ten public university business schools in the nation, and its programs in quantitative analysis and management information systems were gaining national recognition.

The progress did not go unnoticed. In 2012, alumnus Ernest Scheller, Jr., a man I admired very much, gifted the college $50 million for its endowment, and in recognition, it is now known as the Scheller College of Business. Dean Salbu and his successor Maryam Alavi continued to sharpen its focus. By 2020, the college ranked among the top five public business schools in the nation and had become number one in quantitative analysis and number three in management information systems.

It was a long journey from the 1930s when our business school was almost eliminated to achieving a top national ranking, but it was worth the wait. The high esteem was earned by being tough in the face of challenges and developing a creative and adaptive strategy to stand out among the best of the best.

*The Specialty Rankings*

As if rankings for universities and colleges are not enough, additional rankings focus on disciplines and interdisciplinary programs. Lurking among them is the granddaddy of them all, the National Research Council's ranking of PhD programs. The only one published during my presidency was in 1995. The NRC expected to produce another about a decade later, and the process of data collection was begun in 2005. However, it lost its way to good intentions. In an attempt to increase fairness, the National Research Council decided to use a new approach designed to provide a statistical view of more than forty parameters that were said to characterize the perceived strengths and weaknesses of programs vis-à-vis their peers. This idea proved to be confusing for just about everyone. The data were not published until 2010, and they had to be amended and republished in 2011.

Instead of a single numerical ranking, the bottom line for any given program was a ranking range for each of several groups of parameters. However, by my interpretation, the news for Georgia Tech was good. More than 70 percent of the Tech PhD programs that were ranked by the NRC had ranges that reached up into the top twenty, and half fell within ranges that included the top ten. Of course, engineering programs have always been Tech's strong suit and these continued to do well. The improvement for the PhD program in biology, though was especially pleasing. In 1995, the program was still new, producing only a small handful of graduates, and thus it appeared at the bottom of the list of more than a hundred programs. In the 2010 rankings, the average of its statistical range was forty-third of 124 programs, a substantial advance over what was a short time in the academic world. The 2010 ranges for Tech's PhD programs in computer science and public policy moved up to include the nation's top ten, and applied mathematics and chemistry also advanced.

In their own way, the 2010 *USNWR* rankings of graduate disciplines largely agreed with the findings of the National Research Council. In both sets of rankings, Georgia Tech's individual engineering programs were in or near the top ten. Chemistry, physics, biology, and mathematics had improved considerably compared to their rankings in 1995, moving from also-rans to respectability. But it was in the niche rankings that Georgia Tech found a place to shine, reflecting places where schools had chosen to make strategic investments. Both industrial and organizational psychology and discrete mathematics and combinatorics ranked in the top ten. The School of Public Policy's program in environment policy and management ranked twelfth. The School of History and Sociology's program in the history of science ranked fifteenth.

Other specialty rankings of note from the Academic Ranking of

World Universities placed Georgia Tech fifth in the world for nano-technology and nanoscience and eighth in the world for energy sciences and engineering—two areas in which Georgia Tech chose to make a mark.

*Rankings beyond Academics*

While rankings, especially those of *USNWR,* got most of the attention, I was always pleased when our progress was recognized in other places that reflected the deliberate investments we had made. In 2004, the year after we moved our business incubator, the Advanced Technology Development Center (ATDC), to Technology Square, it was recognized by the U.S. Department of Commerce with their national award for Excellence in Technology-Led Economic Development. Only one of these is given each year.

That same year, the Southern Growth Policy Board report *Innovation U: New University Roles in a Knowledge Economy* stated, "Perhaps more than any other research university in North America, economic development is an integral, critical component of the mission of the Georgia Institute of Technology." This statement recognized not only the work of ATDC but also the assistance provided to rural areas of Georgia through Georgia Tech's network of technology transfer stations and the commercialization of intellectual property developed from research.

Although patents are not a direct indicator of economic development activity, Georgia Tech focused on increasing its activity in this area during my tenure. Patents for university intellectual property provide private investors with secure knowledge that investments made during the development phase of a product will be protected until they reach the point of making a profit. Across the span of my presidency from 1994 to 2008, the annual number of patents issued to Georgia Tech faculty increased from 17 to 49, and annual patent disclosures increased from 132 to 323. Taken together, these recognitions and benchmarks of Georgia Tech's work in economic development confirmed our efforts to make the university more than just another research university. Tech was fulfilling its mission to help create jobs and economic prosperity for its community and state.

*Going Global*

Given the popularity of the *USNWR* rankings of American universities, it was inevitable that the rankings game would expand to the global stage. Several contenders emerged in the early 2000s, but it was a difficult playing field. Finding a workable set of parameters for comparing universities within the United States was difficult enough; defining them for the radically different university models that existed around the world proved almost impossible. The magazine *Times Higher Education* created its World University Rankings in 2004, and they are one of the most respected. However, their methodology has been criticized over the years, and they have changed their ranking parameters in response. Fortunately, those changes have largely worked in Georgia Tech's favor. In 2006, Georgia Tech was ranked number 145 in the world, which was something of a shock. But by 2008, Tech had improved to eighty-third. Although I was not there to see it, the 2010 rankings placed Georgia Tech at twenty-seventh. I would love to take at least some of the credit for Georgia Tech's meteoric rise from number 145 to number 27 in just four years, but I am sure this radical improvement was largely due to changes in the ranking parameters.

So where does Georgia Tech actually stand among universities worldwide? I do not think anyone really knows with any degree of accuracy, but given that it is one of the best universities in the United States, and the American university system is considered the best in the world, I believe that Georgia Tech is right up there with the best worldwide. That's my story and I'm sticking to it.

## REFERENCES

"Best Colleges and Universities." *U.S. News and World Report*. http://www.us-news.com/best-colleges.

"Georgia Tech Ranks #1 for Hispanic Engineering Graduate Programs." Georgia Institute of Technology press release, September 9, 2008. https://news.gatech.edu/2008/09/09/georgia-tech-ranks-1-hispanic-engineering-graduate-programs.

Gladwell, Malcolm. "The Order of Things." *The New Yorker*, February 7, 2011.

National Science Foundation. "Faculty Early Career Development Programs (CAREER)." http://www.nsf.gov/career.

National Science Foundation Higher Education Research and Development Survey Data: Public University Honors. *U.S. News Rankings of 57 Leading Universities,* *1983–2007.* http://www.publicuniversityhonors.com/2017/09/13/u-s-news-rankings-for-57-leading-universities-1983-2007/.

"Table 11: "Total R&D Expenditures at Universities and Colleges Fiscal Years 1988–95." *Selected Data on Academic Science and Engineering R&D Expenditures: FY 1995.*

"Table 20: Higher Education R&D Expenditures Ranked by FY 2018 R&D Expenditures: FYs 2009–18." *Higher Education Research and Development Survey Fiscal Year 2018.*

"Table 27: R&D Expenditures at Universities and Colleges Ranked by FY 2008 R&D Expenditures: FY 2001–08." *Academic R&D Expenditures, FY 2008.* www.nsf.gov/statistics/srvyherd/.

*Top 100 Worldwide Universities Granted U.S. Utility Patents, 2016.* National Academy of Inventors and Intellectual Property Owners Association.

*World University Rankings.* Times Higher Education. http://www.timeshighereducation.com/world-university-rankings.

*Chapter 11*

# A PROMISE MADE, A PROMISE KEPT

In 2006, I was chairing a meeting with deans of colleges of engineering. Our discussion focused on the question of why nearly 50 percent of the students who enrolled in engineering left school before they graduated. I thought I understood this issue because we had faced up to it at Georgia Tech and improved our retention rates. But I was struck by a comment made by a dean whose college served a large percentage of students from low-income families. He said, "Contrary to many of your students, the ability of my students to stay the course is driven by financial issues. They are on the edge all the time. If they get sick and cannot work, they cannot pay their tuition. If their parents lose their jobs, the students may not have the money they need to stay in school."

My initial reaction was that this comment did not apply to Georgia Tech. After all, we had the largest voluntary cooperative education program in the nation, enabling students to work their way through school, and our Georgia students had HOPE Scholarships as long as they maintained a 3.0 grade point average. But the comment stuck with me.

When I returned to campus, I gathered a group of Georgia Tech professionals who oversaw financial aid and served as student advisors. I asked them, "Are we losing students for financial reasons?" Not only was the answer yes, but there was more. In addition to those who dropped out because they could not afford the cost, we had students who were borrowing money to stay in school. In 2006, the average student graduating from Georgia Tech was $16,000 in debt. While this number was better than the national average of $19,600, it was still a lot. In addition, I learned that we were losing potential students who did not apply simply because they were afraid they could not afford Georgia Tech.

I knew then that we needed to address this problem, not only for the sake of deserving students but also for the sake of Georgia Tech itself. For students who had to scrape their money together to earn a degree, graduating from Georgia Tech had historically been a ticket to success. I had been one of those students. If Georgia Tech stepped away from helping students like me, it was at risk of becoming a different institution and, in my view, a diminished one.

## MY STORY

In 1959, I applied to Georgia Tech and was accepted. My parents had a strong belief in education. After making their tithe for church, they set aside money for their children's education. With both of them working, they believed they could pay my college expenses. However, by that time my family had moved to Chattanooga, Tennessee, ten miles north of the Georgia border, and I was considered a non-resident student. In 1959, tuition for non-residents was about $600 a year, compared to $200 a year for Georgia residents. It doesn't sound like a lot of money either way today, but it was for my parents, who would have to pay an additional $800 a year for room and board above the tuition.

To help pay for my education, I applied to Georgia Tech's Cooperative Education Program in my freshman year. To be accepted in those days, a student had to complete their freshman year with a 2.0 grade point average. Despite a rough start, I cleared this hurdle, and in my sophomore year I was hired by the Louisville and Nashville Railroad Company to work on a survey team. As was the pattern for co-op students, I alternated quarters between working on the railroad and studying on campus.

My survey team was based in Knoxville, Tennessee, but our work took us anywhere along the line from Marietta, Georgia, to Cincinnati,

Ohio, mostly in small railroad towns in Appalachia that had seen better days. My job was actually one of the better-paying co-op jobs and came with a generous reimbursement policy for travel, which allowed me to save more money for my time on campus. All in all, my co-op job covered the costs for me to attend Georgia Tech for my sophomore and junior years. It helped that even for out-of-state students such as me, tuition and fees were quite low.

Love intervened when I married Anne Robinson in the spring of my junior year, and I dropped out of the co-op plan. Anne got a job, and I helped out by delivering furniture for Sears, Roebuck and Company. In those days, Atlanta had a lot of four-story apartment buildings with no elevators and no air conditioning. I earned every dollar I was paid lugging sofas up the stairs. Then in my senior year Civil Engineering School Chair Bill Schultz took pity on me and hired me to work part-time. Carrying paper and pencils to faculty members was a lot easier than delivering furniture for Sears, and I was grateful. I received my bachelor's degree in Civil Engineering in summer 1963. Looking back, I realized that while I had worked hard, I had also been lucky that Georgia Tech was so affordable.

When I returned to Georgia Tech as president in 1994, I discovered that the Cooperative Education Program was still the largest voluntary program in the country, with more than 3,000 undergraduate students participating. However, two things had changed. First, the cost of attending Georgia Tech was considerably higher. Tuition was now $1,845 per year for Georgia residents and $6,300 for non-residents, and room and board charges totaled almost $5,000 per year. On the positive side, Governor Zell Miller had created the HOPE Scholarship Program in 1993. At its inception, it used state lottery funds to pay tuition, books, and fees for Georgia residents who maintained at least a 3.0 grade point average. Although the costs were higher than in my days as a student, it still seemed to me that the combination of the HOPE Scholarship Program and the co-op option would make it possible for most students from families of modest means to attend.

## LOOKING FOR ANSWERS

After I returned to campus from the deans' meeting in 2006, I took a second look at my assumptions about the affordability of a Georgia Tech education. When I met with the Georgia Tech professionals who were knowledgeable about student finances, I learned that while the HOPE Scholarship covered the cost of tuition, books, and fees, it did not address the cost of room and board, which could total more than tuition, books, and fees. In addition, Georgia Tech's academic rigor meant that more than half of our Georgia students had trouble maintaining a 3.0 grade point average in their freshman year and lost their HOPE Scholarship. That was a blow, especially for students on the edge of financial instability. Of course, the Cooperative Education Program provided job earnings to offset the costs of education. However, co-op students did not start working until they were sophomores, and they spent their senior year back on campus. The coverage was good while it lasted, but it did not extend through all four years to graduation. The bottom line was that our system was full of holes through which students could fall, and the lack of a safety net could be devastating for those with limited financial resources.

I began by pulling together a working group to help sort through the issues. Key players were Provost Gary Schuster along with Marie Mons and Jerry McTier, both seasoned staff members in the Office of Financial Aid. At our first meeting, we reviewed existing programs around the country that had been created to address student financial problems. We immediately saw a dichotomy between private and public universities. Private universities were well ahead of public universities in providing special programs for students from low-income families, supported by endowments they had developed through fundraising campaigns. Public universities, having long believed that their low tuition model took care of the matter, were only now beginning to realize the game had changed as state allocations stagnated or diminished and tuition rates increased. Some had recently introduced need-based assistance programs, but most were limited in scope and none operated in Georgia.

The most impressive of the new programs at public institutions was the Carolina Covenant Program at the University of North

Carolina, begun in 2004. According to the university literature, "The Covenant offers a debt-free path to graduation through a combination of grants, scholarships and a work-study job." While some private money was available to support the program, it was largely funded using set-asides from the general tuition pool, which was allowed under North Carolina state law. Roughly 500 students at each class level were enrolled in the program.

We were impressed by the Carolina Covenant Program, but Georgia's higher education policy differed from North Carolina's in two respects. First, the HOPE Scholarship Program helped to meet the financial aid needs of many students who were Georgia residents. It was not a catchall, but it played a role in the ability of many students to remain at Georgia Tech. Second, Georgia state law prevented the redirection of tuition funds to financial aid, so anything we tried would require private funding. At the time, Georgia Tech's endowment was close to a billion dollars, but it was largely restricted by legally binding gift agreements and long-standing commitments to other good causes. The general principles of the Carolina Covenant Program were appealing, but we faced the challenge of finding a new source of significant private funding if we were to do anything similar.

## WHERE THERE IS A WILL THERE IS A WAY

It was time to nail down the specifics of what we wanted to do. The first decision was the underlying principle for our program. My goal, like that of the Carolina Covenant, was that any student in our program would be able to graduate from Georgia Tech without incurring debt. I wanted to find a way to pay for all of the costs of education, including tuition, fees, and room and board. In 2006, this amount was about $15,000 per year for an undergraduate Georgia resident. However, we knew that inflation and tuition increases would cause it to rise over the course of a four-year program of study. The bottom line was that in 2006, about $90,000 would be needed to carry a freshman to graduation in four years.

I proposed that our commitment to low-income Georgia students would be to meet whatever cost remained after the application of any financial support they brought with them, such as the HOPE

Scholarship, federal Pell Grants, or other grants and scholarships. Like the Carolina Covenant, we would include a federal work-study component. Recognizing the possibility that a student might lose their HOPE Scholarship by not meeting the required 3.0 grade point average, we would promise to pick up the difference, ensuring that there never would be a gap in funding that would cause the student to drop out or borrow money. A guarantee like the one I was proposing was not just important unto itself, but it said to our low-income students that from day one the burden of paying for their education at Georgia Tech was lifted off of their backs.

To implement such a program, we needed a workable and sustainable financial model. In the beginning, the only available source of money was the undesignated funding the Georgia Tech Foundation provided to the president for discretionary use. These funds were in high demand already, so we obviously needed to undertake a new fundraising campaign specifically directed at supporting low-income students. It would not be simple, but I believed in the power of ideas and in the remarkable willingness of our alumni, who knew firsthand the value of a Georgia Tech degree, to help students in need. We had to succeed or the program would ultimately not be sustainable.

Not knowing how things would actually play out, we had to make educated guesses. We decided to define eligibility by an annual family income that fell at or below the federal poverty line ($30,000 in 2006). Estimates showed that fifty to sixty students at each class level would qualify. Once we had students at all four levels of study, we estimated the program would have 200 or so students. At that level, the full cost for their education would be about $4 million per year. However, because students would bring some funding with them from sources such as the HOPE Scholarship or other scholarships or grants and would participate in federal work-study, the demand on Georgia Tech's private funds would be less than the full $4 million, possibly as little as half. Still, half would call for $2 million a year—money we did not have.

As I looked around the room at Schuster, McTier, and Mons, I knew all of us realized we had reached the point of a decision. If we were going to recruit students for fall 2007, we had to get the message out quickly. As I hesitated, Schuster said, "Go ahead. We will figure

226

out how to make it work." The others' faces broke into smiles.

Now it fell to me and our public relations staff to arrange a kickoff. Simultaneously, our Office of Development needed to begin raising endowment funds to make the program sustainable. Because an endowment usually spins off about 4 percent of its corpus for expenditure, generating $2 million a year would require a $50 million endowment. We had our work cut out for us.

### KICKING IT OFF: 2007–2008

On February 1, 2007, we announced the Georgia Tech Promise Program, and as part of our efforts to get the word out, I did an interview with Georgia Public Radio. Two things that followed shortly after the interview reinforced my faith in our assumptions. One led to our first Promise Scholar and the other to our first donor to the Promise Program.

A counselor at Brunswick High School in Brunswick, Georgia, heard my radio interview and placed a call asking to speak to the president of Georgia Tech. I picked up the phone and said, "Hello, this is Wayne Clough." The counselor told me she had a student whom she thought fit the profile of the Promise Program. His name was Duane Carver. He was a senior who had taken honors courses in mathematics and physics and had a high grade point average. But, she said, what was unique about his academic achievements was that he and his family had gone through some hard times financially, even to the point of being homeless for periods of time. I immediately made arrangements for the counselor to speak to our admissions staff.

Duane Carver became our first Promise Scholar, choosing to major in computer engineering. In fall 2007, he joined 185 other students in our first cohort of Promise Scholars. Few of the first group of scholars were recruited like Duane was; there was just not enough time to get it done. Instead, Jerry McTier and Marie Mons made a group of students who were already enrolled at Georgia Tech very happy. They were chosen because the financial statements they had filed in applying for financial aid showed that they met the profile for the Promise Program.

Our first major gift for the Promise Program arrived without fanfare on April 12, 2007. Without any formal solicitation on our part, Jenny and Mike Messner sent us a check for $1 million. Mike Messner was a Georgia Tech civil engineering alumnus who grew up in Georgia, but after obtaining his degree, he established a successful investment business in New York City. As he explained, "I have been in the investment business for a long time, and my Georgia Tech degree is the best investment I ever made. My wife Jenny and I are grateful to be able to help students obtain their Tech degrees, especially those in the Promise Program." Mike and Jenny would become lifelong friends to both Anne and me. Because of their commitment to helping students at Georgia Tech and schools where they live, hardly anyone could set a better example for Promise Scholars.

We were now off and running, with students and a start on our fundraising campaign. When I left Georgia Tech in summer 2008 to become secretary of the Smithsonian Institution, the Georgia Tech Foundation honored me with a gift of $5 million in my name for the Promise Program endowment, for which I will be eternally grateful. It was also an honor to have the program named for me.

While no Promise Scholars had yet graduated by the time I left, we already knew this much:

- Counting the Messner gift and the contribution from the Georgia Tech Foundation, we had more than $9 million in hand to help fund the program.

- Retention of the Promise Scholars was equal to or better than the average for all Georgia Tech students.

- Promise Scholars came from more than fifty counties in Georgia, many from rural areas where Georgia Tech had had difficulty recruiting before.

- Promise Scholars as a group were more diverse than the Georgia Tech student body as a whole.

- The average annual family income for students who enrolled as Promise Scholars was $22,000.

Although I was not there to see the Promise Program reach maturity, Promise Scholars continued to send me notes each year, thanking me for the scholarship. Once a colleague at the Smithsonian walked into my office, noticed I had tears in my eyes, and asked if something was wrong. I said, "No. I have just been reading letters from some remarkable students at Georgia Tech."

In spring 2010, I received word that Duane Carver had graduated with honors, earning his degree in computer engineering in three years. He was quoted as saying, "I don't think the people who give money to the Tech Promise Program realize how huge this is for us. Receiving a Tech Promise Scholarship literally changed my life.... I have a chance to help my family make their dreams come true."

## THE PROMISE PROGRAM, POST-2008

When G. P. "Bud" Peterson was selected as my successor, he and I already knew each other from having served together on the board of the National Science Foundation. He was a good choice for Georgia Tech because of his experience and the fact that he had received his degrees in mechanical engineering. What pleased me even more was the support that he and his wife Val gave to the Promise Program, not only verbally but also in fundraising.

In 2015, after I retired from the Smithsonian and returned to Georgia Tech as a part-time faculty member, Peterson asked me to chair a committee to consider two questions: how to celebrate the tenth anniversary of the Promise Program in 2017 and how to ensure that the program was sustainable going forward. Even though fundraising for the program had been successful, the question of sustainability was real because the dynamics had changed. On the one hand, the cost of tuition, fees, and room and board kept increasing, which put more pressure on the available funds. On the other hand, competition had grown as private schools sought to admit talented young men and women from rural areas. As a result, the number of students participating in the Promise Program had declined over time. My committee consisted of individuals from the financial side of the house, the Alumni Association, the Office of Development, and the Office of Admissions and Financial Aid. I was glad to see my two old friends, Jerry McTier and

Marie Mons, there.

To help us understand how Promise Scholars saw the program from their perspective, McTier and I arranged four luncheons with some of them. Each of the four groups was impressive. Their stories of overcoming obstacles in high school and gaining admission to Georgia Tech were powerful. More than a few came from families that had fallen on hard times through no fault of their own, often because of the illness of one or even both parents. In some cases, their parents had immigrated to the United States and been unsuccessful at obtaining regular work. In other cases, opioid addictions had led parents to pass their children to grandparents to raise. But the consistent, recurring theme in their stories was that these students were determined to create a better life for themselves and their families, and that gave them the will to stay the course.

Among the insights gleaned from our luncheons were that Georgia Tech needed to get more information about the Promise Program to high schools in rural areas and then improve the overall experience of Promise Scholars once they got to campus. These students told us they would like to meet other Promise Scholars so that they would realize they were not alone and could encourage each other. Finally, they said that as they advanced through their courses of study, they gained confidence and were proud to be known as Promise Scholars.

The message was that we needed to ramp up our efforts to reach the Promise Scholars as a group, beginning when they were still in high school and continuing all the way to graduation from Georgia Tech. One place for improvement was providing funds for Promise Scholars to study abroad. McTier and Mons had already found ways to enable selected students to study abroad, and the stories were so positive that we knew we had to offer this option to all Promise Scholars.

As for celebrating the program's tenth anniversary, we felt the best idea was to hold a special reception for Promise Scholars and their families at graduation. Because Georgia Tech has three graduation ceremonies each year, this proposal would call for three receptions.

Our committee met with President Peterson and his staff to present our report. He agreed with our recommendations, and we saw the initial results almost immediately in the form of graduation receptions and "Welcome to Tech" receptions for incoming Promise Scholars to meet each other. We invited Promise Program donors to join us for these events and to speak about their own struggles at Georgia Tech, especially if they had had financial challenges. It helped for the Promise Scholars to hear from someone who had been in their shoes and had worked hard, earned a Georgia Tech degree, and achieved success.

The graduation receptions were a high point, especially because we met the families of the scholars. The receptions have continued beyond the tenth anniversary year, and I have attended all of them to date. Every one has reinforced in a personal way how important the Promise Program is. To hear the families speak about what the Promise Program meant not only to their children but also to them is powerful. At these receptions we also enjoy hearing about the future plans of the scholars, with more than a few going on to graduate school and some heading off to medical school. Finally, to our surprise and delight, some Promise Scholars brought along the person they planned to marry and with whom they would begin their own families.

The implementation of the findings of the committee put the Promise Program on its way to sustainability and created a more holistic Georgia Tech experience for the scholars. Testimony from Promise Scholars indicates not only the impact of the program on its students but also the ripples it sends through their families. In their own words:

"I was shocked," said Milton James on hearing that he had received a Tech Promise Scholarship. Although he had been recruited by Ivy League schools, the Promise Program allowed him to earn a degree at Tech's number-one ranked School of Industrial and Systems Engineering while staying close to his mother, who was on dialysis. "I want to come back as a mentor to students who are having a hard time.... I want to show other students they can do it," he said.

Sarah Banks: "I am not sure I would be at Tech if it were not for the Tech Promise." Her father, the breadwinner for the family, was diagnosed with cancer when she was eleven years old. He passed away after Sarah was accepted into the Promise Program. According to her mother Penny Banks, "After her father was diagnosed with cancer, we had to dip into Sarah's college fund just to make ends meet. So I became worried sick that she wouldn't be able to get an education. You have no idea how grateful I am for Tech Promise. There's no way Sarah would've been able to get into Tech without it. Yes, she had the academic ability to get in, but I couldn't afford to send her."

Steven Webber: "Tech Promise allowed me to have an amazing experience and fall in love with Georgia Tech without worrying about how much my education is costing me and my family."

Marquetta and Marteisha Griffin (twins): "We are from Rochelle, Georgia, a small rural town in South Georgia with two traffic lights. It is known as the watermelon capital of the world. Our mom and dad did not get to go to college, but did their very best to prepare us for it. We had the HOPE Scholarship, but still would have had to take out loans, and we did not want to put the responsibility for this debt on our parents. We could not believe what the Georgia Tech Promise Program is doing for us. It is a life-changing opportunity."

The Promise Program had another unexpected side effect, this one for the donors. In their words:

Robert Stargel: "My wife Jocelyn and I are proud donors to the Promise Program. Having a chance to meet with the scholars and their families at the graduation reception is a moving experience. Time and time again they say their children could not have gone to Georgia Tech without the Promise Program, and now they have unlimited horizons ahead of them."

Charlie Moseley: "My interest in the Promise Scholarship Program came from my experience growing up in a small town in Georgia, and knowing that if you graduate from Georgia Tech you have a world of previously unobtainable opportunities. When I learned Promise Scholars come from families with less than $30,000 annual income, I realized the transformative power of this program for the students and their families."

John Staton: "It has been my pleasure to meet and get to know a number of Promise Scholars and their families. Every one of them, without exception, has a great story to tell. I am always overwhelmed by the pride that each of the students describes in telling us how much the Promise Program means to them and their families."

Francis Lott: "My endowment [gift] to the Promise Scholarship Program has been a singularly uplifting and rewarding experience.

Three Coffee High graduates currently attend Tech on Promise, and one recently graduated. None would have likely been able to attend any college, but all are thriving. I could not be more pleased or proud to know my commitment is changing the lives of these outstanding students."

Kathy Betty: "My late husband Garry Betty and I believed that one of the root causes of poverty is lack of education. When Dr. Clough started the Promise Program, it provided a way to put action behind our passion, and to repay the gratitude Garry had for the education he received from Georgia Tech. As the years have passed, what a joy it has been to watch, meet and hear the stories from the recipients of the Promise Program. There is no greater gift than the gift of hope for the future. That is what the Promise Program is accomplishing."

Wick Moorman: "My wife Bonnie and I have always believed in giving to causes for education. When we first heard about the Promise Program, we were immediately taken by it, both rationally and emotionally. The result was our commitment, which was the largest charitable donation we had made. Not long after, in my role as CEO of Norfolk Southern, I met a young woman, Amelia Joyner, at a safety meeting. She was wearing a hardhat and safety glasses and a Georgia Tech polo shirt. She was a co-op student and her supervisors told me she was so competent, she filled in for them from time to time. Sometime later I received an email from Georgia Tech saying they wanted to let me know about a Promise Scholar working for Norfolk Southern. Attached was a photograph of Amelia Joyner standing in front of an enormous steam locomotive. I admit I became emotional and realized the power of the Promise Program to change people's lives."

Even the people who have made the Promise Program work at the ground level right from the start have been touched and changed by the program and its participants:

Marie Mons: "In 2007 some folks called the Promise Program an experiment, others folly. Those of us working with the students and their families every day called it the most significant commitment to access that Georgia Tech ever attempted. For me, working with and for this program, and seeing firsthand the impact on individuals that are now Tech grads, has been the most rewarding opportunity of my student service career."

Jerry McTier: "For the past fourteen years I had the privilege to work with the Promise Scholars, every one of them—an incredible group, diverse in every way imaginable. Kids too shy to even look at me when I met them are now making their way through the world as Tech grads. I have been in the business of assisting students and their families to find ways to finance their higher education dreams for more than forty-eight years. Seeing these young people who were not born with a silver spoon in their mouths exceed the expectations of others (not theirs) has been the highlight of those forty-eight-plus years. One of my favorite quotes comes from a Promise Scholar: 'It's not where I'm from that matters; it's where I am going.'"

## POSTSCRIPT

As I write this chapter, it is fourteen years since the Georgia Tech Promise Program was initiated, and it now has a track record. More than 850 students have benefitted from the program—605 have graduated and 170 are still working on their degrees. Assuming all of those still in school graduate, Promise Scholars will have a graduation rate of 91 percent. As a group, Promise Scholars are more diverse than the Georgia Tech student body as a whole. Of those who have participated in the program, 34 percent are White; 28 percent are Asian American; 21 percent are African American; 11 percent are Hispanic; and 6 percent are from other ethnic groups. The average annual family income for all of the Promise Scholars is about $21,000.

After I retired from Georgia Tech in 2008, Bud Peterson and Georgia Tech continued to press forward with fundraising efforts to support the Promise Program. While individual donors continued to be the backbone of the fundraising, willing corporations and foundations, including Southern Company Charitable Foundation, the Woodruff Foundation, Aaron's Inc., and the Coca-Cola Company stepped up. As I write this book, almost $55 million has been raised, exceeding the goal we set back in 2007.

The statistics are telling, but the real story lies with the Promise Scholars. I often explain the importance of something in terms of its absence. What would the world be like if the Georgia Tech Promise

234

Program did not exist? Most obviously, 850 students from low-income families would never have gone to Georgia Tech. But there is more to the story. At Georgia Tech they learned to compete against some of the brightest students in the nation. This level of confidence in their own ability to succeed is big for students whose only prior experience is in small rural schools. I know something about it because it happened to me. At Georgia Tech, each Promise Scholar grows into a capable, confident person who will make a difference in our country. They know what it means to overcome the hardest challenges life can throw at you and still come back fighting and succeeding.

To conclude this story, I return to the very first Promise Scholar who launched the program. Duane Carver came to our attention because, when I was interviewed on Georgia Public Radio about the program, his high school counselor in Brunswick, Georgia, was listening. She knew he was special because he excelled at his coursework, even though he and family were homeless at times. He matriculated at Georgia Tech in fall 2007, and I did not have a chance to meet him before I left the following summer. That situation was rectified in June 2016 when the Georgia Tech Foundation held its annual meeting at Sea Island, Georgia. This meeting was special because it celebrated the successful conclusion of Georgia Tech's second national campaign. The campaign had raised $1.8 billion, a part of which was dedicated to student scholarships, including the Promise Program. Because the quiet phase of the campaign had begun on my watch in 2004, I was invited to speak. After I concluded my remarks, there was a surprise in store. A young man walked up through the audience and introduced himself as Duane Carver, now a successful intellectual property lawyer in Atlanta.

In his remarks, Carver described what his Promise Scholarship had meant for him and his family—a story I had never heard. After he graduated from Georgia Tech in three years with a degree in computer engineering, he took a job with IBM in the Research Triangle. He saved his money and helped his sister pay her way through college. After she had earned her degree, he and his sister saved their money to pay for their mother to earn her degree in secondary education and her teaching certificate. When these family obligations were taken care of,

Carver enrolled at the University of California, Berkeley School of Law, one of the top-ranked schools in the nation, where he studied intellectual property law. He concluded his remarks this way: "The Promise Program did not just help me earn a degree from Georgia Tech; it helped my family out of poverty." The audience was quiet for a moment as everyone absorbed what he had just said, and then they burst into applause.

Of all the accomplishments that have been attributed to me for my service at Georgia Tech, few can be guaranteed to last. But no circumstances can ever take away the students who have received their degrees with the help of the Promise Program. I'll take that as a legacy anytime.

## REFERENCES

Bailey, Kristen. "Futures Filled with Promise: 10 Years of Tech Promise." Georgia Institute of Technology press release, May 1, 2017. http://www.news.gatech.edu/features/10-years-tech-promise/.

Davis, Janel. "Tech Promise: Georgia Tech Aid Program Guarantees Degree without Debt." *Atlanta Journal Constitution*, December 24, 2016. https://www.ajc.com/news/education/tech-promise-georgia-tech-aid-program-guarantees-degree-without-debt/yLgub6rfV1IgZIGPXkHSrM/.

"Georgia Tech Financial Aid Program to Provide Access to a Debt-Free Degree." *Philanthropy News Digest*, February 5, 2007.

*Chapter Twelve*

## SUMMING UP

Seven years into the job as Georgia Tech president, I was asked to write a short play that would be performed as part of a fundraiser for Atlanta's wonderful Horizon Theater. The producers encouraged me to sprinkle in a bit of humor. My play, titled "A Half-Day in the Life of a President," was intended to be a spoof of those instances in which a university president gets caught in the crossfire over a decision that he or she must make. The story begins with an urgently requested 7:30 a.m. meeting with a group of important alumni who tell the president they have information from trusted sources that the football coach, whom they greatly admire, might leave. They say the only way to ensure he will stay is for the university to undertake a multi-million-dollar renovation of the football stadium. As they leave the meeting, they demand an answer by noon. At 9:00 a.m. another group of equally important alumni arrives. They state that they will give no money toward renovating the football stadium unless the football coach, whom they dislike intensely, is fired. They also demand an answer by noon. And so it goes throughout the morning of the benighted president. Most of the play was fictional, but I did not entirely make up the incident about the football coach. In real life, we did renovate the football stadium, but the coach left anyway.

As my little play illustrated, all university presidents face dozens of decisions, often under difficult circumstances. However, only a few of those decisions make a lasting difference. This book is about the decisions of my tenure as president of the Georgia Institute of Technology that I believe made a difference. I did not include any decisions about athletics, not because I do not enjoy collegiate athletics or because I think them unimportant to the university and the students, alumni, and fans. In fact, they play a significant role for the student athletes who compete, enhance the student experience, and contribute to the image of the university. But at Georgia Tech, athletics have not shaped the course of the university's history any more than they have shaped the course of history at Cambridge, Oxford, Stanford, or MIT. Rather, the decisions that have shaped the course of Georgia Tech's history have centered on the mission of the university—a well-rounded, high-quality education with a strong academic work ethic; discovery, innovation, and entrepreneurship; and service to the community and the world.

Because I wrote this book more than a decade after my tenure as president of Georgia Tech had ended, I had the advantage of a longer perspective regarding which decisions made a difference. Time and history will be the ultimate judge. My purpose is to provide insights into why and how the decisions were made and then detail how we implemented them. Getting decisions right is one thing; seeing them through is quite another. Sometimes I had to spend considerable time convincing others of the virtues of my decisions, and then I spent even more time raising the money required to make a reality of them. After all, a good decision is not worth much if it is never executed.

With the passage of the years, I found it interesting that most of the decisions that stood out, and thus were included in this book, were based to a large degree on fundamentals and philosophical principles I had gained from my journey through life. It helped that I had loving parents and spent my childhood in a rural South Georgia town where my love of reading and nature nurtured my sense of curiosity. But my childhood home was also the South of the 1940s, where tenant farmers, both White and African American, struggled to make a life, and opportunity was lost to poverty and a lack of access to education.

As a seventeen-year-old, I was accepted at Georgia Tech, and there I learned the importance of hard work and never giving up, all the while honing my competitive edge. Along my way through life, I learned from mentors whom I chose myself because they were good at making decisions and getting others to go along with them. My experiences as a civil engineering consultant for large infrastructure projects and as an earthquake engineer who traveled the world gave me tools to deal with complex problems and explain them to laypeople. Finally, time spent on the faculty of four different universities before returning to Georgia Tech was valuable in providing a perspective that others did not have.

Coming back to Georgia Tech as the first alumnus to be its president was an unexpected coincidence. It almost did not happen. But it gave me a chance to repay an institution that had helped lift my sights and taught me that I had something to offer. My motivation was high to do the job right.

What lessons does this book offer for others?

1. Time spent reimagining what an institution and its purposes should be is well spent. No matter how big the problems an institution faces, it needs a framework for what it should become at the end of the day, and its leader should never lose sight of this goal.

2. Do not let a lack of resources deter you from thinking big. State your purpose in terms of aspirations; they inspire people. Without aspirations, our campus infrastructure would not have doubled in size; we would not have risen into the top ten public universities in the nation; and our biotechnology program would not have been launched.

3. Calculated risk is your friend. Without it we would never have borrowed $320 million to build Technology Square or launched two national capital campaigns and raised $1.5 billion in gifts over the course of my tenure.

4. Seize opportunities and run with them. Without this attitude, we would not have launched the Sam Nunn School of International Affairs or formed our biomedical partnership with Emory University, which then rose to the top of the national rankings.

5. Base your decisions on the right motivations; it will increase the likelihood that you will make the right choices. Having the right

motivations aided the creation of a sustainable campus and was at the root of our work to make Georgia Tech a place where all students had a fair chance to grow as human beings and to graduate.

6. Recognize that not all decisions will be right or have the impact you are hoping for. I regret that we were not more successful in creating a more inclusive campus and that I was not able to advance the cause of the humanities farther.

7. Finally, remember that public universities have an obligation to help the United States live up to the ideals on which it was founded. No matter how far down the ladder young people begin, they deserve an opportunity to climb as far as their talents and aspirations can take them. That is the American dream, and public universities have an important role to play in making it come true. The Georgia Tech Promise Program demonstrates the power of this idea.

From time to time, I have had the privilege of speaking to groups of university faculty and administrators about serving in leadership roles. A central thrust of my message is this enduring paradox: On the one hand, the time frame of their opportunity to make a difference will likely be short compared to the life span of their university. On the other hand, bringing about lasting change at a university takes time.

In my own case, it helped that at the outset we had only two years to prepare to serve as the Olympic Village for the 1996 Centennial Olympic Games. I had to work twice as hard to keep a focus on what was really important for the growth of Georgia Tech in the long run and make progress on those things, even as we scrambled to get our Olympic preparations done on time. My goal was that in the end, Georgia Tech's integrity as an academic institution would be untouched by the disruption of the Olympics; that when we came out the other end of the Olympics, it would be as if the Games had never occurred. I know that goal concentrated my attention, and I think we succeeded. The unexpected and lasting benefit from the Olympics experience was that we saw how much could be accomplished through focus, hard work, teamwork, multitasking, and a "no challenge is too big" attitude.

Looking back, I believe that in total the decisions made during my tenure as president led to a Georgia Tech based on the right values and poised to contribute to its home community as well as to the global community. We now know from experience that the graduates from this new, reimagined Georgia Tech are better prepared for life and more motivated to make a difference for the right reasons. I like to think the lessons we learned along the way can be translated to other universities, particularly those that, like Georgia Tech, focus on technology.

It was a great honor for a boy born in rural South Georgia to have become the man who served as the first alumnus to be president of Georgia Tech. If I made a difference, it was because of the many great mentors and colleagues I was fortunate to have throughout my life. My achievements as president were a tribute to them and paid forward the debt I felt I owed them and Georgia Tech.

# ACKNOWLEDGMENTS

Acknowledgments to those who helped me with this book are a testament to the large number of people who helped make my tenure as president of Georgia Tech a success.

To my wife Anne, and to my children and family, thanks for your love and support throughout my tenure as president of Georgia Tech.

I owe an enormous debt to Sandra Bramblett, whom I hired in 1994 to head up Georgia Tech's institutional research program. Fortunately, she was still there in 2015 when I returned to campus after serving as Secretary of the Smithsonian. She singlehandedly served as the key source of information, data, and chronology for the book.

Sarah Eby-Ebersole, who was my speechwriter when I was president and edited four of my books, edited this one with her usual care and professionalism. Carol Hogan, my assistant, helped coordinate and schedule interviews, conducted research, and gave advice throughout.

Then there are those who freely gave their time through interviews, finding photographs and resource documents, reviewing chapters, and answering my innumerable questions. These include Paul Benkeser, Yves Bertholet, Brett Boatright, Barrett Carson, Marc Dash, Travis Denton, Marta Garcia, Elizabeth Gallant, Sam Graham, Tom Hall, Amy Bass-Henry, Nolan Hertel, Mellisa Kemp, Scott Levitan, Donna Lewellan, Bill Long, Frank Mann, Pete McTier, Jerry McTier, Bob McMath, Bill Miller, Christopher Moore, Marie Mons, Wendy Newstetter, Dan Papp, Bill Ray, Mark Sanders, Gary Schuster, Andy Smith, John Staton, John Taylor, Bob Thompson, Ashely Toomey-Flinn, John Toon, Bill Todd, Al Trujillio, Jerry Ulrich, Tom Ventulett, Betsy Verner, Pat Wichmann, JulieAnne Williamson, and Tony Zivalich. To all I owe sincere thanks. Without their help I could not have completed this book.

I need to express my gratitude to Georgia Tech and presidents Bud Peterson and Angel Cabrera, who supported my work for over three years. Also to the Georgia Tech Foundation for its role in helping invest wisely in the future of Georgia Tech.

To the editors and staff of the Mercer University Press and its director, Marc Jolley, I express my appreciation for encouraging the publication of the book and in providing the editing and design support needed to create a beautiful finished product.

Finally, I thank the remarkable students, faculty, staff, and alumni of Georgia Tech who are committed to making my alma mater one of the best universities in the world.

# INDEX